A MODERN INTRODUCTION TO BIBLICAL HEBREW

A MODERN INTRODUCTION
TO
BIBLICAL HEBREW

by

JOHN F. A. SAWYER

ORIEL PRESS LTD

First published 1976
Reprinted with minor corrections 1976
Reprinted 1980, 1984 and 1987

Publication of this book has been generously assisted by the Sponsorship Committee for Publications of the University of Newcastle upon Tyne

A Teaching Cassette is available on request
from the author at £3.70 ($7.00) plus postage

ISBN 0 85362 159 4

Published by Oriel Press Ltd
An imprint of Routledge & Kegan Paul Ltd
11 New Fetter Lane, London EC4P 4EE

Printed in Great Britain by
Redwood Burn Limited, Trowbridge, Wiltshire

PREFACE

The primary aim of this book is to provide students of the Hebrew Bible, who may have no other experience of, and possibly very little interest in, learning a foreign language, with a comprehensive description of the basic structures of Biblical Hebrew grammar and syntax, sufficient for their needs. But in attempting to simplify matters for the non-linguist, it was found desirable to move away from the rather esoteric methods and terminology of traditional grammars, and it is hoped that the alternative presented here may also contribute something to the wider field of Hebrew and Semitic linguistics.

Emphasis throughout is on the *meaning* of Hebrew. The starting point is always the sentence, and words are thus analysed or discussed only in actual contexts. Close attention has been paid to translation, and discrepancies in the semantic range of Hebrew terms (like -וְ, -בְּ and כִּי) and their closest English equivalents have been consistently noted where they occur. Special religious factors operating in the massoretic text of the Bible have also been fully discussed, and the meaning of prefixes and suffixes, which occur more frequently in a given text than any other lexical items, has been given as much space as their form. The semantic theory outlined briefly in Appendix B is directed primarily towards the needs of students consulting Biblical commentaries, dictionaries and word-studies, but some of the phenomena discussed there, notably semantic fields and word-types, also provide valuable ways of arranging vocabulary as part of the learning process: geographical terms, parts of the body, and words for "to help, save", for example, could be collected and examined, as could taboo words, loanwords, transparent terms, and examples of extension and restriction of meaning (pp.169-173).

Secondly, the book concentrates on regularities in the grammar and syntax rather than on phonetic and orthographic variation. For example, the verb forms וַיֹּאמֶר "and he said", וַיַּעַשׂ "and he did" and וַיָּבֹא "and he came" are all introduced together in Chapter VI as one part of the grammar, not split up for phonological reasons and dealt with in three separate chapters, as they are in traditional grammars. Similarly, there is one chapter on Number, one on Gender, and so on, because for the beginner the similarities between דְּבָרִים and עָרִים, אִשָּׁה and גְּדוֹלָה and the like are more important than the differences. The complexities of massoretic phonology have been relegated to Appendix A.

This led to a third innovation. All the basic grammatical forms and structures are introduced in the first ten chapters (Part One). These chapters are, of course, for that reason highly concentrated; but Part Two, *Syntax and Word-formation* constantly revises the grammar of Part One, as it arises in different contexts. For example, all the Derived Stems of the verb are introduced together in Chapter X, but are examined again in Part Two, under the headings "Active and Passive", "Causative Constructions" and "Reflexive Constructions". This means that useful work on the text of the Hebrew Bible can begin at an early stage, not in spite of the grammar-book, but in conjunction with it.

A fourth break with tradition is in terminology. Immediately transparent terms, or terms widely used outside Hebrew grammars as well, have been substituted for some of the traditional terms. The value of the massoretic shorthand and the reasons for retaining it intact for so many centuries are appreciated. But against it, are its quaintness, which is a distraction and a stumbling-block to many students faced with a language that is foreign enough without it, and the fact that it inevitably gives the impression that there is something peculiar about Hebrew which sets it apart from other languages. It may be argued that the student brought up on this new grammar will be unable to follow commentaries and lexica which still use the traditional terminology. There are three answers to this. First, not all the traditional terms have been dropped, only those found to be unnecessary or misleading. Second, the General Index includes most of the traditional terms which the student is likely to come across. Thirdly, the avoidance of quaint but familiar terms, admittedly an extreme measure in the realm of Biblical Hebrew, was undertaken for the specific purpose of helping students at an elementary stage. There is no reason why later on students should not become familiar with the entire thesaurus of Latin and Hebrew technical terms, although it is perhaps not premature to express the hope that, for the benefit of the general linguist and semitist, as well as the elementary student, Hebrew grammar will not always be decorated so richly with these antique conventions.

Finally, all comparative philology and historical linguistics, which help and interest some students but confuse others, are "optional extras" excluded from the main part of the grammar. Discussion of how the letters Ayin and Qoph were once pronounced, for example, or what the reconstructed original form of the noun מֶ֫לֶךְ or the verb יָלַד was, is confined to an Appendix on "The History of the Hebrew Language" (pp. 182f).

It remains to say a word on how the grammar may best be used.

PREFACE

Each chapter begins with a set of Hebrew sentences, taken as a rule *verbatim* from the Hebrew Bible. These examples are then analysed and every new feature described. The analysis is followed by a summary of the material covered in the chapter, and there is often a table presenting some of it in graphic form. Each chapter ends with exercises in which the 300 most frequently occurring items of Biblical Hebrew vocabulary are introduced at the rate of 15 per chapter. Students should be encouraged to study each chapter thoroughly on their own first, before dealing with it in class, because as well as teaching the theory, this method gives them practice from the start in tackling an unseen Hebrew text. An intensive two-week course at the rate of approximately one chapter per day would provide a comprehensive grounding in the grammar by covering the whole of Part One. Where timetables allow, reading-practice, either in the class room or the language laboratory, is valuable. The grammar is also suitable for use as a "teach yourself" book, a biblical concordance (such as Mandelkern) providing a key to the exercises if required.

My thanks are due especially to Chaim Rabin, Takamitsu Muraoka and Henry Hart for their detailed criticisms and suggestions; also to Peter Ackroyd, J.H. Hospers, C.-A. Keller, Richard Coggins, John Pellowe and Margaret Jervis for advice and encouragement at various stages; and to the many students, both in the Department of Religious Studies and the Adult Education Department at the University of Newcastle upon Tyne, who have, either wittingly or unwittingly, provided valuable consumer research data over the years. In the task of getting an unusually complicated typescript printed and published at a time of national economic crisis, I am indebted to Bruce Allsopp; and for Nechamah Inbar, who typed the whole book impeccably, I have nothing but praise. Lastly, I gladly acknowledge generous assistance from this University's Sponsorship of Publications Committee and Research Fund.

Newcastle Upon Tyne J.F.A.S.
October, 1975

TABLE OF CONTENTS

TABLE OF CONTENTS

TABLE OF CONTENTS

ABBREVIATIONS AND SYMBOLS

AV	King James' Authorised Version of the Bible (1611)
BH	Biblical Hebrew
C	Consonant
D-stem	Doubled Stem (Piel) (X)
f	feminine
fpl	feminine plural
fs	feminine singular
H-stem	Hiphil stem (X)
JB	The Jerusalem Bible (1966)
K	Kethīb (p. 6)
mpl	masculine plural
ms	masculine singular
N	Noun
NEB	The New English Bible (1970)
Np	proper name
N-stem	Niphal stem (X)
PC	Prefix Conjugation (VI)
PG	Pregenitive (V)
P-S	Proto-Semitic (Appendix C)
Q	Qerē (p.6)
RSV	Revised Standard Version of the Bible (1952)
SC	Suffix Conjugation (IV)
T-stem	Hithpael stem (X)
V	Vowel
Ø	zero
*	reconstructed form; form not attested.
>	develops into; is reduced to.

Roman numerals I-XX refer to relevant chapters.

SCRIPT AND PRONUNCIATION

The original pronunciation of Biblical Hebrew is not normally advocated in the grammar books for several reasons. First, there is not enough evidence to reconstruct it convincingly. Second, the Hebrew Bible was composed over a period of about 1000 years, and the complexities of phonetic variation over that period would be immense. Third, modern editions of the Hebrew text, with very few exceptions, are based on massoretic tradition, and while the massoretes no doubt have preserved some original features quite correctly, they cannot be said to have recovered the original text or pronunciation in every case (cf. p. 181).

It is customary, therefore, to take the Massoretic Text as the starting-point for the study of Biblical Hebrew; but even here there are problems, because several distinct pronunciations of this are in use at the present time. On the one hand, there are the two Jewish traditions, Sephardi (oriental) and Ashkenazi (European) (p. 186). Several varieties of the former are current in Israel, where Hebrew has been the official language since 1948, and are steadily superseding the latter in Jewish communities all over the world. On the other hand, there is a "scientific pronunciation", mainly confined to the British Isles, which is an attempt to realize all the phonetic oppositions represented in the massoretic script as precisely as possible. This often involves an "orientalizing" pronunciation intended to highlight certain phonetic correspondences between Hebrew and modern spoken Arabic.

In favour of an Israeli pronunciation are the following considerations: (a) it is the simplest; (b) it is the most widely used; and (c) it is the pronunciation of a living language. The variety of Israeli pronunciation recommended here may best be described as a "citation style": that is, a pronunciation characterized by clear and studious articulation which emphasizes grammatical and lexical distinctions, and facilitates aural communication between teacher and student. For a description of the phonology of this variety of Hebrew, see Appendix A.

Transliteration from Hebrew into a more familiar script is kept to a minimum, and used only as an aid to pronunciation, alongside the corresponding Hebrew script. For the consonants, the conventional transliteration system, which is designed to be autonomous and indicates the form of the Hebrew rather than how to pronounce it, is therefore unsuitable for beginners and a simpler system is used here instead. Only two letters require comment: χ is the final sound in Scots *loch*, and an apostrophe stands for the glottal stop heard in some dialects of English in place of intervocalic *t* in words like *metal (me'al)* and *butter (bu'er)*. Where transliterated Hebrew is used on its own, however, the conventional system (given in the tables on pp. 8 and 189) must be adhered to.

For the vowels, the conventional system has been adopted without the distinction between the three short vowels *a*, *e*, *o* and the three corresponding "compound shwas" (p. 4), and that between long vowels and vowel-letters. Neither of these distinctions is perceptible in pronunciation. ə stands for the short unstressed vowel in, for example, the four unstressed syllables of *William the Conqueror*. ē is the final vowel in *café* (as opposed to *e* in *bed*), and ī is the second vowel in *grand prix*, (as opposed to *i* in *pig).*

Main stress is marked by an accent written over the vowel of the stressed syllable: e.g. *méleχ* "king". Doubling (p. 5) is not normally indicated in transliteration since it is purely orthographic. Transliterations are printed in italics; English translations within quotation marks.

SCRIPT

Hebrew is read from right to left. The alphabet consists of 22 letters which stand for consonants. Five of these have special *final forms*, which are mostly characterized by a flourish or "tail" below the line: ךּ, ם, ן, ף, ץ. Four consonants, א, ה, ח and ע, are called "gutturals" (p.158).

Letters liable to be confused in the printed script are distinguished by the following features:

1. length of horizontal stroke: ו/ך נ/כ ו/ר ז/ד ג/ב
2. length of vertical stroke: ד/ך ו/ן י/ו
3. shape of corner: ת/ח/ה ס/ם מ/ט ו/ז ר/ד נ/ג כ/ב
4. dots: שׁ/שׂ ו/ךּ

The modern cursive characters (see p. 190) are formed as follows

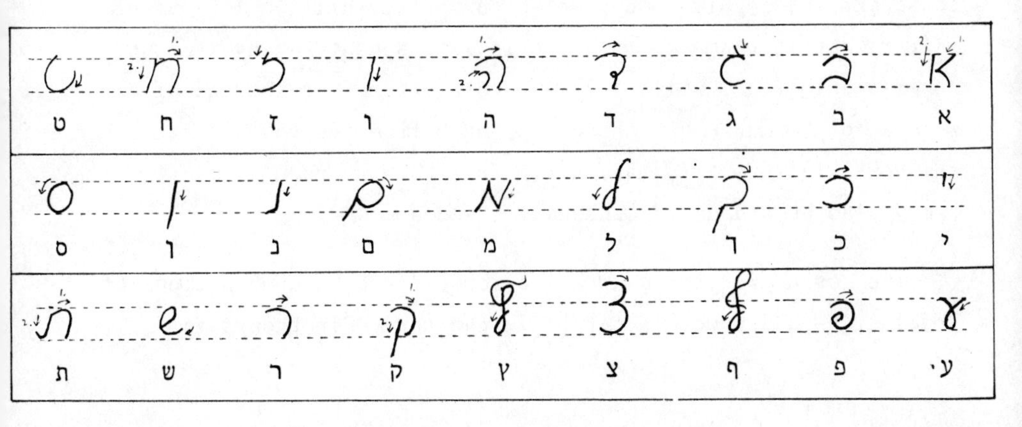

There are twelve *vowel signs*. Ten of these are written below their letter: e.g. סֵ֫פֶר מְלָכִים. Of the *compound shwas*, ֱ occurs only with gutturals, ֲ and ֳ mainly with gutturals but occasionally elsewhere: e.g. וּזֲהַב (Gen. 2:12) and קֳדָשִׁים (Lev. 22: 7). The sign for *ō* is written above the left side of its letter, but when it precedes שׁ or follows שׂ it is sometimes not written to avoid the awkwardness of two points very close together: thus מֹשֶׁה *mōshe* "Moses" and שֹׂנֵא *sōnē* "hating". The sign for *ū* consists of the vowel-letter ו (see below) with an inner dot: וּ.

The sign ְ ("shwa") is not pronounced except at the beginning of a word (e.g. לְדָוִיד *lədāvīd* "to David"), when it is the second of two shwas (e.g. יִמְלְכוּ *yimləχū* "they reign"), and between two identical consonants (e.g. נְרַנְּנָה *nəranənā* "let us shout for joy").

There are three *vowel-letters* ו, י and ה. As well as standing for consonants like the rest of the alphabet, these may also stand for vowels (see p. 191). They combine with five of the vowel-signs as follows: וֹ (*ō* as opposed to וּ *ū*), ִי *(ī)*, ֵי *(ē)*, and, at the end of a word, ֶה *(-e)*, ֵה *(-ē)*, ֹה *(-ō)*, ָה *(-ā)*. Inside a word, vowel-letters can be distinguished from the corresponding consonants by the absence of their own vowel-sign: thus in מִצְוָה *mitsvā* ו is a consonant, having its own vowel-sign ָ *(ā)*, while ה is a vowel-letter; but in הַמַּצּוֹת *ha-matsōt* ה is a consonant having its own vowel-sign ַ *(-a)*, while וֹ is a vowel-letter. At the end of a word a dot distinguishes the consonant הּ from the vowel-letter, and the vowel-letters וֹ *(ō)* and וּ *(ū)* from the consonant ו *(v)*. (The sign וּ may also be a doubled consonant : see below).

The seven *diphthongs* are also represented by combinations of vowel-signs and vowel-letters. In the three diphthongs וּי *(ūi)*,

וֹי *(ōi)* and ַי, ָי *(ai)* the second element, represented by the letter י, is vocalic although no second vowel-sign is written. In the other four diphthongs, which occur only before final ה, ח and ע, the second element, a short back vowel, is represented by a vowel-sign written under the final consonant, but pronounced before it: e.g. גָּבוֹהַּ *gāvōa* (not * *gāvōha*); נֹחַ *nōaχ* (not * *nōχa*); מוֹשִׁיעַ *mōshīa* (not * *mōshī'a*).

An *inner dot* distinguishes the six letters בּ, גּ, דּ, כּ, פּ, תּ ("Beghadhkephath") from their post-vocalic forms ב, ג, ד, כ, פ, ת (p. 157). In these six letters, in a post-vocalic position, and in other letters, the inner dot also indicates *doubling*. Doubling occurs under the following conditions:

1. in nouns, after the prefix הַ "the" (p. 18).
2. in verbs, after the prefix וַ "and" (p. 39).
3. as the second root-letter in the Doubled Stem (p. 62)
4. where a preceding *n* (or *l*) has been omitted by assimilation (p. 161).
5. in a number of other words (for historical reasons): e.g. אַתָּה "you", עַמִּי "my people".

Doubling never occurs at the beginning or end of a word, except in אַתְּ "you (f)" and נָתַתְּ "you (f) gave". In several letters with shwa, notably ו, י, ל, מ, נ, ס, פ, ק, doubling is unmarked. Gutturals and ר are never doubled (p.158).

Monosyllabic words are often joined by a *hyphen* to another word in the same phrase. Six prepositions (אֶל־, אֶת־, מִן־, עַד־, עַל־, עִם־), four particles (אַל־, אִם־, אֶת־, פֶּן־) and several other common words (e.g. בֶּן־, בַּת־, כָּל־) are normally, but not always, joined to the next word in the phrase by a hyphen. The hyphen occurs sporadically elsewhere.

Several of the thirty or so other signs in the Biblical text, which function rather like punctuation marks, are useful aids to analysing sentence structure. The text is divided into *verses*, and the end of each verse is marked by the sign ׃ Within a verse the *major pauses* are marked by ֑ under the stressed syllable of the word preceding the pause, and *minor pauses* by ֔ above the stressed syllable of the word preceding the pause, or by ֒ above the last letter of the word preceding the pause. The books of Psalms, Job and Proverbs have a separate system in which the word preceding the major pause is marked by ֭ ֫ on the stressed syllable and the syllable before it.

The main *stress* within a word is thus often indicated by these pause-markers. In the last word of a verse the main stress is marked by the sign ֽ under the stressed syllable. Elsewhere this sign normally marks a secondary stress. In modern grammar-books, including this one, ֫ is a convenient way of marking stress where it is not marked in any other way.

A small circle ֯ above a word in the text refers the reader to a *marginal note*. The most important of these marginal notes are the early Jewish textual emendations known as *Qerē* readings. These had to be given in the margin because alterations to the consonantal text of the Bible were forbidden. The pronunciation of the text, however, was less sacrosanct, and the result is that we frequently find in the text the consonants of one word (*Kethīb* "that which is written") with the points and vowel-signs of another (*Qerē* "that which is to be read"). The consonants of the *Qerē* word are then normally given in the margin: e.g. at Psalm 54:7 יָשְׁו֯ב is made up of K. יָשׁוּב (cf. NEB) and Q. יָשִׁיב (cf. RSV). There are a number of frequent, conventional *Qerē* readings which are not explained in the margin. Most important of these is the name of Israel's God יְהֹוָה or יְהֹוִה (see p. 12).

Before the introduction of chapter divisions, taken over from the Vulgate in the fourteenth century, the text was divided in the following ways, still indicated in most editions of the Hebrew Bible. The Pentateuch is divided into 54 weekly portions, indicated by the word פרש ("Parash") printed in the margin, or by the initials פ פ פ at the head of each portion (Gen. 6:9; 12:1; 18:1; etc.). A word or phrase from the beginning of each portion serves as its title: e.g. נח "Noah" is the title of Gen. 6:9-11: 32;. and משפטים "ordinances" is the title of Ex. 21-24. The Hebrew titles of the "Five Books of Moses" are similarly formed: בראשית (Genesis), שמות (Exodus), ויקרא (Leviticus), במדבר (Numbers), דברים (Deuteronomy). Other liturgical divisions in the text are marked by ס̇ (for סדר "Seder" or "Sidra") or שני "second", שלישי "third", etc. (i.e. subsections of each portion) in the margin. Short paragraphs are separated by a space containing the symbol פ (for פתוח "open") or ס (for סתום "closed").

SCRIPT AND PRONUNCIATION

Printed	Cursive	Trans-lit.*	Name	Pronunciation
א		ʾ	Aleph	not pronounced, except between vowels where it stands for a glottal stop (p.153): e.g. הָאָרֶץ *hāʾāreṯs* "the earth, the land."
בּ		*b*	Beth	*b* as in *big*.
ב		*bh*		*v* as in *never* (only after a vowel).
ג		*g,gh*	Gimel	*g* as in *golf*.
ד		*d,dh*	Daleth	*d* as in *dog*.
ה		*h*	He	*h* as in *hat*, except at the end of a word where it is not pronounced.
ו		*w*	Waw	1. *v* as in *vote* (consonant). 2. *ū* or *ō* (vowel-letter).
ז		*z*	Zayin	*z* as in *size*.
ח		*ḥ*	Ḥeth	χ like final sound in Scots *loch*.
ט		*ṭ*	Ṭeth	*t* as in *tap*.
י		*y*	Yodh	1. *y* as in *yawn* (consonant). 2. *ī* or *ē* (vowel-letter).
כּ (fin. form ךּ)		*k*	Kaph	*k* as in *kitten*.
כ		*kh*		χ like final sound in Scots *loch* (only after a vowel).
ל		*l*	Lamedh	*l* as in *lip*.
מ (fin. form ם)		*m*	Mem	*m* as in *milk*.
נ (fin. form ן)		*n*	Nun	*n* as in *nice*.
ס		*s*	Samekh	*s* as in *salt*.
ע		ʿ	Ayin	not pronounced, except between vowels where it stands for a glottal stop (p.153): e.g. לְעוֹלָם *ləʿōlām* "for ever".
פּ (fin. form ף)		*p*	Pe	*p* as in *pink*.
פ		*ph*		*f* as in *fox* (only after a vowel).
צ (fin. form ץ)		*ṣ*	Ṣadhē	*t͜s* as in *cats*.
ק		*q*	Qoph	*k* as in *kitten*.
ר		*r*	Resh	*r* as in Scots *Murray*.
שׁ		*š*	Shin	*sh* as in *shop*.
שׂ		*ś*	Sin	*s* as in *salt*.
ת		*t,th*	Taw	*t* as in *tap*.

* Conventional Transliteration (see p.2).

VOWEL-SIGNS

Sign	Name	Pronunciation	
ִ	Ḥireq	*ī* as in *grand prix* (except in unstressed position before doubled consonant or vowelless consonant, when it is pronounced as *i* in *pig*: e.g. (מִצְוָה *mitsvā* "commandment") (p.156).	
ֵ	Ṣerē	*ē* as in *café*.	
ֶ	Seghol	*e* as in *bed*.	
ֻ	Qibbuṣ	*u* as in *soon*.	
וּ	Shureq	*ū* as in *soon*.	
ֹ	Ḥolem	*ō* as in *more*.	
ָ	Qameṣ	*ā* as in *car* (except in unstressed position before doubled consonant or vowelless consonant, when it is pronounced like *o* in *hot*: e.g. חָכְמָה *χoχmā* "wisdom") (p.156).	
ַ	Pathaḥ	*a* as in French *chat* (almost *u* in *shut*).	
ְ	Shwa	not pronounced, except at the beginning of a word, after a vowelless consonant and between two identical consonants (p. 154).	
ֱ	Ḥaṭeph Seghol	*e* as in *bed*.	Compound Shwas
ֳ	Ḥaṭeph Qameṣ	*o* as in *hot*.	Compound Shwas
ֲ	Ḥaṭeph Pathaḥ	*a* as in French *chat* (almost *u* in *shut*).	Compound Shwas

DIPHTHONGS

וּי	*ūi* as in *chop-suey*.
וֹי	*ōi* as in *joy*.
ַי ָי	*ai* as in *tie*.
ִיהַ ִיחַ ִיעַ	*īa* as in *idea*.
ֵהַ ֵחַ ֵעַ	*ēa* as in *mea culpa*.
וּהַ וּחַ וּעַ	*ūa* as in *Rotorua*.
וֹהַ וֹחַ וֹעַ	*ōa* as in *Samoa*.

OTHER COMMON SIGNS

המּלך	inner dot denoting doubling (p.5).	Daghesh forte
בּית	inner dot distinguishing the six letters בּ,גּ,דּ,כּ,פּ,תּ from their post-vocalic forms (p. 157).	Daghesh lene
גבוהּ	in final הּ distinguishes the consonant from the vowel-letter ה.	Mappiq
על־פני	hyphen.	Maqqeph
הארץ׃	the end of a verse.	Soph Pasuq
אלה֑ים	a major pause within the verse.	Athnaḥ
וב֔הו	a minor pause within the verse.	Zaqeph Qaṭon
הרקיע֒	the first of two major pauses in a verse.	Segholta
ה֫אר֥ץ	a major pause within a verse (in the books of Psalms, Job and Proverbs only).	Olē we-Yoredh
הארֽץ׃	main stress on the last word of a verse.	Silluq
היֽתה	in other positions, secondary stress.	Metheg
ב֯ראשית	marginal note.	

PART ONE
BASIC GRAMMAR

CHAPTER I. WORDS AND ROOTS

EXAMPLES

1. The Lord is king for ever (Ps. 29:10).	יְהוָה מֶלֶךְ לְעוֹלָם:	א.
2. By me kings reign (Prov. 8:15).	בִּי מְלָכִים יִמְלֹכוּ:	ב.
3. The Lord gave sovereignty to David (II Chr. 13:5).	יְהוָה נָתַן מַמְלָכָה לְדָוִיד:	ג.

ANALYSIS

1. יְהוָה is the name of Israel's God. According to an early religious tradition the name, probably "Yahweh", was never to be pronounced. To preserve this tradition, it was written with the vowels of another word, either אֲדֹנָי *a-dō-nāi* "the Lord" or אֱלֹהִים *elōhīm* "God," and this is how it is to be pronounced. The usual English translation of יְהוָה is "the Lord", although JB has "Yahweh" (cf. AV "Jehovah": Ex. 6:3).

מֶלֶךְ *mé-leχ* is the Hebrew for "king". The *root* of this word, like many Hebrew roots, consists of three consonants called root-letters: מ-ל-ךְ (ךְ is a final form: p. 3). The first consonant with its vowel-sign ֶ gives the syllable -מֶ *me-*; the second has the same vowel-sign and the third has no vowel (p. 3), giving the syllable -לֶךְ *leχ*; the stress is on the first syllable. This is then the *citation-form* of the word (i.e. the form cited in the dictionary). There are many nouns of the type CéCeC (C = consonant): cf. דֶּרֶךְ *déreχ* "way"; עֶבֶד *éved* "servant"; אֶרֶץ *érets* "land, earth".

WORDS AND ROOTS

לְעוֹלָם *lə-ō-lām* "for ever": this five-letter word is made up of two different lexical items which will be found under separate entries in the dictionary:

(1) the first consonant with its vowel sign (shwa at the beginning of a word: p.4) gives the syllable -לְ *lə*-, which is the citation-form of a preposition meaning "to, for". There are four prepositions, like לְ, prefixed to their noun or pronoun (XV).

(2) the next consonant ע (a glottal stop) is followed by the vowel-letter ו -*ō* (p.4) giving the syllable -עוֹ *ō*-; and the last syllable לָם- is made up of the consonant ל, its vowel sign ָ and the consonant ם (final form) pronounced -*lām*. עוֹלָם is the citation-form of another noun, like מֶלֶךְ consisting of three root-letters, ם-ל-ע, but of a different and less common type.

2. בִּי *bī* "by me" is made up of -בְּ *bə*, the citation-form of another preposition like -לְ *lə*-, and ִי- -*ī*, one of the suffix pronouns (VIII). It refers to the speaker, in this context wisdom personified (Prov. 8:15). The vowels of a citation-form change according to certain rules (pp. 155f.): -בְּ *bə* "by" (citation-form); but בִּי *bī* "by me" (no vowel); בָּהֶם *bāhem* "by them (the vowel of the preposition has become *ā*). The consonants of a citation-form, however, normally remain the same.

מְלָכִים *mə-lā-χ́īm* "kings" is the plural of מֶלֶךְ. Before the plural suffix ִים- -*īm*, which is stressed, the vowels of the citation-form have changed: cf. דֶּרֶךְ *dérex* "way" (citation-form), but דְּרָכִים *də-rā-χ́īm* "ways"; עֶבֶד *éved* "servant" (citation-form), but עֲבָדִים *a-vā-d́īm* "servants".

יִמְלֹכוּ *yim-lṓ-χū* is a verb. This word has no separate entry in the dictionary since the first letter is not part of the citation-form. It is a grammatical prefix which identifies the subject of the verb as "he" or "they". Similarly the final vowel-letter וּ- *ū* is a grammatical suffix which defines the subject as plural ("they", not "he") (VI). There is a "vocabulary" of such prefixes and suffixes on pp.209ff . The three remaining letters make up the root מ-ל-ךְ, with which we are already familiar from the noun מֶלֶךְ "king", and thus the verb means "to be king, to reign". מָלַךְ *mālaχ* is the citation-form of the verb (IV), and is related to מֶלֶךְ "a king" in the same way as דָּרַךְ *dā-raχ* "to walk" is related to דֶּרֶךְ "way", and עָבַד *ā-vad* "to serve" is related to עֶבֶד "servant".

3. יְהוָה נָתַן *a-dō-nā̆i nā-tan* "the Lord gave". On יְהוָה see 1. above. נָתַן *nā-tan* is the citation-form of the Hebrew verb for "to give". Cf. the proper name יְהוֹנָתָן *yə-hō-nā-tān* "Jonathan" ("the Lord gave").

מַמְלָכָה *mam-lā-χā* "kingdom, sovereignty" is another word containing the root מ-ל-ךְ. The initial consonant מ is not a separate prefix like -בְּ "in" (see 2. above), but an inseparable part of the citation-form of the noun. It is the chief characteristic of another common noun-type m*VCCV́C* or m*VCCVC*á: e.g. מִזְבֵּחַ "altar" (cf. זָבַח "to sacrifice"); מִשְׁפָּט "judgment" (cf. שָׁפַט "to judge"); מַעְבָּרָה "ford" (cf. עָבַר "to cross").

לְדָוִד *lə-dā-vīd* is made up of the lexical prefix -לְ "to, for", which is the citation-form of the preposition discussed in 1. above and the proper name דָּוִד "David". Notice how the initial ד in דָּוִד (with inner dot) has become ד after the vowel of לְ (cf. p.5).

I

WORDS AND ROOTS

SUMMARY

A. Many words are not cited in the dictionaries in the form in which they appear in any given Hebrew text. *Citation-forms* may have grammatical prefixes or suffixes attached to them, like -י *y-* "he, they" (prefixed to verbs), the suffixes ִים- *-īm* (a plural-marker in nouns) and וּ- *-ū* (a plural-marker in verbs), and the lexical prefixes -בְּ *bə-* "in, by, with" and -וְ *və-* "and".

B. The addition of prefixes and suffixes frequently brings about internal vowel-changes in the citation-form of a word, but the consonants, which are naturally more conspicuous than the vowels in the Hebrew script, normally remain the same.

C. The citation-form of a noun consists of *root-letters*, all of them consonants, and *formatives*, like the inseparable prefix -מ in מַמְלָכָה "kingdom" and the vowel pattern CéCeC in מֶלֶךְ "king".

VOCABULARY

אֱלֹהִים	"God"	דָּוִד	"David"	מֶ֫לֶךְ	"king"
אֶ֫רֶץ	f."earth, land"	-וְ	"and"	נָתַן	"to give"
אֶת־	object-marker	יְהוָה	"the Lord, YHWH"	עֶ֫בֶד	"servant"
-בְּ	"in, by, with"	יִשְׂרָאֵל	"Israel"	עוֹלָם	"all time"
בָּרָא	"to create"	מָלַךְ	"to be king"	שָׁמַ֫יִם	"heaven"

EXERCISES

1. Write out in Hebrew and read aloud:

א. זֶה סֵפֶר תּוֹלְדוֹת אָדָם (Gen. 5:1).

ב. נֹחַ אִישׁ צַדִּיק תָּמִים הָיָה בְּדוֹרוֹתָיו (Gen. 6:9).

ג. כִּי בְּצֶלֶם אֱלֹהִים עָשָׂה אֶת־הָאָדָם (Gen. 9:6).

ד. וּרְדוּ בִדְגַת הַיָּם וּבְעוֹף הַשָּׁמַיִם (Gen. 1:28).

ה. וְעֵץ הַחַיִּים בְּתוֹךְ הַגָּן וְעֵץ הַדַּעַת טוֹב וָרָע (Gen. 2:9).

2. Translate and write down the citation-form of each of the following:

וּבְיִשְׂרָאֵל, אֶרֶץ וְשָׁמַיִם, יִבְרָא, מְלָכִים, נָתְנוּ, וְדָוִד.

CHAPTER II. VERBLESS SENTENCES. DEFINITE AND INDEFINITE.

EXAMPLES

1.	The Lord is one (Deut. 6:4).	יְהוָה אֶחָד׃	א.
2.	The word is good (Deut. 1:14).	טוֹב הַדָּבָר׃	ב.
3.	The man Moses was very great (Ex.11:3)	הָאִישׁ מֹשֶׁה גָּדוֹל מְאוֹד׃	ג.
4.	God is not a man (Num. 23:19)	לֹא אִישׁ אֵל׃	ד.
5.	But king Solomon will be blessed (I Kgs. 2:45).	וְהַמֶּלֶךְ שְׁלֹמֹה בָּרוּךְ׃	ה.

ANALYSIS

1. This is a *verbless sentence*. The *subject* is יְהוָה "the Lord" and the *predicate* is אֶחָד *exād* "one". Verbless sentences do not occur in English, and in translating from Hebrew the appropriate form of the verb "to be" must be added: "The Lord (is) one".

יְהוָה "the Lord" is a proper name, and therefore definite.

2. In this example the predicate טוֹב *tōv* "good" precedes the subject הַדָּבָר *ha-dāvār* "the word". The order Predicate-Subject is as common as Subject-Predicate in verbless sentences.

הַדָּבָר "the word" is made up of two elements:

(1) the prefix -הַ *ha-* "the"

(2) the noun דָּבָר "word". Words of the type *CaCVC* are as common as those of the type *CéCeC* (p. 12): e.g. גָּדוֹל "great"; נָבִיא "prophet".

The prefix makes the noun *definite*: it is not דָּבָר "a word", "any word you like" (indefinite), but הַדָּבָר "the word, the one we have been thinking about, the one just mentioned" (definite). The first consonant of the noun is *doubled* (p. 5) after this prefix: cf. הַמֶּלֶךְ "the king"; הַשָּׁמַיִם "the heavens"; הַכֹּהֵן "the priest".

3. Here the order is Subject-Predicate again. The subject consists of two terms: הָאִישׁ *hā-īsh* "the man" (before the consonant א, which is never doubled, הַ is written -הָ: p. 158); and מֹשֶׁה *Mōshe* "Moses". Both are definite.

גָּדוֹל מְאוֹד *gādōl mə'ōd* "very great" is the predicate. The adverb מְאוֹד "very" comes after the word it modifies, unlike English "very". גָּדוֹל is similar in type to דָּבָר *(CāCVC)*.

As there is no time reference in this sentence, past-time is deduced from the context (Ex. 11:3).

4. The order is the same as in 2. The negative particle לֹא "not" always precedes the word it negates. אִישׁ "a man" is indefinite.

אֵל *ēl* "God" is a proper name here, but it also occurs in Biblical Hebrew as a noun, either definite or indefinite (cf. English *god* and *God*).

5. This sentence is similar to 3. וְהַמֶּלֶךְ *və-ha-méleχ* "but the king" is made up of three elements: the citation-form of the lexical prefix -וְ *və-* "and", the grammatical prefix expressing definiteness -הַ *ha-* "the", and the citation-form of the noun מֶלֶךְ "king". -וְ has a much wider range of meaning than "and" in English, and in some contexts is best translated "but", "so", "then" or the like (cf. XIX).

VERBLESS SENTENCES

There is again no time reference (cf. 3. above), but the context suggests that it refers to future time (I Kings 2:45).

SUMMARY

A. The verbless sentence is an important feature of Hebrew syntax, corresponding to English sentences with the verb "to be" in the predicate.

B. Nouns with the prefix -הַ *ha*- are definite, like nouns with "the" in English. Proper names are also definite. Hebrew has no precise equivalent to English "a, an" to denote indefiniteness.

C. Hebrew word-order frequently differs from English: e.g. מְאוֹד "very" comes after the word it modifies, and the order Predicate-Subject is as common in verbless sentences as Subject-Predicate.

VOCABULARY

אִישׁ	"man"	טוֹב	"good"	נָבִיא	"prophet"
בָּרוּךְ	"blessed"	כֹּהֵן	"priest"	צַדִּיק	"righteous, just"
גָּדוֹל	"great"	-לְ	"to, for"	צִיּוֹן	f. "Zion"
דָּבָר	"word, thing"	לֹא	"no, not"	קָדוֹשׁ	"holy"
-הַ	"the"	מְאוֹד	"very"	רַע	"bad"

EXERCISES

1. Put into the indefinite:

הַנָּבִיא, הַקָּדוֹשׁ, הַשָּׁמַיִם, הָאִישׁ, הַמֶּלֶךְ.

DEFINITE AND INDEFINITE

2. Write in Hebrew and translate:

א. לֹא טוֹב הַדָּבָר׃

ב. בָּרוּךְ יְהוָה לְעוֹלָם׃

ג. וְהָאִישׁ נָבִיא לֵאלֹהִים׃

ד. דָּוִד הַמֶּלֶךְ כֹּהֵן בְּיִשְׂרָאֵל׃

ה. גָּדוֹל בְּצִיּוֹן יְהוָה׃

ו. יְהוָה הַצַּדִּיק׃

3. Read the Hebrew aloud.

CHAPTER III. PRONOUNS. ADJECTIVES. MASCULINE AND FEMININE.

EXAMPLES

1.	I am the Lord (Isa. 42:8).	אֲנִי יְהוָֹה׃	א.
2.	You are a people holy to the Lord (Deut. 7:6)	עַם קָדוֹשׁ אַתָּה לַיהוָֹה׃	ב.
3.	A wealthy woman was there (II Kgs. 4:8).	וְשָׁם אִשָּׁה גְדוֹלָה׃	ג.
4.	It is the great city (Gen. 10:12).	הִיא הָעִיר הַגְּדוֹלָה׃	ד.
5.	God is in heaven, and you upon earth (Eccl. 5:1).	אֱלֹהִים בַּשָּׁמַיִם וְאַתָּה עַל־הָאָרֶץ׃	ה.

ANALYSIS

1. The subject of this verbless sentence is the First Person Singular *(1s)* pronoun אֲנִי "I". Personal pronouns are described as First Person when they refer to the speaker(s) (*I*, *we*, etc.), Second Person when they refer to the person(s) addressed (*you*), and Third Person when they refer to the person(s) being spoken about (*he*, *they*, etc.). There are separate singular and plural forms, and, in the Second and Third Person, masculine and feminine forms are also distinguished.

Personal pronouns are represented in Hebrew either by separate words ("independent pronouns"), or by prefixes and suffixes attached to nouns, verbs and prepositions (VIII). The independent pronouns occur mainly as the subjects of verbless sentences, like אֲנִי "I" in the present example, but also, in some contexts, for emphasis (XX).

ADJECTIVES

The predicate is the proper name יְהוָה.

2. The subject is the second person singular masculine (2 *ms*) pronoun אַתָּה "you", referring to Israel (Deut. 7:6). In English "you" may refer to masculine or feminine, singular or plural persons; in Hebrew there are four distinct pronouns.

The predicate is made up of the noun עַם "a people" and the adjective קָדוֹשׁ "holy". In Hebrew an adjective comes after its noun, and agrees with it in gender, number and definiteness: thus, in the present example, both words in the phrase עַם קָדוֹשׁ are masculine, singular and indefinite.

לַיהוָה "to the Lord" is made up of the preposition -לְ "to, for", and the proper name יְהוָה. On the various spellings of -לְ see p.23.

3. -וְ "and" is sometimes best left untranslated (cf. XIX).

שָׁם "there, in that place" is an adverb, functioning here as the predicate of a verbless sentence (XV).

אִשָּׁה גְדוֹלָה " a wealthy woman" is similar to the phrase עַם קָדוֹשׁ "a holy people" in the previous example, but the noun and the adjective in this case are both feminine.

There are two genders in Hebrew, so that all nouns, even those denoting things, are either masculine or feminine. Nouns with the stressed suffix ָה (*-ā*) are feminine. (There is one masculine noun ending in ָה, לַ֫יְלָה "night", but here the suffix is unstressed). Nouns ending in ת are also feminine, and so are nouns denoting females (e.g. אֵם "mother"), some parts of the body (e.g. יָד "hand", עַיִן "eye"), and a number of common nouns including עִיר "city", רוּחַ

"wind, spirit", נֶ֫פֶשׁ "soul, living person", and אֶ֫רֶץ "earth, land".

Adjectives agreeing with feminine nouns mostly end in ָה but there are some with feminine forms in ת (cf. p.59).

The addition of a stressed suffix like ָה *(-ā)* brings about vowel-changes in the citation-form (cf.I). In nouns of the type *CāCVC* (גָּדוֹל, נָבִיא, דָּבָר, etc.) the long vowel in the first syllable is reduced *(ā>ə)*: e.g. גָּדוֹל "great" (citation-form) as opposed to גְּדוֹלָה (feminine form); נָבִיא "prophet" as opposed to נְבִיאָה "prophetess". The pattern *CəCVCV́(C)* is extremely common (p. 156).

4. The subject of this sentence is the third person feminine singular (3*fs*) pronoun הִיא referring to the feminine singular noun הָעִיר "the city". Like all singular pronouns referring to things, הִיא corresponds in this example to English "it". There are no neuter forms in Hebrew.

In the phrase הָעִיר הַגְּדוֹלָה "the great city", both terms are feminine, singular and definite. -הַ is attached to the adjective as well as the noun to denote definiteness (cf. II).

All names of cities are feminine.

5. Two verbless clauses are linked by the conjunction -וְ "and". The predicate of the first clause is the word בַּשָּׁמַ֫יִם, which is made up of three elements:

(1) the preposition -בְּ "in".

(2) the definite prefix -הַ "the".

(3) the noun שָׁמַיִם "heaven".

In combination with -הַ, -בְּ and -לְ become -בַּ *(ba-)* and -לַ *(la-)* (or variants before gutturals: p. 159): לְמֶ֫לֶךְ "to a king" (indefinite) as opposed to לַמֶּ֫לֶךְ "to the king" (definite); בְּעִיר "in a city" as opposed to בָּעִיר "in the city".

The predicate of the second clause consists of the preposition עַל "upon", and the noun הָאָ֫רֶץ "the earth" (definite). עַל- is normally attached to its noun by a hyphen (p.5).

The citation-form of the Hebrew for "earth" is אֶ֫רֶץ; but the first vowel is always written ָ after הַ-, not just in pause (p. 157). On the spelling of the definite prefix הַ- before א, see p. 158.

SUMMARY

A. The independent personal pronouns occur mainly as the subjects of verbless sentences. The commonest forms are:

	Singular	Plural
1st	אָנֹכִי or אֲנִי "I"	אֲנַ֫חְנוּ "we"
2nd masc.	אַתָּה "you" (sing.)	אַתֶּם "you" (plur.)
2nd fem.	אַתְּ "you" (fem. sing.)	אַתֶּן "you" (fem.plur.)
3rd masc.	הוּא "he, it"	הֵם or הֵ֫מָּה "they"
3rd fem.	הִיא "she, it"	הֵ֫נָּה "they" (fem.)

B. There are two genders in Hebrew, masculine and feminine. The stressed suffix ָה- indicates feminine gender. Many other nouns are feminine.

MASCULINE AND FEMININE

C. An adjective comes after its noun, and agrees with it in number, gender and definiteness.

VOCABULARY

אֲנִי	"I"	בָּמָה	f. "high place"	עִיר	f. "city"
אַתָּה	"you (m)"	הוּא	"he"	עַל־	"upon"
אַתְּ	"you (f)"	הִיא	"she"	עַם	"people"
אִשָּׁה	f. "woman"	הִנֵּה	"behold"	רוּחַ	f. "wind, spirit"
בַּ֫יִת	"house"	נֹחַ	"Noah"	שָׁם	"there"

EXERCISES

1. Write in Hebrew and translate

א. אַתָּה הָאִישׁ:

ב. יְהוָֹה הוּא הָאֱלֹהִים:

ג. נֹחַ אִישׁ צַדִּיק:

ד. לֹא בַשָּׁמַיִם הִיא:

ה. אָנֹכִי אָנֹכִי יְהוָֹה:

ו. בְּרוּכָה אַתְּ לַיהוָֹה:

ז. וְשָׁם הַבָּמָה הַגְּדוֹלָה:

ח. אֲנִי יְהוָֹה קָדוֹשׁ בְּיִשְׂרָאֵל:

ט. טוֹבָה הָאָרֶץ מְאוֹד מְאוֹד:

י. הִנֵּה רוּחַ גְּדוֹלָה וְלֹא בָרוּחַ יְהוָֹה:

2. Read the Hebrew aloud.

CHAPTER IV. VERBAL SENTENCES. THE SUFFIX CONJUGATION

EXAMPLES

1.	I have not dwelt in a house (II Sam. 7:6).	לֹא יָשַׁבְתִּי בְּבַיִת׃	א.
2.	A prophet has not arisen in Israel like Moses (Deut. 34:10).	לֹא קָם נָבִיא בְּיִשְׂרָאֵל כְּמֹשֶׁה׃	ב.
3.	They will know that a prophet was in the city (Ezek. 2:5).	וְיָדְעוּ כִּי נָבִיא הָיָה בָּעִיר׃	ג.
4.	You will take a wife for Isaac from there (Gen. 24:7).	וְלָקַחְתָּ אִשָּׁה לְיִצְחָק מִשָּׁם׃	ד.
5.	We saw the land and behold (it was) very good (Judg. 18:9).	רָאִינוּ אֶת־הָאָרֶץ וְהִנֵּה טוֹבָה מְאוֹד׃	ה.

ANALYSIS

1. This is a verbal sentence. The verbal form יָשַׁבְתִּי is made up of three distinct elements:

(1) a suffix תִּי- referring to the subject of the sentence ("I");

(2) the root י-שׁ-ב which identifies the verb יָשַׁב "to dwell" (p.116);

(3) the form of the verbal stem -יָשַׁב which in this context (II Sam. 7:6) points to past time (cf. English suffix *-t* in *dwelt*).

There are two basic sets of verbal forms called "conjugations": the *Suffix-Conjugation (SC)*, in which the person of the subject is represented by suffixes, and the *Prefix-Conjugation (PC)* in which it is represented by prefixes (VI). Neither conjugation corresponds exactly to any of the tenses in the English system.

SUFFIX CONJUGATION

On the Hebrew verb system, see Chapter XII.

The conventional citation-form of a Hebrew verb is the *3ms* SC: thus the Hebrew for "to dwell" is יָשַׁב (literally "he dwelt"). Both vowels are normally *-a-* in this form.

2. קָם "he arose, has arisen" is *3ms* SC of the verb קָם "to get up". On monosyllabic verbs like קָם, see Chapter XVII.

The noun נָבִיא "a prophet" is added in extension or clarification of the subject. Such a noun normally comes after the verb.

כְּמֹשֶׁה "like Moses": the preposition -כְּ "like, as" is always attached to its noun (cf. -בְּ and -לְ).

3. וְיָדְעוּ is made up of -וְ "and", and *3pl* SC of the verb יָדַע "to know". וְ + SC points to future time. In this construction *1s* and *2s* suffixes are normally stressed: יָשַׁבְתִּי (cf.1) but וְיָשַׁבְתִּי.

In the suffix conjugation *3fs* and *3pl* suffixes are stressed and the second vowel of the stem reduced to shwa: יָדַע "he knew", but יָדְעוּ "they knew"; יָשַׁב "he sat", but יָשְׁבָה "she sat".

כִּי "that" is a subordinating conjunction after verbs of saying, knowing, hearing, etc. (XIX).

הָיָה is *3ms* SC of the verb הָיָה "to be". Without -וְ "and", SC often points to past time (cf. 1). הָיָה is of the same type as רָאָה in that it ends in a vowel (XVIII).

4. וְלָקַחְתָּ is made up of -וְ "and" and *2ms* SC of the verb לָקַח "to take". -וְ + SC points to future time (cf. 3).

VERBAL SENTENCES

מִשָּׁם is made up of the preposition מִן- "from" and the adverb שָׁם "there, that place". The second consonant of מִן- is usually omitted by assimilation: cf. מִדָּוִד "from David"; מִבֵּית לֶחֶם "from Bethlehem" (XV.3).

5. This sentence is divided in two by the pause marked at הָאָֽרֶץ (p. 6). רָאִ֫ינוּ is *1pl* SC of the verb רָאָה "to see". In verbs of this type, final $\bar{a}$ becomes $\bar{\imath}$ before 1st and 2nd person SC suffixes: cf. רָאִ֫יתִי "I saw"; הָיִ֫ינוּ "we were" (XVIII).

אֶת־הָאָ֫רֶץ "the land" is the *object* of the verb. The verb in a verbal sentence may require an additional expression before it makes sense: e.g. **why did you not send*? requires the addition of an object (*the letter, a messenger*). In Hebrew a grammatical distinction is made between definiteness and indefiniteness in the object of a verb: if the object is definite (II), it is preceded by the particle אֵת : רָאִ֫ינוּ אֶת־הַמֶּ֫לֶךְ "we saw the king". The object is then clearly identifiable in a verbal sentence. Otherwise the object is not marked (לֹא אָמְרוּ דָּבָר "they did not say a word").

הִנֵּה טוֹבָה מְאוֹד is a *quasi-verbal clause*, introduced by one of the quasi-verbals "behold" (X).

SUMMARY

A. In a verbal sentence subject and predicate are both contained in the verbal form. A noun or noun-phrase is often added, usually after the verb, in extension or clarification of the subject.

B. When the object of a verb is definite it is marked by the particle אֶת־. Otherwise it is unmarked.

SUFFIX CONJUGATION

C. There are two conjugations in Hebrew: the Suffix Conjugation and the Prefix Conjugation.

D. -וְ + SC usually points to future time ("Waw Consecutive").

SUFFIX CONJUGATION

SUFFIX	EXAMPLES	REMARKS
-tī *1s* "I"	יָשַׁבְתִּי "I dwelt"	suffix unstressed
-tā *2ms* "you"	רָאִיתָ "you saw"	final *-ā* > *-ī-* (XVIII)
-t *2fs* "you" (fem.)	קַמְתְּ "you (fem. sing.) got up"	*-ā-* > *-a-* (XVII)
-Ø *3ms* "he, it"	בָּרָא "he created"	final aleph silent.
-ā *3fs* "she, it"	נָתְנָה "she gave"	suffix stressed: second vowel reduced to shwa
-nū *1pl* "we"	בָּאנוּ "we came"	suffix unstressed
-tem *2mpl* "you"	יְדַעְתֶּם "you (masc. pl.) knew"	suffix stressed; first vowel reduced to shwa (p.156)
-ten *2fpl* "you" (fem.)	אֲמַרְתֶּן "you (fem. pl.) said"	suffix stressed; first vowel reduced to shwa
-ū *3pl* "they"	לָקְחוּ "they took"	suffix stressed: second vowel reduced to shwa.

VERBAL SENTENCES

VOCABULARY

אֶל־	"to"	לָקַח	"to take"	קָם	"to get up"
בָּא	"to come"	מִדְבָּר	"wilderness"	רָאָה	"to see"
הָיָה	"to be"	מִן־	"from"	שָׁלוֹם	"peace"
יָדַע	"to know"	עָבַד	"to serve"	שָׁמַע	"to hear"
יָצָא	"to go out"	עָלָה	"to go up"	תֹּהוּ וָבֹהוּ	"formless void"

EXERCISES

1. Give the citation-forms and English equivalents of the following: עָבְדָה, שָׁמַעְתָּ, בָּאתִי, וְיָצָא, לָקְחוּ, וְעָלִינוּ.

2. Write in Hebrew and translate:

א. לֹא יָדַעְתִּי:
ב. וְיָצָא מִשָּׁם בְּשָׁלוֹם:
ג. וְהַנָּבִיא בָּא אֶל־הַמֶּלֶךְ:
ד. וַעֲבַדְתֶּם אֶת־יְהוָֹה אֱלֹהִים:
ה. וּבָאוּ וְרָאוּ אֶת־הַבַּיִת הַגָּדוֹל:
ו. וְהִנֵּה רוּחַ גְּדוֹלָה בָּאָה מִן־הַמִּדְבָּר:
ז. רָאִיתִי אֶת־הָאָרֶץ וְהִנֵּה תֹּהוּ וָבֹהוּ:
ח. וְלָקְחוּ אֶת־הָאִישׁ וְהָיָה לְכֹהֵן:
ט. לֹא שָׁמַעְנוּ אֶל־יְהוָֹה אֱלֹהִים:
י. וְקַמְתָּ וְעָלִיתָ אֶל־הָעִיר:

3. Read the Hebrew aloud.

CHAPTER V. THE GENITIVE

EXAMPLES

1. And they will dwell in Jerusalem, the city of holiness (Neh. 11:1).	א. וְיָשְׁבוּ בִּירוּשָׁלַ͏ִם עִיר הַקֹּדֶשׁ׃
2. You have built the house of the Lord, and the house of the king (I Kgs. 9:1).	ב. בָּנִיתָ אֶת־בֵּית יְהוָה וְאֶת־בֵּית הַמֶּלֶךְ׃
3. The word of the Lord is good (II Kgs. 20:19).	ג. טוֹב דְּבַר יְהוָה׃
4. And you shall keep the law of God, which he gave by the hand of Moses (Neh. 10:30).	ד. וְשָׁמַרְתָּ אֶת־תּוֹרַת הָאֱלֹהִים אֲשֶׁר נָתַן בְּיַד מֹשֶׁה׃
5. The name of Abram's wife is Sarai (Gen. 11:29).	ה. שֵׁם אֵשֶׁת אַבְרָם שָׂרָי׃

ANALYSIS

1. The suffix conjugation with -וְ "and" points to future time (IV).

In בִּירוּשָׁלַ͏ִם the preposition -בְּ "in" loses its vowel before -יְ (p. 160).

עִיר הַקֹּדֶשׁ "the city of holiness" is made up of two nouns in the *genitive relationship*. This relationship in English is marked either by the preposition *of* (*the wisdom of Solomon*) or by the suffix *-s'/'s* (*Solomon's wisdom*). In Hebrew the relationship is not marked by a single grammatical feature. Often, as in this example, it is simply a sequence of nouns N_1 + *ha*-N_2, or N_1+ Np:

THE GENITIVE

e.g. יוֹם יְהוָֹה "the day of the Lord". The first term in this structure is called the *pregenitive* (PG). It never takes -הַ, even when it is definite, and is inseparable from the second term: e.g. יוֹם יְהוָֹה הַגָּדוֹל "the great day of the Lord" (the adjective הַגָּדוֹל agrees with PG יוֹם, but cannot break the sequence N_1+Np).

The relationship expressed by the genitive is often one of possession, but not always: in the present example, N_2 describes or qualifies N_1 so that the phrase might be translated "the holy city". The genitive relationship is probably rather more common in Hebrew than it is in English, where adjectives and compound-nouns often take its place: thus עִיר הָאֱמֶת "the faithful city"; סֵפֶר הַתּוֹרָה "the law-book"; רֹאשׁ הַפִּנָּה "the cornerstone"; נִשְׁבְּרֵי לֵב "heartbroken".

2. בָּנִיתָ is *2ms* SC of בָּנָה "to build" (cf. רָאָה: XVIII). The structure of the phrases בֵּית יְהוָֹה (N_1 + N_p) and בֵּית הַמֶּלֶךְ (N_1 + *ha*-N_2) marks them out as expressing a genitive relationship. But there are two other genitive-markers:

(1) the first term is definite, as the particle אֶת- shows, but does not take -הַ (cf. 1 above);

(2) בֵּית "the house of" is the PG form of the noun בַּיִת "house" (citation-form).

Many nouns have no separate PG form in the singular: e.g. עִיר, קוֹל, אִישׁ, and nouns like מֶלֶךְ. But many like בַּיִת have a PG form which involves vowel-reduction (p.161). The commonest nouns of this type (*CáyiC*, *CáweC*), in which the second root-letter is a semi-vowel (p.160), are the following:

אַיִן "nothing" (PG אֵין quasi-verbal: X)
בַּיִת "house" (PG בֵּית)
חַיִל "strength, power" (PG חֵיל)
יַיִן "wine" (PG יֵין)
עַיִן "eye" (PG עֵין)
מָוֶת "death" (PG מוֹת)

V

THE GENITIVE

3. In the phrase דְּבַר יְהוָה "the word of the Lord" the genitive markers are

(1) the structure $N_1 + N_p$,

(2) דְּבַר, the PG form of דָּבָר "word, thing".

In words of this type (*CāCV́C* III.3), the first vowel is reduced to shwa in the PG forms: cf. נָבִיא "prophet" (PG נְבִיא); מָקוֹם "place" (PG מְקוֹם); צָבָא "host, army" (PG צְבָא).

In this example the genitive relationship expresses authorship or origin.

4. The structure of the phrase תּוֹרַת הָאֱלֹהִים (N_1 + *ha*-N_2) marks this phrase as expressing a genitive relationship. In addition תּוֹרַת is the PG form of תּוֹרָה "law". All nouns ending in ָה *(-ā)* (which are feminine: III) have PG forms ending in ת- *(-t)*: cf. שָׁנָה (PG שְׁנַת) "year": חָכְמָה (PG חָכְמַת) "wisdom"; מִצְוָה (PG מִצְוַת) "commandment".

אֲשֶׁר corresponds to the English relative words "who/whom/which" and "that", as well as to the "*wh*-words" in phrases like "the time *when*..", and "the place *where*.." (XIX;XX.4).

In the phrase בְּיַד מֹשֶׁה "by the hand of Moses", the genitive is marked in the same three ways as in תּוֹרַת הָאֱלֹהִים. יַד is the PG form of יָד (vowel-reduction: p.161).

5. In the first phrase, both the first two terms are pregenitives: שֵׁם "the name of" has no separate PG form; but אִשָּׁה "woman, wife" becomes אֵשֶׁת in the PG position. In English both terms are definite ("*the* name of *the* wife of.."). In Hebrew the entire phrase is definite when the last term is definite.

THE GENITIVE

SUMMARY

A. The genitive expresses a relationship between nouns or noun-like words. As well as possession, it may express comparison ("a wild ass of a man": Gen. 16:12), definition ("the land of Egypt"), description ("the city of holiness"), extent ("a day's journey": Jon. 3:4), and the like.

B. The structure N_1 + *ha*-N_2 (or N_1 + N_p) usually indicates a genitive relationship. The two terms are inseparable.

C. The first term in such a relationship is called the Pregenitive (PG) and may be marked in two ways:

(1) PG never takes the prefix -הַ "the" although it is usually definite.

(2) there are special PG forms for many nouns (but not all), notably nouns like דָּבָר, בַּ֫יִת, and תּוֹרָה.
There is a separate PG plural suffix (VII).

PREGENITIVE FORMS IN THE SINGULAR

TYPE	CITATION FORM	PREGENITIVE
בַּ֫יִת	בַּ֫יִת "house"	בֵּית הָאֱלֹהִים "the house of God"
	מָ֫וֶת "death"	מוֹת מֹשֶׁה "the death of Moses"
דָּבָר	דָּבָר "word"	דְּבַר יְהוָה "the word of the Lord"
	נָבִיא "prophet"	נְבִיא יְהוָה "the prophet of the Lord"

THE GENITIVE

TYPE	CITATION FORM		PREGENITIVE	
תּוֹרָה	תּוֹרָה	"law"	תּוֹרַת מֹשֶׁה	"the law of Moses"
	חָכְמָה	"wisdom"	חָכְמַת שְׁלֹמֹה	"the wisdom of Solomon"
	אִשָּׁה	"woman, wife"	אֵשֶׁת אַבְרָהָם	"the wife of Abraham"
מֶ֫לֶךְ	מֶ֫לֶךְ	"king"	מֶלֶךְ יִשְׂרָאֵל	"the king of Israel"
Mono-syllable	עִיר	"city"	עִיר הַקֹּדֶשׁ	"the city of holiness"
	יָד	"hand"	יַד מֹשֶׁה	"the hand of Moses"

VOCABULARY

אֲשֶׁר relative word: "that, which", etc. (XIX)

בֵּן "son"

בָּנָה "to build"

הָלַךְ "to go"

יָד f. "hand"

יוֹם "day"

יָשַׁב "to dwell, sit"

מָ֫וֶת "death"

נָתַן "to give"

עַד- "up to, until"

פְּלִשְׁתִּי "Philistine"

רֹאשׁ "head"

שֵׁם "name"

שָׁנָה f. "year"

תּוֹרָה f. "law, instruction"

EXERCISE

Translate:

א. הָלַךְ בְּתוֹרַת אֱלֹהִים׃

THE GENITIVE

ב. נָתַן יְהוָה אֶת־עַם יִשְׂרָאֵל בְּיַד הַפְּלִשְׁתִּי:

ג. שֵׁם הָאִישׁ אֱלִימֶּלֶךְ וְשֵׁם אֵשֶׁת אֱלִימֶלֶךְ נָעֳמִי:

ד. לֹא נָבִיא אָנֹכִי וְלֹא בֶן־נָבִיא אָנֹכִי:

ה. בָּאוּ אֶל־בֵּית הַנָּבִיא אֲשֶׁר בָּעִיר:

ו. וְיָשַׁב שָׁם עַד־מוֹת הַכֹּהֵן הַגָּדוֹל:

ז. הִנֵּה בָּא יוֹם יְהוָה עַל־עַם יִשְׂרָאֵל:

ח. בִּשְׁנַת מוֹת הַמֶּלֶךְ עֻזִּיָּהוּ רָאִיתִי אֶת־יְהוָה:

ט. עָלָה מֵעִיר דָּוִד אֶל־הַבַּיִת אֲשֶׁר בָּנָה:

י. לָקַח דָּוִד אֶת־רֹאשׁ הַפְּלִשְׁתִּי:

CHAPTER VI. THE PREFIX CONJUGATION. THE IMPERATIVE

EXAMPLES

1.	But the word of the Lord will stand for ever (Isa. 40:8).	וּדְבַר יְהוָה יָקוּם לְעוֹלָם׃	א.
2.	You will dwell in the land of Goshen (Gen. 46:34).	תֵּשְׁבוּ בְּאֶרֶץ גֹּשֶׁן׃	ב.
3.	And he said, "Now you will see what I shall do to Pharaoh" (Ex. 6:1).	וַיֹּאמֶר עַתָּה תִרְאֶה אֲשֶׁר אֶעֱשֶׂה לְפַרְעֹה׃	ג.
4.	And Noah did all that God said (Gen. 6:22).	וַיַּעַשׂ נֹחַ אֶת־כָּל־אֲשֶׁר אָמַר אֱלֹהִים׃	ד.
5.	And Solomon came to Jerusalem and reigned over all Israel (II Chr.1:13).	וַיָּבֹא שְׁלֹמֹה לִירוּשָׁלִַם וַיִּמְלֹךְ עַל־כָּל־יִשְׂרָאֵל׃	ה.
6.	And God said to Jonah "Arise, go to Nineveh" (Jon. 1:2).	וַיֹּאמֶר אֱלֹהִים אֶל־יוֹנָה קוּם לֵךְ אֶל־נִינְוֵה׃	ו.

ANALYSIS

1. In this context (Isaiah 40:8) -וְ is best translated "but" (cf. II.5). On the form -וּ before another consonant with shwa, see p.160.

דְּבַר יְהוָה "the word of the Lord" is a genitive phrase (V). On the abnormal word-order (Subject-Verb), see below on 4.

יָקוּם is the verb in this verbal sentence. It is *3ms* Prefix Conjugation of the verb קָם "to stand". As in the Suffix Conjugation (IV), it is made up of three elements:

(1) a prefix -י referring to the subject.

(2) a root ק-ם which gives the meaning of the particular verb;

(3) a verbal form -קום indicating tense, mood or aspect (XII). In the Prefix Conjugation the person of the subject is determined by a set of *prefix consonants*: -א "I", -ת "you", -י "he, it, they", -ת "she, it", and -נ "we". In the second and third persons the subject is more closely defined by suffixes: -וּ *mpl*(or -וּן, -ןְ) -נָה *fpl*, and -ִי *2fs*. (Out of context there is ambiguity between *2ms* and *3fs*, and between *2fpl* and *3fpl* because they are identical in form). The *prefix-vowel* varies according to stem (X) and verb-type (XI). In verbs of the type קָם (XVII) it is *-ā-* : cf. אָמוּת "I will die", תָּבוֹא "you will come".

This PC form is best considered an integral part of the citation-form of each verb (as it is in the Hebrew-English vocabulary), and memorized along with the conventional SC form : thus יָקוּם/קָם "to stand"; יֵשֵׁב/יָשַׁב "to dwell"; יֹאמַר/אָמַר "to say".

2. תֵּשְׁבוּ is *2mpl* PC of the verb יָשַׁב "to dwell, sit". In the PC of five common verbs beginning with י and הָלַךְ "to go" the first root-letter, which is a semi-vowel (p. 160), combines with the prefix-vowel to become *-ē-*; the second vowel is also *-ē-* (XVI).

Before the suffixes *-ī* (*2fs*) and *-ū* (*2mpl, 3mpl*) the second vowel is reduced (p. 161): e.g. יֵשֵׁב "he will dwell", but יֵשְׁבוּ "they will dwell".

3. וַיֹּאמֶר is made up of -וַ "and", the *3ms* PC prefix י "he" and the verb אָמַר "to say".

אָמַר is one of three common verbs beginning with א in which the prefix vowel is *-ō-* and the א is not pronounced. The other two are אָבַד "to die, to perish" and אָכַל "to eat" (XII).

PREFIX CONJUGATION

וַיֹּאמֶר illustrates a very important feature of Hebrew narrative style: -וַ + *PC points to past time*. The prefix consonant is doubled, and the prefix stressed with reduction of the unstressed syllable: e.g. יֹאמַר "he will say" but וַיֹּאמֶר *va-yṓmer* "and he said": יָקוּם "it will stand" but וַיָּקָם *va-yā́kom* "and it stood". (Vowel-reduction: p. 161).

תִּרְאֶה is *2ms* PC of רָאָה "to see". Verbs of this type (XVIII) have only two root-letters and end in a vowel. In the prefix tense the prefix vowel is *-i-* and the second vowel is *-e*. The second vowel, however, is lost before the suffixes *-ī* and *-ū* , and in the prefix-stressed forms with -וַ (p. 161).

A pause before the noun clause "what I shall do..." is marked at תִּרְאֶה.

אֶעֱשֶׂה is *1s* PC of עָשָׂה "to make, do". It is similar to רָאָה in type. Verbs beginning with ע, however, have other characteristics (XII).

4. וַיַּעַשׂ (like וַיֹּאמֶר in the previous example) is made up of -וַ "and", the *3ms* prefix -יַ *(ya-)* "he" and the verb עָשָׂה "to do". After -וַ the prefix consonant is doubled, the prefix is stressed, and in verbs of the type רָאָה the second vowel is lost (cf. 3). According to the rule that -וַ + PC points to past time, this is translated "and he did". The word-order in verbal sentences is normally Verb-Subject.

אָמַר is *3ms* SC of the verb אָמַר "to say". It points to past time here.

5. וַיָּבֹא from בָּא "to come" is made up of the same elements as וַיֹּאמֶר and וַיַּעַשׂ, and points to past time (3). בָּא is a monosyllabic verb like קָם (XVII).

The sentence is divided into two clauses by a minor pause at לִירוּשָׁלָם. On the spelling of לִירוּשָׁלָם "to Jerusalem" see p.160.

וַיִּמְלֹךְ is *3ms* PC of the verb מָלַךְ "to rule" with -וַ "and", and points to past time. Verbs of the type שָׁמַר have prefix vowel *-i-* (*-e-* in *1s*) and second vowel *-ō-* (XI).

כָּל־ *-(kol)* "all, every" is normally joined to its noun by a hyphen (p.5).

6. On וַיֹּאמֶר see 3 above.
A pause before the command is marked at יוֹנָה.

קוּם is the *ms* imperative of קָם "to arise" (XVII). Commands to the second person are expressed by the *imperative*. In Hebrew this "mood" (XIII) is marked in the verb by a set of imperative forms, which consist of the four second person PC forms *without the prefixes*: e.g. תָּקוּם "you will get up" as opposed to קוּם "get up!" (imperative); תֵּלֵךְ "you will go" as opposed to לֵךְ "go!" (imperative); תִּרְאוּ "you will see" as opposed to רְאוּ "see!" (imperative).

לֵךְ is similarly the *ms* imperative of הָלַךְ "to go" (XVI).

SUMMARY

A. In the Prefix Conjugation the person of the subject is determined by a set of prefix consonants.

B. -וַ + PC points to past time ("Waw Consecutive").

C. In the second person, PC without the prefixes expresses commands (imperative).

PREFIX CONJUGATION.

PREFIXES			EXAMPLES		VERB-TYPE	
1s	א__	*V*__	אָמוּת	"I shall die"	מֵת	XVII
2ms	תּ__	*t*__	תִּרְאֶה	"you will see"	רָאָה	XVIII
2fs	(ִ__ין) תּ__ִי	*t*__*ī*(*n*)	תֵּשְׁבִי	"you will dwell"	יָשַׁב	XVI
3ms	י__	*y*__	יֹאמַר	"he will say"	אָמַר	XII
3fs	תּ__	*t*__	תִּתֵּן	"she will give"	נָתַן	XIV
1pl	נ__	*n*__	נֵלֵךְ	"we shall go"	הָלַךְ	XVI
2mpl	(__וּ, __ֻן) תּ__וּ	*t*__*ū*(*n*)	תָּבוֹאוּ	"you will come"	בָּא	XVII
2fpl	תּ__נָה	*t*__*nā*	תֹּאמַ֫רְנָה	"you will say"	אָמַר	XII
3mpl	(__וּ, __ֻן) י__וּ	*y*__*ū*(*n*)	יִמְלְכוּ	"they will rule"	מָלַךְ	XI
3fpl	תּ__נָה	*t*__*nā*	תִּשְׁמַ֫עְנָה	"they will hear"	שָׁמַע	XIII

THE IMPERATIVE

SUFFIXES			EXAMPLES		VERB-TYPE	
ms	–	__ø	שְׁמַע	"hear"	שָׁלַח	XIII
fs	ִי-	__*ī*	לְכִי	"go"	יָשַׁב	XVI
mpl	וּ-	__*ū*	רְאוּ	"see"	רָאָה	XVIII
fpl	-נָה	__*nā*	שֹׁ֫בְנָה	"go back"	קָם	XVII

IMPERATIVE

VOCABULARY

אָמַר	"to say"	מַמְלָכָה	f. "kingdom, rule"	עַתָּה	"now"
אֲנַ֫חְנוּ	"we"	מֹשֶׁה	"Moses"	פַּרְעֹה	"Pharaoh"
הַר	"mountain"	מֵת	"to die"	קוֹל	"voice, sound"
כָּבוֹד	"glory"	עָמַד	"to stand"	שָׁב	"to return"
כָּל־	"all, every"	עָשָׂה	"to make, do"	שְׁלֹמֹה	"Solomon"

EXERCISES

1. Give the citation-form of the following:

וַיִּתְּנוּ, תֵּשֵׁב, נָבוֹא, וַתִּרְאוּ, יַעֲלוּ, תֵּלְכוּ, וַיֹּאמֶר.

2. Translate:

א. וַיֹּאמֶר אֱלֹהִים אֶל־מֹשֶׁה אֶהְיֶה אֲשֶׁר אֶהְיֶה:

ב. עַתָּה תִרְאוּ אֶת־כָּל־אֲשֶׁר אֶעֱשֶׂה לְפַרְעֹה:

ג. וַיַּעַל מֹשֶׁה אֶל־הַר הָאֱלֹהִים:

ד. עַתָּה תָּשׁוּב הַמַּמְלָכָה לְבֵית דָּוִד:

ה. שְׁמַע בְּקוֹל הָעָם לְכָל־אֲשֶׁר יֹאמְרוּ:

ו. וַיָּקָם וַיֵּצֵא מִשָּׁם וַיָּבֹא אֶל־הָאִישׁ:

ז. וַאֲנַחְנוּ נֵלֵךְ בְּשֵׁם יְהוָה אֱלֹהִים:

ח. וַיַּעַל כְּבוֹד יְהוָה מִן־הָעִיר וַיַּעֲמֹד עַל־הָהָר:

ט. וַיִּבֶן שְׁלֹמֹה אֶת־הַבָּיִת:

י. וְעַתָּה שׁוּב וְלֵךְ בְּשָׁלוֹם:

CHAPTER VII. SINGULAR AND PLURAL. THE DUAL. DEMONSTRATIVES.

EXAMPLES

1. These are the things which you will do on that day (Zech. 8:16).	א. אֵלֶּה הַדְּבָרִים אֲשֶׁר תַּעֲשׂוּ בַּיּוֹם הַהוּא:
2. And you will dwell in great and good cities which you did not build (Deut. 6:10).	ב. וְיָשַׁבְתָּ בְּעָרִים גדולות וְטוֹבוֹת אֲשֶׁר לֹא בָנִיתָ:
3. Fathers will not die on account of (their) sons (II Kgs. 14:6).	ג. לֹא יָמוּתוּ אָבוֹת עַל-בָּנִים:
4. And he walked in the way of the kings of Israel (II Kgs. 8:18).	ד. וַיֵּלֶךְ בְּדֶרֶךְ מַלְכֵי יִשְׂרָאֵל:
5. The voice is the voice of Jacob, but the hands are the hands of Esau (Gen. 27:22).	ה. הַקּוֹל קוֹל יַעֲקֹב וְהַיָּדַיִם יְדֵי עֵשָׂו:

ANALYSIS

1. הַדְּבָרִים אֵלֶּה "these are the things" is a verbless sentence (II) in which the demonstrative pronoun אֵלֶּה "these" is the subject. There are two sets of demonstratives in Hebrew. They function both as pronouns and as adjectives. As pronouns they agree in number and gender with the noun they refer to: thus אֵלֶּה is the masculine plural form of the demonstrative זֶה "this", referring to הַדְּבָרִים "the things".

דְּבָרִים is the plural form of the noun דָּבָר "word, thing". ־ִים -*īm* is one of three suffixes by which a plural noun is marked.

DEMONSTRATIVES

Most nouns, and all adjectives with this plural suffix are masculine. The suffix is stressed and in nouns of this type (*CāCVC*: III.3) the long vowel in the first syllable is reduced: e.g. דָּבָר "word", but דְּבָרִים "words".

תַּעֲשׂוּ is *2mpl* PC of the verb עָשָׂה "to make, do".

The phrase בַּיּוֹם הַהוּא "on that day" illustrates the second function of the demonstratives. The demonstrative הַהוּא "that" functions as an adjective here, coming after its noun and agreeing with it in number, gender and definiteness. הוּא, הִיא etc. are identical in form with the third person pronouns (cf. III), but as demonstrative adjectives they always have the definite prefix: e.g. הוּא הַיּוֹם "that (it) is the day", but הַיּוֹם הַהוּא "that day".

2. -וְ + SC points to future time (IV).

עָרִים is the plural of עִיר f. "city" (cf. *-ā-* in בָּנִים "sons" from בֵּן and יָמִים "days" from יוֹם). עָרִים is feminine in spite of the plural suffix -ִים (cf. 1).

גְּדוֹלוֹת "great" and טוֹבוֹת "good" are feminine, plural and indefinite, agreeing with עָרִים "cities". With the plural suffix -וֹת *-ōt*, many nouns and all adjectives are feminine. The suffix takes the place of the feminine singular suffix -ָה *-ā* (III): e.g. תּוֹרָה "law", plural תּוֹרוֹת.

בָּנִיתָ "you built" is *2ms* SC of the verb בָּנָה "to build" (cf. רָאָה : XVIII).

3. אָבוֹת is the plural of אָב "father". Some masculine nouns take the plural suffix -וֹת : cf. שֵׁמוֹת "names" from שֵׁם ; קוֹלוֹת "voices"

from קוֹל; מְקוֹמוֹת "places" from מָקוֹם.

בָּנִים is the plural of בֵּן "son". cf. 2.

4. -וַ + PC points to past time (VI). יֵלֶךְ is *3ms* PC of the verb הָלַךְ "to go". The first root-letter in this type of verb (cf. יָשַׁב: XVI) is omitted in the Prefix Conjugation.

מַלְכֵי "the kings of" is the pregenitive plural of מֶלֶךְ "king". -ֵי -*ē* (like the final vowel in *today*: p. 154) is the last of the three plural suffixes, and occurs only in the PG position. Most nouns with this suffix are masculine. There is no special PG plural suffix for feminine nouns.

In nouns of the type *CéCeC* (like מֶלֶךְ) (p. 12) the addition of this stressed suffix brings about vowel changes:
(1) the first vowel becomes *-a-*, *-i-* or *-o-* (חֵלֶק "portion" is an exception: PG plural חֶלְקֵי); (2) the other vowel is shwa:

דֶּרֶךְ	"way"	דַּרְכֵי	"the ways of ..." (a)
זֶבַח	"sacrifice"	זִבְחֵי	"the sacrifices of ..." (i)
אֹהֶל	"tent"	אָהֳלֵי	"the tents of ..."(o)

5. The two halves of this sentence are divided by the pause marked at יַעֲקֹב. The predicate (קוֹל יַעֲקֹב "the voice of Jacob") is definite, but קוֹל is without -הַ, because it is in the pregenitive position (p. 34).

יָדַיִם is composed of the feminine noun יָד "hand" and the dual suffix -ַיִם *-áyim*. In addition to singular and plural forms, a few nouns, most of them denoting pairs of things, take dual forms (e.g. יָדַיִם "hands"; עֵינַיִם "eyes"). Verbs and adjectives associated with these forms are in the plural.

THE DUAL

The PG dual form is identical with that of the PG plural: thus יְדֵי עֵשָׂו "the (two) hands of Esau", beside יְדֵי אַנְשֵׁי הַמִּלְחָמָה "the (many more than two) hands of the soldiers". (Jer. 38:4).

SUMMARY

A. Demonstratives function both as pronouns (in particular as subject of a sentence) and as adjectives.

זֶה "this" — הוּא "that"

	Masc.	Fem.
Sing.	זֶה "this"	זֹאת "this"
Plur.	אֵלֶּה "these"	

	Masc.	Fem.
Sing.	הוּא "that"	הִיא "that"
Plur.	הֵם "those"	הֵן "those"

B. The plural is marked by three suffixes:

(1) masculine plural ִ-ים *(-īm)*

(2) feminine plural -וֹת *(-ōt)*

(3) pregenitive plural (masculine) ֵ-י *(-ē)*

They are all stressed. Many masculine nouns take the *fpl* suffix; a few feminine nouns take the *mpl* and PG *pl* suffixes. The feminine singular suffixes ָ-ה, ֶ-ת, etc. are omitted before plural suffixes.

C. The dual is marked by the suffix ַ-יִם *-áyim* (with feminine nouns in *-a*: ָ-תַיִם *-ātáyim*). It is rare in Hebrew, the numeral שְׁתַּיִם "two" being preferred in most cases (XVII).

SINGULAR AND PLURAL

PLURAL AND DUAL FORMS

MASCULINE NOUNS

	Suffix	דָּבָר "word"	מֶ֫לֶךְ "king"	יוֹם "day"	אָב "father"
Plural	־ִים -*īm*	דְּבָרִים	מְלָכִים	יָמִים	
	־וֹת -*ōt*				אָבוֹת
Dual	־ַ֫יִם -*áyim*			יוֹמַ֫יִם	
Pregenitive Plural	־ֵי -*ē*	דִּבְרֵי	מַלְכֵי	יְמֵי	
	־וֹת -*ōt*			(יְמוֹת)	אֲבוֹת

FEMININE NOUNS

	Suffix	תּוֹרָה "law"	שָׁנָה "year"	עִיר "city"	יָד "hand"
Plural	־וֹת -*ōt*	תּוֹרוֹת	(שָׁנוֹת)		(יָדוֹת)
	־ִים -*īm*		שָׁנִים	עָרִים	
Dual	־ָתַ֫יִם *ātáyim*		שְׁנָתַ֫יִם		
	־ַ֫יִם -*áyim*				יָדַ֫יִם
Pregenitive Plural	־וֹת -*ōt*	תּוֹרוֹת	שְׁנוֹת		(יְדוֹת)
	־ֵי -*ē*		שְׁנֵי	עָרֵי	יְדֵי

VII

DEMONSTRATIVES

VOCABULARY

אַחֲרֵי	"after, behind"	זֶה, זֹאת	"this"	מִצְוָה	f. "commandment"
אֵ֫לֶּה	"these"	חֶ֫סֶד	"love, loyalty"	מִצְרַ֫יִם	"Egypt"
אַתֶּם	"you (pl)"	כָּרַת	"to cut"	רַב	"much, many"
בֹּ֫קֶר	"morning"	כָּרַת בְּרִית	"to make a covenant"	שָׁלַח	"to send"
בְּרִית	f. "covenant"	לִפְנֵי	"before, in front of"	שָׁמַר	"to keep"
הֵם	"they, those"				

EXERCISES

1. Put into the singular:

שְׁנָתַ֫יִם, רַבִּים, הָאֵ֫לֶּה, מִצְוֹות, אֲרָצוֹת, שָׁנִים, אָבוֹת.

2. Translate into English:

א. שִׁמְעוּ אֶת־דִּבְרֵי הַבְּרִית הַזֹּאת׃

ב. אֵ֫לֶּה שְׁמוֹת הָאֲנָשִׁים אֲשֶׁר שָׁלַח מֹשֶׁה אֶל־הָאָ֫רֶץ׃

ג. הִנֵּה שָׁמַ֫עְנוּ כִּי מַלְכֵי בֵּית יִשְׂרָאֵל מַלְכֵי חֶ֫סֶד הֵם׃

ד. וַיְהִי בַבֹּ֫קֶר וַיֵּצֵא וַיַּעֲמֹד וַיֹּ֫אמֶר אֶל־כָּל־הָעָם צַדִּיקִים אַתֶּם׃

ה. יֵדְעוּ כָּל־עַמֵּי הָאָ֫רֶץ אֶת־יַד יְהוָה׃

ו. קְדֹשִׁים תִּהְי֫וּ כִּי קָדוֹשׁ אָ֫נִי׃

ז. אַחֲרֵי שָׁנִים רַבּוֹת תֵּצְאוּ מִמִּצְרַ֫יִם וּמִבֵּית עֲבָדִים׃

ח. תַּעֲשׂוּ אֶת־כָּל־הַמִּצְוֹות הָאֵ֫לֶּה אֲשֶׁר נָתַן יְהוָה לְמֹשֶׁה׃

ט. וַיִּכְרֹת הַמֶּ֫לֶךְ אֶת־הַבְּרִית לִפְנֵי יְהוָה׃

י. זֹאת הַבְּרִית אֲשֶׁר תִּשְׁמְרוּ׃

CHAPTER VIII. SUFFIX PRONOUNS

EXAMPLES

1. And he heard my voice from his temple (Ps. 18:7).	וַיִּשְׁמַע מֵהֵיכָלוֹ קוֹלִי׃	א.
2. And you will rejoice in all the goodness which the Lord your God has given you and your household (Deut. 26:11).	וְשָׂמַחְתָּ בְכָל־הַטּוֹב אֲשֶׁר נָתַן לְךָ יְהוָה אֱלֹהֶיךָ וּלְבֵיתֶךָ׃	ב.
3. Their king will pass on before them, the Lord at their head (Mic. 2:13).	יַעֲבֹר מַלְכָּם לִפְנֵיהֶם וַיהוָה בְּרֹאשָׁם׃	ג.
4. The Lord is my god and the rock of my salvation (Ps. 89:27).	יְהוָה אֱלֹהַי וְצוּר יְשֻׁעָתִי׃	ד.
5. Because you are my kinsman, should you therefore serve me for nothing? (Gen.29:15).	הֲכִי אָחִי אַתָּה וַעֲבַדְתַּנִי חִנָּם׃	ה.
6. And he was no more, because God had taken him away (Gen. 5:24).	וְאֵינֶנּוּ כִּי לָקַח אֹתוֹ אֱלֹהִים׃	ו.

ANALYSIS

1. הֵיכָלוֹ "his temple" consists of two elements: the noun הֵיכָל "temple" and the *3ms* suffix pronoun וֹ- *(-ō)* "his, him". Similarly קוֹלִי "my voice" is made up of the noun קוֹל "voice" and the *1s* suffix pronoun ־ִי *(-ī)* "my, me". These two elements are in a kind of genitive relationship ("the temple of him", "the voice of me"); but in English correspond to adjectival phrases ("his temple", "my voice"). For the omission of the object-marker אֶת־ with קוֹלִי, see Chapter XVI on poetic style.

SUFFIX PRONOUNS

2. לְךָ "to you" is made up of the preposition -לְ "to" and the *2ms* suffix pronoun ךָ- *(-χā)* "your, you". When they are attached to prepositions, the suffix pronouns correspond to pronouns in English.

אֱלֹהֶיךָ "your god": the same *2ms* suffix pronoun is attached to a plural form אֱלֹהִים. In the plural, suffix pronouns are attached to a PG form. The connecting vowel is not always *-ē-*, but varies according to the suffix (Table). The PG plural vowel-letter י (cf. V), however, is constant in all plural forms with suffix pronouns and is usually stressed (not in *2pl* and *3pl*).

וּלְבֵיתֶךָ "and to your household" is made up of -וְ "and" (*ū* before a shwa: p. 159), -לְ "to", בֵית the PG form of בַּיִת "house", with the *2ms* suffix ךָ- *-χā* "your".

The stressed connecting vowel *-e-* before the suffix is a phonetic variant required before the main pause (p.157).

3. The main clause is separated from the circumstantial clause (XIX) by the pause marked at לִפְנֵיהֶם.

מַלְכָּם "their king" consists of the noun מֶלֶךְ "king" and the *3mpl* suffix pronoun ָם- *-ām*. Nouns like מֶלֶךְ do not normally have a special PG form in the singular, but before the suffix pronouns, the two vowels of the citation-form are reduced to one: מֶלֶךְ "king" beside מַלְכִּי "my king"; עֶבֶד "servant" beside עַבְדְּךָ "your servant". The vowel in these forms is usually *-a-*, but often *-i-* and occasionally *-o-* (cf. p.45). Notice the inner dot in the third root-letter: מַלְכִּי *malkī* "my king" as opposed to PG מַלְכֵי *malχē* "kings of" (VII. 4).

SUFFIX PRONOUNS

לִפְנֵיהֶם "before them" is made up of the preposition לִפְנֵי "before" and the *3mpl* suffix pronoun הֶם- *-hem*. The *3pl* suffixes have two forms: (1) ָם- *-ām*, ָן- *-ān* attached to singular forms (cf. רֹאשָׁם, מַלְכָּם), and (2) הֶם- *-hem*, הֶן- *-hen* attached to plural forms (לִפְנֵיהֶם). Both forms are stressed.

רֹאשׁ "head" has no special PG form in the singular.

4. אֱלֹהַי "my god" is similar in form to אֱלֹהֶיךָ "your god" in 2 above, but the connecting vowel is *-a-*, instead of *-e-*. This vowel connects the *1s*, *2fs* and *3ms* suffixes to plural forms (Table): cf. אֱלֹהַיִךְ "your (*fs*) god"; אֱלֹהָיו "his god" (pronounced *e-lō-hāv*).

יְשֻׁעָתִי "my salvation" consists of the PG form of יְשׁוּעָה "salvation" (cf. V. 4) with the *1s* suffix pronoun ִי- *-ī* "my". The vowel in the prestress syllable is lengthened (p. 156); thus יְשֻׁעַת "the salvation of (PG form)", but יְשֻׁעָתוֹ "his salvation".

The relationship between a noun and its suffix pronoun is not always one of possession (cf. the Genitive: V). In יְשֻׁעָתִי, for example, the suffix refers to the object of a verb implied by the noun: I am the object of the saving act of which God, the "Rock", is subject.

5. הֲכִי "is it because...?" consists of the interrogative prefix -הֲ *ha-* and the conjunction כִּי "because" (XIX). A sentence is made into a question by prefixing -הֲ to the first word. There is no change in word-order as there is in English (XI).

The two clauses are separated by the pause at אָתָּה (note change of stress in pausal form: p. 157).

SUFFIX PRONOUNS

אָח "brother", like אָב "father", apparently has no special PG singular form before the *1s* suffix pronoun ־ִי. Before all the other singular suffixes and *1pl* suffix, however, the PG forms אֲבִי- and אֲחִי- occur.

וַעֲבַדְתַּ֫נִי "and you will serve me": ־ְו "and" (*va-* before compound shwa: p. 159) with Suffix Conjugation points to future time (IV); the *2ms* suffix ־תָ "you" refers to the subject of the verb עָבַד "to serve"; and the *1s* pronoun ־נִי *-nī* "me" to the object. Attached to verbs, some of the suffix pronouns have variant forms: where a connecting vowel is required, it is *-a-* in SC and *-e-* in PC (Table).

On the conjunction ־ְו between subordinate and main clauses, see Chapter XIX.

6. וְאֵינֶ֫נּוּ is made up of ־ְו "and", the quasi-verbal אֵין "there is not" (X), and ־ֶ֫נּוּ *-énū*, a variant form of the *3ms* suffix pronoun. The n-form of the singular suffix pronouns occurs with certain verb forms, the quasi-verbals and the preposition ־מִן "from": cf. יִשְׁמָעֲךָ֫ "he will hear you"; הִנֶּ֫נּוּ "behold him"; מִמֶּ֫נִּי "from me". A pause before the subordinate clause is marked at אֵינֶ֫נּוּ.

אֹתוֹ consists of the definite object-marker ־אֶת with the *3ms* suffix pronoun ־וֹ. Before all the suffixes except *2mpl* and *2fpl*, ־אֶת becomes ־אֹת.

SUMMARY

A. Suffix Pronouns attached to nouns correspond to possessive adjectives in English ("my", "your", "his" etc.). With these suffixes some nouns have a special form in the singular closely resembling the PG form; in the plural and dual, masculine

PRONOMINAL SUFFIXES (THE COMMONEST FORMS)

SUFFIX			NOUNS		VERBS (AND QUASI-VERBALS)	PREPOSITIONS
			SINGULAR	PLURAL		
1s	־ִי	*-ī*	רֹאשִׁי "my head"	אֱלֹהַי "my God"		לִי "to me"
	־נִי	*-nī*			יְקָחֵנִי "he took me"	
	־ֶנִּי	*-énī*			אֵינֶנִּי "I am not"	
2ms	־ךָ	*-χā*	בֵּיתְךָ "your house"	בָּנֶיךָ "your sons"	רְאִיתִיךָ "I saw you"	לְךָ "to you"
	־ֶךָּ	*-ékā*			אַיֶּכָּה "where are you?"	מִמְּךָ "from you"
2fs	־ךְ	*-χ*	מַלְכֵּךְ "your king"	בְּנוֹתַיִךְ "your daughters"	יַצִּילוּךְ "they will deliver you"	בָּךְ "in you"
3ms	־וֹ	*-ō*	תּוֹרָתוֹ "his law"		יְדָעוֹ "he knows him"	בּוֹ "in him"
	־הוּ	*-hū*	אָבִיהוּ "his father"		יִמְצָאֵהוּ "he found him"	כָּמֹהוּ "like him"
	־ו	*-v*	אָבִיו "his father"	עֲבָדָיו "his servants" (*avādāv*)	יְדַעְתִּיו "I know him"	
	־ֶנּוּ	*-énū*			אֵינֶנּוּ "he is not"	מִמֶּנּוּ "from him"
3fs	־ָהּ	*-ā*	אִישָׁהּ "her husband"		בְּרָאָהּ "he created her"	לָהּ "to her"
	־הָ	*-hā*	אָחִיהָ "her brother"	פָּנֶיהָ "her face"	רְאִיתִיהָ "I saw her"	עָלֶיהָ "on her"
1pl	־נוּ	*-nū*	קוֹלֵנוּ "our voice"	יָדֵינוּ "our hands"	עָזְרֵנוּ "help us"	לָנוּ "to us"
2mpl	־כֶם	*-χem*	קוֹלְכֶם "your voice"	אֲבֹתֵיכֶם "your fathers"		לָכֶם "to you"
2fpl	־כֶן	*-χen*	אֲבִיכֶן "your father"	עֵינֵיכֶן "your eyes"		לָכֶן "to you"
3mpl	־ם	*-m*	עֲוֹנָם "their sin"		יוֹשִׁיעֵם "he saved them"	בָּם "in them"
	־הֶם	*-hem*		יְדֵיהֶם "their hands"		לָהֶם "to them"
3fpl	־ן	*-n*	קוֹלָן "their voice"			
	־הֶן	*-hen*		אֱלֹהֵיהֶן "their god"		לָהֶן "to them"

and feminine, all nouns have the PG plural vowel-letter י.

B. Attached to verbs and prepositions, the suffix pronouns function like English personal pronouns "me, you, him" etc. A verb may have two suffixes, the first one referring to the subject (Suffix Conjugation forms: IV), the second to the object (C. below).

C. If the object of a verb is a pronoun, it is represented by suffix pronouns, attached either directly to the verb, or to the definite object-marker אֹת־/אֶת־.

VOCABULARY

אָב	"father"	כֹּה	"so, thus"	נָפַל	"to fall"
אַבְרָהָם	"Abraham"	כָּתַב	"to write"	נָשָׂא	"to lift, carry"
בַּת	f. "daughter"	לֵבָב (לֵב)	" heart"	סֵפֶר	"book"
-הֲ	mark of interrogation (XI)	מָה	"what?"	עַיִן	f. "eye, spring"
יוֹסֵף	"Joseph"	מָקוֹם	"place"	קָרָא	"to call"

EXERCISES

Translate:

א. אֶקְרָא לֵאלֹהִים יִשְׁלַח מִשָּׁמַיִם יִשְׁלַח אֱלֹהִים חַסְדּוֹ:

ב. תֹּאמְרוּ לְיוֹסֵף אֲנַחְנוּ עֲבָדֶיךָ תִּקַּח (לָקַח) אֹתָנוּ אֶל־בֵּיתֶךָ:

ג. מָה תִּתֵּן (נָתַן) לִי:

ד. הִנֵּה יִפְּלוּ (נָפַל) כָּל־מַלְכֵי הָאָרֶץ לְפָנָיו וְהוּא יֹאמַר לָהֶם שָׁלוֹם:

ה. וַאֲמַרְתֶּם לְבָנֶיךָ וְלִבְנוֹתֶיךָ וְהֵם יִשְׁמְרוּ אֶת־כָּל־מִצְוֹתָי:

ו. אֶת־כָּל־אֲשֶׁר תִּכְתֹּב בַּסֵּפֶר נִשְׁמֹר בְּכָל־לְבָבֵנוּ:

ז. כֹּה תֹאמַר אֶל־בְּנֵי יִשְׂרָאֵל יְהוָה אֱלֹהֵי אֲבוֹתֵיכֶם שְׁלָחַנִי אֲלֵיכֶם:

ח. וַיִּשָּׂא (נָשָׂא) אַבְרָהָם אֶת־עֵינָיו וַיַּרְא אֶת־הַמָּקוֹם:

ט. הֲלֹא כָל־הָאָרֶץ לְפָנֶיךָ:

י. וּשְׁלַחְתֶּם בְּיָדָם אֵלַי כָּל־דָּבָר אֲשֶׁר תִּשְׁמָעוּ:

CHAPTER IX. PARTICIPLES. VERBAL NOUNS.

EXAMPLES

1.	The man who did this deserves to die (II Sam. 12:5).	בֶּן־מָוֶת הָאִישׁ הָעֹשֶׂה זֹאת׃	א.
2.	Blessed be he who comes in the name of the Lord (Ps. 118:26).	בָּרוּךְ הַבָּא בְּשֵׁם יְהוָה׃	ב.
3.	The Lord preserves all who love him (Ps 145:20).	שׁוֹמֵר יְהוָה אֶת־כָּל־אֹהֲבָיו׃	ג.
4.	It is not good that the man should be alone (Gen. 2:18).	לֹא־טוֹב הֱיוֹת הָאָדָם לְבַדּוֹ׃	ד.
5.	Will you build me a house to dwell in? (II Sam. 7:5).	הַאַתָּה תִּבְנֶה־לִּי בַיִת לְשִׁבְתִּי׃	ה.
6.	And the waters gradually ebbed from the earth (Gen. 8:3).	וַיָּשֻׁבוּ הַמַּיִם מֵעַל־הָאָרֶץ הָלוֹךְ וָשׁוֹב׃	ו.

ANALYSIS

1. בֶּן־מָוֶת "a son of death" is an idiom best translated "deserving death": cf. בֶּן־שָׁנָה "one year old"; בֶּן־אָדָם "son of man, a member of the human race".

הָעֹשֶׂה is the *active participle* of the verb עָשָׂה "to do, make" with definite prefix -הַ "the". The characteristic vowel of the active participle is -ō- in the first syllable.

There are two participles in Hebrew, an active participle and a passive participle. In form these are noun-like: gender, number, definiteness and the genitive relationship are marked in the same way as in the noun (cf. adjectives). The active participle, however, is sometimes also verb-like. In the present example הָעֹשֶׂה is masculine singular and definite, agreeing like an adjective with הָאִישׁ "the man", but it is verb-like also, in having a direct object, namely, the demonstrative pronoun זֹאת "this". It is usually helpful to translate active participles, in the first instance, as nouns in *-er*: הָעוֹשֶׂה "the doer (of this)".

Tense is unmarked in the participle: in this context it points to past time (II Sam. 12:5).

2. בָּרוּךְ is a passive participle. The rounded vowel *-ū-* in the second syllable is the chief characteristic of a passive participle (cf. the passive "rounded stems": X.6).

בָּרוּךְ functions as the predicate of a verbless sentence, agreeing in number and gender with the subject הַבָּא. Tense and mood are unmarked (cf. 1) but the context suggests a prayer for the future (Ps. 118:26).

בָּא is the *ms* active participle of the verb בָּא "to come" (XVII). The *ms* active participle of verbs of the type קָם is identical with the citation-form of the verb. They have no passive participle.

הַבָּא is noun-like ("the comer") in that it is masculine, singular and definite, and functions as subject of the sentence; it is verb-like in being accompanied by the adverbial expression בְּשֵׁם יְהוָֹה "in the name of the Lord". Tense is unmarked.

3. שׁוֹמֵר is the active participle of the verb שָׁמַר "to keep, watch". It is noun-like ("keeper, preserver") and functions as predicate

of a verbless sentence with the subject יְהוָה, and verb-like in having a direct object (אֶת־כָּל־אֹהֲבָיו). The statement is intended to hold good for all time (Ps. 145:20), and corresponds to an English present tense.

אֹהֲבָיו is the *mpl* active participle of the stative verb אָהֵב "to love" (XV), with the *3ms* suffix pronoun ו- "him, his". It is noun-like ("lovers of him") in function as well as in form, being object of שׁוֹמֵר. The suffix pronoun refers to יְהוָה, the object of the verb אָהֵב. This construction is normally represented in English by a subordinate clause: "those who love him".

4. לֹא טוֹב is the predicate of this verbless sentence. The subject is the phrase הֱיוֹת הָאָדָם לְבַדּוֹ.

הֱיוֹת is a verbal noun from הָיָה "to be". It functions like an English gerund (form with suffix *-ing*). It is both noun-like in being in a genitive relationship to הָאָדָם, and verb-like in being accompanied by the adverbial phrase לְבַדּוֹ. In other words the phrase might be translated "the being alone of the man".

The suffix וֹת- is characteristic of PG verbal nouns from verbs of the type רָאָה (XVIII): cf. רְאוֹת from רָאָה, עֲשׂוֹת from עָשָׂה. The first vowel in these forms is normally shwa (Table).

5. -הֲ is the interrogative prefix (XI). The independent pronoun אַתָּה emphasises the subject of the verb תִּבְנֶה "Will you build ...?" (XX).

לְשִׁבְתִּי is the verbal noun from יָשַׁב "to dwell", with the preposition לְ "for, to" and the *1s* suffix pronoun ִי- "me, my". The suffix refers to the subject of the verb (cf. 2): "for my dwelling, for me to dwell in".

The characteristics of PG verbal nouns from this type of verb (XVI) and some others are the loss of the first root-letter, the suffix ת ֶ and the stressed first syllable. The form resembles nouns of the type *CéCeC* (cf. מֶלֶךְ): שֶׁ֫בֶת (from יָשַׁב), with suffix שִׁבְתִּי; לֶ֫כֶת (from הָלַךְ), with suffix לֶכְתִּי (Table).

6. The verbal nouns הָלוֹךְ וָשׁוֹב function as adverbs modifying the verb וַיָּשֻׁבוּ "and they abated" (XV). This construction enriches the meaning of the verb, and is best represented by an appropriate adverb in English (e.g. "surely, certainly, gradually"): cf. הָלוֹךְ וּבָכוֹ יֵלֵ֫כוּ "continually weeping shall they go" (Jer. 50:4).

This form of the verbal noun ("Infinitive Absolute") differs from the PG form already discussed: characteristic of all verb-types are the vowels *-ā-* in the first syllable and *-ō-* in the second.

SUMMARY

A. The Hebrew verb has an active participle and a passive participle. In form they resemble nouns. Active participles for convenience may be translated in the first instance as nouns in *-er*.

B. In function they are both nounlike and verblike, and correspond to a large variety of English constructions:

(a) nouns in *er*/*-or* and other agent nouns (עֹשֶׂה "maker"; שׁוֹפֵט "judge").

(b) adjectives (מִשְׁפָּט כָּתוּב "written judgment"; אִישׁ זָקֵן "an old man").

(c) relative clauses (הָאִישׁ הָעוֹשֶׂה זאת "the man who did this").

(d) noun-phrases containing a relative clause (הַבָּא "he who comes").

(e) the main verb in a clause (יְהוָה נֹתֵן לְךָ "the Lord gives you").

ACTIVE AND PASSIVE PARTICIPLES.

	ACTIVE	PASSIVE
masc. sing.	שׁוֹמֵר "keeper, watchman" בָּא "one who comes"(XVII) בּוֹנֶה "builder" (XVIII)	בָּרוּךְ "blessed" בָּנוּי "built"
fem. sing.	מֹלְכָה מֹלֶכֶת "ruler" שָׁרָה "singer" (XVII) עוֹשָׂה "maker" (XVIII)	שְׁמוּרָה "kept" בְּנוּיָה "built"
masc. plur.	שֹׁפְטִים "judges" מֵתִים "dead" (XVII) רֹאִים "seers" (XVIII)	כְּתוּבִים "written" עֲשׂוּיִם "made, done"
fem. plur.	שֹׁמְעוֹת "hearers" שָׁרוֹת "singers" (XVII) רֹאוֹת "seers" (XVIII)	כְּתוּבוֹת "written" רְאוּיוֹת "seen"

C. Verbal nouns in Hebrew correspond to a variety of English constructions:

(1) gerunds (forms with suffix *-ing*): e.g. צֵאתְךָ וּבוֹאֶךָ "*your going out* (from יָצָא) and *your coming in* (from בָּא)". (Psalm 121:8).

(2) infinitives (with or without *to*): e.g. לֹא יָכֹלְתִּי לִרְאוֹת "I am unable *to see* (from רָאָה), I cannot *see*".

(3) nouns: e.g. דַּעַת אֱלֹהִים "the *knowledge* (from יָדַע) of God".

(4) subordinate clauses: e.g. בְּשִׁבְתְּךָ בְּבֵיתְךָ "*when you sit*, lit. "in

your *sitting* (from יָשַׁב) in your house" (Deut. 6:7).

(5) adverbial expressions: e.g. אָכוֹל תֹּאכֵל "you may certainly eat" (from אָכַל) (Gen. 2:16) ("Infinitive Absolute") (XX).

VERBAL NOUNS

CITATION FORM	VERBAL NOUNS	WITH SUFFIX
שָׁמַר "to keep" (XI)	שָׁמֹר PG שְׁמֹר	שָׁמְרוֹ
נָתַן "to give" (XII)	נָתוֹן PG תֵּת	תִּתִּי
הָלַךְ "to go" (XVI)	הָלוֹךְ PG לֶכֶת	לֶכְתְּךָ
שָׁב "to return" (XVII)	שׁוֹב PG שׁוּב	שׁוּבֵנוּ
רָאָה "to see" (XVIII)	רָאֹה PG רְאוֹת	רְאֹתְךָ

VOCABULARY

אָהֵב	"to love"	גּוֹי	"nation"	נָגַע	"to touch"
אָכַל	"to eat"	יְהוּדָה	f. "Judah"	נֶפֶשׁ	f."self,person"
אֲרוֹן	"box, ark"	יְרוּשָׁלַ͏ִם	f. "Jerusalem"	שָׂם	"to put"
בָּחַר	"to choose"	כְּ-	"like, as"	שָׂמַח	"to rejoice"
בְּתוֹךְ	"in, inside"	כִּסֵּא	"throne"	שָׁתָה	"to drink"

EXERCISES

1. Translate:

א. כָּל־יְהוּדָה וְיֹשְׁבֵי יְרוּשָׁלַ͏ִם נָפְלוּ לִפְנֵי יְהוָה׃

ב. שֹׁמֵר מִצְוָה שֹׁמֵר נַפְשׁוֹ׃

ג. עֹשֶׂה שָׁלוֹם וּבֹרֵא רָע אֲנִי יְהוָה עֹשֶׂה כָּל־אֵלֶּה׃

ד. בָּרוּךְ יְהוָה אֲשֶׁר נָתַן יוֹשֵׁב כִּסְאִי וְעֵינַי רֹאוֹת׃

ה. הַנֹּגֵעַ בָּאִישׁ הַזֶּה וּבְאִשְׁתּוֹ מוֹת יָמוּת׃

ו. אַתָּה יָדַעְתָּ שִׁבְתִּי וְקוּמִי׃

PARTICIPLES

ז. תִּשְׁמֹר לַעֲשׂוֹת כְּכָל־הַכָּתוּב בְּסֵפֶר הַתּוֹרָה:

ח. וַיֵּלְכוּ כָּל־הָעָם לֶאֱכֹל וְלִשְׁתּוֹת וְלַעֲשׂוֹת שִׂמְחָה גְדוֹלָה:

ט. מָלַךְ בֶּן־דָּוִד בִּירוּשָׁלַיִם הָעִיר אֲשֶׁר בָּחַר יְהוָה לָשׂוּם אֶת־שְׁמוֹ שָׁם:

י. וַיִּרְאוּ אֶת־הָאָרוֹן וַיִּשְׂמְחוּ לִרְאוֹת:

2. Write down the citation-form of all participles and verbal nouns.

CHAPTER X. DERIVED STEMS OF THE VERB. QUASI-VERBALS

EXAMPLES

1.	I shall come down and speak with you there (Num 11:17).	וְיָרַדְתִּי וְדִבַּרְתִּי עִמְּךָ שָׁם׃	א.
2.	They took Jeremiah the prophet and threw him into the pit (Jer. 38:6).	וַיִּקְחוּ אֶת־יִרְמְיָהוּ וַיַּשְׁלִכוּ אֹתוֹ אֶל־הַבּוֹר׃	ב.
3.	There was no-one to declare it, no-one to proclaim it (Isa. 41:26).	אֵין מַגִּיד וְאֵין מַשְׁמִיעַ׃	ג.
4.	You will go with us and fight against the Ammonites (Judg. 11:8).	וְהָלַכְתָּ עִמָּנוּ וְנִלְחַמְתָּ בִּבְנֵי עַמּוֹן׃	ד.
5.	He will come and pray towards this house (I Kgs. 8:42).	וּבָא וְהִתְפַּלֵּל אֶל־הַבַּיִת הַזֶּה׃	ה.
6.	Therefore by this the guilt of Jacob will be expiated (Isa. 27:9).	לָכֵן בְּזֹאת יְכֻפַּר עֲוֹן יַעֲקֹב׃	ו.

ANALYSIS

1. וְיָרַדְתִּי is *1s* SC of יָרַד "to go down", with וְ- "and" pointing to future time (IV).

וְדִבַּרְתִּי is *1s* SC of the verb דִּבֶּר "to speak", with וְ- "and". דִּבֶּר is the "Doubled Stem" of a less common verb with similar meaning דָּבַר (Simple Stem). Up to now, the stem of every verb-form has consisted simply of the root-letters (cf. I). In the *derived stems*, now to be discussed, the root-letters are augmented in various ways by "stem-formatives". In verbs like דִּבֶּר "to speak", for example, the second root-letter is doubled (p. 5), and the vowel pattern is *-i-e/a-*. Other common Doubled Stem ("D-stem") verbs are: בִּקֵּשׁ "to look for"; הִלֵּל "to praise"; צִוָּה "to command".

D-stems are often causative in meaning (XVII), especially when the simple stem of the same verb is also in common use:

SIMPLE STEM	DOUBLED STEM
אָבַד "to perish"	אִבֵּד "to destroy"
חָיָה "to live"	חִיָּה "to give life to"
קָדַשׁ "to be holy"	קִדֵּשׁ "to make holy, sanctify"
שָׂמַח "to rejoice"	שִׂמַּח "to make happy, gladden"

Suffixes and Prefixes are added to the derived stems in the same way as in the SC and PC of the simple stem: וְאִבַּדְתִּי "I shall destroy"; יְדַבְּרוּ "they will speak". The Prefix vowel in the D-stem is always shwa (or compound shwa: אֲדַבֵּר "I speak").

2. וַיַּשְׁלִכוּ is *3mpl* PC of הִשְׁלִיךְ "to throw" with -וְ "and". This is an H-stem verb, so-called because the citation-form and other SC forms have the prefix -ה. In the PC the -ה is omitted (cf. -הַ "the":II), and the H-stem-formative is the vowel-pattern *-a-ī/ē-*. Other common verbs like הִשְׁלִיךְ are: הֶאֱמִין "to believe", הִגִּיד "to tell" (XIX), הוֹשִׁיעַ "to save", and הִצִּיל "to rescue".

The H-stem is frequently causative in meaning where the simple stem of the same verb is also in common use (cf. D-stem):

SIMPLE STEM	H-STEM
בָּא "to come	הֵבִיא "to bring"
יָדַע "to know"	הוֹדִיעַ "to inform"
מֵת "to die"	הֵמִית "to kill"
עָלָה "to go up"	הֶעֱלָה "to take up, bring up"
רָאָה "to see"	הֶרְאָה "to show"
שָׁמַע "to hear"	הִשְׁמִיעַ "to proclaim"

3. אֵין is Pregenitive in form (cf. V.2), but in function is a *quasi-verbal*, and corresponds to English "there is/are not". Unlike true PG forms, however, it need not come immediately before its noun: e.g. וְאֵין בְּכָל־הָאָרֶץ לֶחֶם "and there was no bread in the whole land". Cf.־יֶשׁ "there is/are".

מַגִּיד is the *ms* active participle of the H-stem verb הִגִּיד "to tell, declare". In three of the derived stems, D-stem, H-stem and T-stem (see below), participles are marked by the prefix -מ: מְדַבֵּר from דִּבֵּר "to speak"; מַשְׁלִיךְ from הִשְׁלִיךְ "to throw"; מִתְפַּלֵּל from הִתְפַּלֵּל "to pray".

The prefix-vowel in the active participle and throughout the PC of H-stem verbs is normally *-a-*.

מַשְׁמִיעַ is the *ms* active participle of the H-stem of the verb שָׁמַע "to hear". הִשְׁמִיעַ is causative in meaning: "to cause to hear, proclaim" (cf. 2).

4. A minor pause is marked at עִמָּנוּ. נִלְחַמְתָּ is *2ms* SC of the N-stem verb נִלְחַם "to fight". Other verbs like נִלְחַם are: נֶאֱמַן "to be faithful", נִמְלַט "to escape", נִפְלָא "to be wonderful", and נִשְׁבַּע "to swear, promise". In the PC, Imperative and Verbal Nouns, the prefix -נ is omitted by assimilation (p.161), and the stem-formative is then the vowel-pattern *-i-ā-e-*.

N-stems are often passive in meaning, especially when an active stem of the same verb is in common use:

SIMPLE STEM	N-STEM
בָּנָה "to build"	נִבְנָה "to be built"
יָלַד "to bear"	נוֹלַד "to be born"
רָאָה "to see"	נִרְאָה "to be seen, appear"
שָׁמַע "to hear"	נִשְׁמַע "to be heard"

The preposition -בְּ frequently occurs in contexts of rebellion and hostility: cf. פָּשְׁעוּ בִי "they have rebelled against me" (Ezek. 2:3); לֹא־תַעֲנֶה בְרֵעֲךָ עֵד שָׁקֶר "you shall not bear false witness against thy neighbour" (Ex. 20:16).

5. הִתְפַּלֵּל is *3ms* SC of the T-stem verb הִתְפַּלֵּל "to pray". The chief stem-formative is the infix -ת-. The prefix *hit-* occurs in SC forms and doubling of the second root-letter in all forms. Other common T-stem verbs like הִתְפַּלֵּל are: הִתְהַלֵּךְ "to walk about" and הִתְנַבֵּא "to prophesy".

T-stems are frequently reflexive in meaning (XVIII), especially when the simple stem of the same verb is also in common use:

SIMPLE STEM		T-STEM	
לָבַשׁ	"to put on"	הִתְלַבֵּשׁ	"to dress (oneself)"
קָדַשׁ	"to be holy"	הִתְקַדֵּשׁ	"to sanctify oneself"
רָאָה	"to see"	הִתְרָאָה	"to look at oneself"

בַּיִת "temple" is common in religious language, and in numerous place-names: בֵּית אֵל "Bethel"; בֵּית לֶחֶם "Bethlehem"; בֵּית שֶׁמֶשׁ "Beth Shemesh"; בֵּית שְׁאָן "Beth Shean".

6. יְכֻפַּר is *3ms* PC of the passive of the D-stem verb כִּפֵּר "to expiate". D-stem and H-stem verbs have special passive forms, the "rounded stems", so called because the stem-formative in both PC and SC is one of the rounded vowels, *o*, *ō*, and *u* (p.154).

ACTIVE		PASSIVE	
דִּבֶּר	"to speak"	דֻּבַּר	"to be spoken"
הֵמִית	"to kill"	הוּמַת	"to be killed"
הִשְׁלִיךְ	"to throw"	הֻשְׁלַךְ	"to be thrown"

The prefix-vowel in the D-stem, both active and passive, is always shwa.

SUMMARY

A. Besides the *Simple Stem* (e.g. שָׁמַר "to keep") Hebrew has a number of *Derived Stems*, distinguished from the simple stem by "stem-formatives". The following are the commonest in Biblical Hebrew:

STEM	PREFIX IN CITATION-FORM (SC)
Simple Stem (Qal)	None
Doubled Stem (Piel)	None (second root-letter doubled)
N-stem (Niphal)	-נִ *(ni-)*
H-stem (Hiphil)	-הִ *(hi-)*
T-stem (Hithpael)	-הִתְ*(hit-)*
Rounded D-stem (Pual)	None (second root-letter doubled)
Rounded H-stem (Hophal)	-הָ, -הֻ *(ho-, hu-)*

B. Many D-stem and H-stem forms are causative in meaning, many N-stem forms passive, and many T-stem forms reflexive, in relation to the simple stem forms of the same verb. But there are also many derived stems for which there is no corresponding simple stem in Biblical Hebrew, and such generalizations about their meaning are inappropriate. Rounded stem forms, however, are always passive.

QUASI -VERBALS

STEM	CITATION FORM (SC)	PREFIX CONJUGATION	וַ+PREFIX CONJUGATION	ACTIVE PARTICIPLE	ENGLISH
Simple	שָׁמַר	יִשְׁמֹר	וַיִּשְׁמֹר	שֹׁמֵר	"to keep"
D-stem	דִּבֵּר	יְדַבֵּר	וַיְדַבֵּר	מְדַבֵּר	"to speak"
Rounded D-stem	(דֻּבַּר)	יְדֻבַּר	וַיְדֻבַּר	מְדֻבָּר	"to be spoken"
H-stem	הִשְׁלִיךְ	יַשְׁלִיךְ	וַיַּשְׁלֵךְ	מַשְׁלִיךְ	"to throw"
Rounded H-stem	הֻשְׁלַךְ	יֻשְׁלַךְ	וַיֻּשְׁלַךְ	מֻשְׁלָךְ	"to be thrown"
N-stem	נִלְחַם	יִלָּחֵם	וַיִּלָּחֵם	נִלְחָם	"to fight"
T-stem	הִתְפַּלֵּל	יִתְפַּלֵּל	וַיִּתְפַּלֵּל	מִתְפַּלֵּל	"to pray"

C. Quasi-verbal sentences are sentences in which the "quasi-verbals" (with or without a suffix pronoun referring to the subject) function like the verb in a verbal sentence. The commonest are:

אַיֵּה "where is/are ...?"
אֵין "there is/are not..."
הִנֵּה "behold"
יֵשׁ־ "there is/are..."
עוֹד "still yet"

VOCABULARY

אַהֲרֹן "Aaron"
אֵל "God, El"
דִּבֶּר D. "to speak"
הוֹשִׁיעַ H. "to save"
הִתְפַּלֵּל T. "to pray"
יַעֲקֹב "Jacob"
כִּפֶּר D. "to expiate"
לָמָּה "why?"
נִלְחַם N. "to fight"
עָוֹן "sin, guilt"
עֹלָה f. "holocaust"
עַמּוֹן "Ammon"
צִוָּה D. "to command"
שֶׁמֶשׁ f. "sun"
תַּחַת "under"

DERIVED STEMS OF THE VERB

EXERCISES

1. Translate the following and identify the stem of each verb:

א. וַיָּבֵא אֶת־כָּל־הַכֹּהֲנִים מֵעָרֵי יְהוּדָה׃

ב. וַיְדַבֵּר יְהוָה אֶל־מֹשֶׁה אַחֲרֵי מוֹת בְּנֵי אַהֲרֹן׃

ג. וְהֵם מִתְפַּלְלִים אֶל־אֵל לֹא יוֹשִׁיעַ׃

ד. בִּדְבַר יְהוָה שָׁמַיִם נַעֲשׂוּ׃

ה. הִנֵּה יְהוָה מְצַוֶּה וַעֲוֹן יַעֲקֹב יְכֻפָּר׃

2. Translate the following and give the citation-form of each verb:

ו. וְאַנְשֵׁי בֵּית־שֶׁמֶשׁ הֶעֱלוּ עֹלוֹת לַיהוָה בַּיּוֹם הַהוּא׃

ז. וְאֶת־בְּנֵיהֶם לֹא הֵמִית כַּכָּתוּב בְּסֵפֶר תּוֹרַת מֹשֶׁה׃

ח. נָתַתִּי אֶת־לִבִּי לְכָל־מַעֲשֶׂה אֲשֶׁר נַעֲשָׂה תַּחַת הַשָּׁמָיִם׃

ט. וַיָּקֶם יְהוָה מוֹשִׁיעַ לִבְנֵי יִשְׂרָאֵל וַיּוֹשִׁיעֵם׃

י. לָמָּה הֶעֱלִיתָנוּ מִמִּצְרַיִם לְהָבִיא אֹתָנוּ אֶל־הַמָּקוֹם הָרַע הַזֶּה׃

PART TWO
SYNTAX AND WORD FORMATION

CHAPTER XI. QUESTIONS. PERSONAL NAMES. VERB-TYPES.

EXAMPLES

1.	Did you say, "Adonijah is to be king after me"? (I Kgs. 1:24)	אָמַרְתָּ אֲדֹנִיָּהוּ יִמְלֹךְ אַחֲרָי׃	א.
2.	Are you not a man? Who is like you in Israel? (I Sam. 26:15)	הֲלֹא אִישׁ אַתָּה וּמִי כָמוֹךָ בְּיִשְׂרָאֵל׃	ב.
3.	Why did you not keep watch over the king? (I Sam. 26:15)	לָמָּה לֹא שָׁמַרְתָּ אֶל־הַמֶּלֶךְ׃	ג.
4.	What is your country and of what people are you? (Jon. 1:8)	מָה אַרְצֶךָ וְאֵי־מִזֶּה עַם אָתָּה׃	ד.
5.	Inquire of Baalzebub whether I shall recover (II Kgs. 1:2).	דִּרְשׁוּ בְּבַעַל־זְבוּב אִם־אֶחְיֶה׃	ה.

ANALYSIS

1. This question is unmarked, but is identified as such by the context (I Kings 1:24). There was no question-mark in the punctuation system of the biblical text, nor any necessary change of word-order. In direct speech no doubt the intonation pattern would have distinguished questions from plain statements.

A pause between the two clauses is marked at אָמַרְתָּ.

אֲדֹנִיָּהוּ "Adonijah" illustrates two very common features of Hebrew personal names: (1) the element יה or יהו, denoting "the Lord, YHWH" (p. 12), as in אֵלִיָּהוּ "Elijah", יְשַׁעְיָה "Isaiah" and הַלְלוּיָה "Praise the Lord!"; (2) the sentence-structure, which may be either verbless (IV), as in אֲדֹנִיָּהוּ "Adonijah (YHWH is my Lord)", or verbal (VI), as in זְכַרְיָ֫הוּ "Zechariah (YHWH remembered)".

יִמְלֹךְ is *3ms* PC of the verb מָלַךְ "to be king" (I). In type, מָלַךְ is like שָׁמַר "to keep". *Verb-types* are distinguished one from another by their phonetic structure, verbs beginning with the semi-vowel י, for example, like יָשַׁב (XVI), from verbs ending in a vowel like רָאָה (XVIII). Verbs of this first type, like שָׁמַר, are distinguished from other verb-types by the absence of any phonetic peculiarity (pp.157ff) and the vowel pattern *-i-ō-* in the Prefix Conjugation.

2. The prefix -הֲ attached to the first word of a sentence marks it out as a question. (Notice the vowel-sign which distinguishes this prefix from -הַ "the": p.17). It requires no change in grammar or word-order.

The second sentence in this example is marked as a question by the question-word מִי "who? whom?". There are twelve common question-words in Hebrew:

אַיֵּה	"where?"	לָ֫מָּה	"why?"
אֵיךְ, אֵיכָה	"how?"	מַדּוּעַ	"why?"
אֵי-מִזֶּה	"where... from?"	מֵאַ֫יִן	"where... from?"
אֵיפֹה	"where?"	מָה	"what?"
אָ֫נָה	"where... to?"	מִי	"who?"
אִם	"whether (reported question: 5)"	מָתַי	"when?"

With the suffix pronouns, the preposition -כְּ "like" has the form -כָּמֹ (XV.4).

3. לָ֫מָּה "why?" is made up of the preposition -לְ "for" and the question-word מָה "what?". The first syllable is stressed and the מ doubled.

שָׁמַ֫רְתָּ is *2ms* SC of the verb שָׁמַר "to keep (watch)". On the verb-type, see above.

4. This sentence is divided into two clauses by the pause marked at אַרְצָה. מָה "what?" is a question-word.

אֵי-מִזֶּה "from what?" is made up of the question word אֵי and the prepositional construction מִזֶּה "from this". There are several אֵי-terms in Hebrew which correspond to English *wh*-terms in the pairs *what/that*, *where/there*, *whence/thence*, etc: cf. זֶה/אֵי־זֶה and פֹּה/אֵיפֹה.

5. דִּרְשׁוּ is *mpl* imperative of the verb דָּרַשׁ "to inquire". Like other verbs of the type שָׁמַר it has an imperative of the form *CəCōC* (PC without prefixes: VI). With the *fs* and *mpl* suffixes the shwa becomes *-i-* (p. 159).

בַּעַל זְבוּב "Baalzebub (Lord of the flies)" is probably a conscious corruption of בַּעַל זְבוּל "Baalzebul" (cf. Matth. 10:25), a divine epithet of Canaanite origin denoting "Lord of the heights". There are many examples of this type of word-formation, motivated by religious purism. בֹּשֶׁת "shame, abomination", for example, is substituted for בַּעַל "Baal" in the personal name יְרֻבַּעַל "Jerubbaal", giving יְרֻבֶּשֶׁת "Jerubbesheth" (II Samuel 11:21; cf. Judg. 6:32).

אִם־אֶחְיֶה "whether I may live" is a reported question. After verbs of asking, knowing, testing and the like, questions are introduced by (i) the prefix -הֲ, (ii) one of the usual direct question-words, or (iii) as here, the conjunction אִם־ "whether".

QUESTIONS

SUMMARY

A. A question may be marked by the prefix -הֲ attached to the first word of a sentence, or by one of the question-words לָמָּה, מָה, מִי, etc. Many questions, however, are unmarked in Biblical Hebrew and are identified from the context.

B. A reported question (after verbs of asking, seeing, knowing, etc.) may also be marked by the conjunction אִם־ "whether".

C. Hebrew personal names are frequently in the form of verbless or verbal sentences containing the element יָהוּ or יָהּ ("the Lord"). Pagan names, containing the element בַּעַל "Baal", may be given derogatory forms such as Baalzebub and Jerubbesheth.

D. There are twelve main verb-types, distinguished from one another as follows, by their phonological structure:

VERB-TYPE	PHONOLOGICAL STRUCTURE	CHAPTER
אָמַר "to say"	initial א : PC prefix-vowel ō.	XII
בֵּרַךְ "to bless"	second root-letter a guttural (which is never doubled).	XVI
הִגִּיד "to tell"	H-stem verb in which the first root-letter is נ.	XIX
זָקֵן "to grow old"	second vowel in PC is *a*, in SC *a*, *ē* or *ō*.	XV
יָשַׁב "to dwell"	first root-letter י : PC prefix vowel *ē* or *ī* (י is omitted).	XVI
נָפַל "to fall"	first root-letter נ (assimilated after most prefixes).	XIV
סָבַב "to go round"	second and third root-letters identical, and not always both written.	XVI

VERB-TYPES

VERB-TYPE	PHONOLOGICAL STRUCTURE	CHAPTER
עָבַד "to serve"	initial guttural: prefix vowel usually *a* (p. 158).	XII
קָם "to stand"	monosyllabic: long vowels in most forms.	XVII
רָאָה "to see"	two root-letters: most PC forms end in *e*, most SC forms in *ā*, both written with vowel-letter ה.	XVIII
שָׁלַח "to send"	final guttural: second vowel in PC forms is *a* (p. 158).	XIII
שָׁמַר "to keep"	normal: 3 root-letters, no gutturals, no semi-vowels, no נ.	XI

VERBS WITH NO PHONOLOGICAL PECULIARITY

	Simple-Stem שָׁמַר "to keep"	N-stem נִסְתַּר "to hide"	H-stem הִשְׁלִיךְ "to throw"	D-stem דִּבֶּר "to speak"	T-stem הִתְלַבֵּשׁ "to dress"
SUFFIX CONJUGATION					
ls "I"	שָׁמַרְתִּי	נִסְתַּרְתִּי	הִשְׁלַכְתִּי	דִּבַּרְתִּי	הִתְלַבַּשְׁתִּי
2ms "you"	שָׁמַרְתָּ	נִסְתַּרְתָּ	הִשְׁלַכְתָּ	דִּבַּרְתָּ	הִתְלַבַּשְׁתָּ
2fs "you"	שָׁמַרְתְּ	נִסְתַּרְתְּ	הִשְׁלַכְתְּ	דִּבַּרְתְּ	הִתְלַבַּשְׁתְּ
3ms "he, it"	שָׁמַר	נִסְתַּר	הִשְׁלִיךְ	דִּבֶּר	הִתְלַבֵּשׁ
3fs "she, it"	שָׁמְרָה	נִסְתְּרָה	הִשְׁלִיכָה	דִּבְּרָה	הִתְלַבְּשָׁה
1pl "we"	שָׁמַרְנוּ	נִסְתַּרְנוּ	הִשְׁלַכְנוּ	דִּבַּרְנוּ	הִתְלַבַּשְׁנוּ
2mpl "you"	שְׁמַרְתֶּם	נִסְתַּרְתֶּם	הִשְׁלַכְתֶּם	דִּבַּרְתֶּם	הִתְלַבַּשְׁתֶּם
2fpl "you"	שְׁמַרְתֶּן	נִסְתַּרְתֶּן	הִשְׁלַכְתֶּן	דִּבַּרְתֶּן	הִתְלַבַּשְׁתֶּן
3pl "they"	שָׁמְרוּ	נִסְתְּרוּ	הִשְׁלִיכוּ	דִּבְּרוּ	הִתְלַבְּשׁוּ
PREFIX CONJUGATION					
ls "I"	אֶשְׁמֹר	אֶסָּתֵר	אַשְׁלִיךְ	אֲדַבֵּר	אֶתְלַבֵּשׁ
2ms "you"	תִּשְׁמֹר	תִּסָּתֵר	תַּשְׁלִיךְ	תְּדַבֵּר	תִּתְלַבֵּשׁ
2fs "you"	תִּשְׁמְרִי	תִּסָּתְרִי	תַּשְׁלִיכִי	תְּדַבְּרִי	תִּתְלַבְּשִׁי

XI

VERBS WITH NO PHONOLOGICAL PECULIARITY: שָׁמַר "TO KEEP", ETC.

3ms "he, it"	יִשְׁמֹר	יִסָּתֵר	יַשְׁלִיךְ	יְדַבֵּר	יִתְלַבֵּשׁ
3fs "she, it"	תִּשְׁמֹר	תִּסָּתֵר	תַּשְׁלִיךְ	תְּדַבֵּר	תִּתְלַבֵּשׁ
1pl "we"	נִשְׁמֹר	נִסָּתֵר	נַשְׁלִיךְ	נְדַבֵּר	נִתְלַבֵּשׁ
2mpl "you"	תִּשְׁמְרוּ	תִּסָּתְרוּ	תַּשְׁלִיכוּ	תְּדַבְּרוּ	תִּתְלַבְּשׁוּ
2fpl "you"	תִּשְׁמֹרְנָה	תִּסָּתַרְנָה	תַּשְׁלֵכְנָה	תְּדַבֵּרְנָה	תִּתְלַבֵּשְׁנָה
3mpl "they"	יִשְׁמְרוּ	יִסָּתְרוּ	יַשְׁלִיכוּ	יְדַבְּרוּ	יִתְלַבְּשׁוּ
3fpl "they"	תִּשְׁמֹרְנָה	תִּסָּתַרְנָה	תַּשְׁלֵכְנָה	תְּדַבֵּרְנָה	תִּתְלַבֵּשְׁנָה
IMPERATIVE					
2ms	שְׁמֹר	הִסָּתֵר	הַשְׁלֵךְ	דַּבֵּר	הִתְלַבֵּשׁ
2fs	שִׁמְרִי	הִסָּתְרִי	הַשְׁלִיכִי	דַּבְּרִי	הִתְלַבְּשִׁי
2mpl	שִׁמְרוּ	הִסָּתְרוּ	הַשְׁלִיכוּ	דַּבְּרוּ	הִתְלַבְּשׁוּ
2fpl	שְׁמֹרְנָה	הִסָּתַרְנָה	הַשְׁלֵכְנָה	דַּבֵּרְנָה	הִתְלַבֵּשְׁנָה
וַ + PC					
3ms "and he..."	וַיִּשְׁמֹר	וַיִּסָּתֵר	וַיַּשְׁלֵךְ	וַיְדַבֵּר	וַיִּתְלַבֵּשׁ
3mpl "and they..."	וַיִּשְׁמְרוּ	וַיִּסָּתְרוּ	וַיַּשְׁלִיכוּ	וַיְדַבְּרוּ	וַיִּתְלַבְּשׁוּ
ACTIVE PARTICIPLE					
ms ("-er")	שֹׁמֵר	נִסְתָּר	מַשְׁלִיךְ	מְדַבֵּר	מִתְלַבֵּשׁ
mpl ("-ers")	שֹׁמְרִים	נִסְתָּרִים	מַשְׁלִיכִים	מְדַבְּרִים	מִתְלַבְּשִׁים
PASSIVE PARTICIPLE					
ms	שָׁמוּר		מֻשְׁלָךְ	מְדֻבָּר	
mpl	שְׁמוּרִים		מֻשְׁלָכִים	מְדֻבָּרִים	
VERBAL NOUN					
Basic form	שָׁמוֹר	נִסְתּוֹר	הַשְׁלֵךְ	דַּבּוֹר	
Pregenitive	שְׁמֹר	הִסָּתֵר	הַשְׁלִיךְ	דַּבֵּר	הִתְלַבֵּשׁ
PG with *1s* suffix	שָׁמְרִי	הִסָּתְרִי	הַשְׁלִיכִי	דַּבְּרִי	הִתְלַבְּשִׁי

QUESTIONS

E. The commonest verbs of the type שָׁמַר are:

דָּרַשׁ	"to seek, inquire"	מָלַךְ	"to rule"	רָדַף	"to pursue"
זָכַר	"to remember"	פָּקַד	"to visit, appoint"	שָׁבַר	"to break"
כָּרַת	"to cut"	קָבַר	"to bury"	שָׁפַט	"to judge"
כָּתַב	"to write"	אָסַף	"to collect, assemble"	שָׂרַף	"to burn"

VOCABULARY

אָדָם	"man"	חַטָּאת	f. "sin"	פָּקַד	"to punish, care for" H "to appoint"
אוֹר	"light"	חָכְמָה	f. "wisdom"	צֶ֫דֶק	"righteousness"
אֱנוֹשׁ	"man"	חֶ֫רֶב	f. "sword"	רָעָב	"famine"
דֶּ֫בֶר	"plague"	כִּי	"because, that, except, but"	שָׁאַל	"to ask"
זָכַר	"to remember"	מִי	"who"	שָׁפַט	"to judge"

EXERCISES

Translate into English:

א. אֲנִי יְהוָה קְרָאתִיךָ בְצֶ֫דֶק וְאֶתֶּנְךָ לְאוֹר הַגּוֹיִם׃

ב. בַּחֶרֶב וּבָרָעָב וּבַדֶּבֶר אֶפְקֹד עַל־הַגּוֹי הַהוּא׃

ג. מָה אֱנוֹשׁ כִּי תִזְכְּרֶ֫נּוּ וּבֶן־אָדָם כִּי תִפְקְדֶ֫נּוּ׃

ד. עַתָּה חָכְמָה תִּתֵּן לִי כִּי מִי יִשְׁפֹּט אֶת־עַמְּךָ׃

ה. רְאוּ מָה אַתֶּם עוֹשִׂים כִּי לֹא לְאָדָם תִּשְׁפְּטוּ כִּי לַיהוָה׃

ו. הֲלֹא הֵם כְּתוּבִים בְּסֵפֶר דִּבְרֵי הַיָּמִים לְמַלְכֵי יְהוּדָה׃

ז. וַיַּפְקִידֵהוּ עַל־בֵּיתוֹ וְכָל־אֲשֶׁר־לוֹ נָתַן בְּיָדוֹ׃

ח. וָאֶשְׁאַל אוֹתָהּ וָאֹמַר בַּת־מִי אַתְּ׃

ט. עַתָּה יִזְכֹּר עֲוֹנָם וְיִפְקֹד חַטֹּאותָם׃

י. שִׁמְרוּ מִצְוֹתַי כְּכָל־הַתּוֹרָה אֲשֶׁר צִוִּיתִי אֶת־אֲבוֹתֵיכֶם׃

CHAPTER XII. TENSE, MOOD AND ASPECT. VERBS BEGINNING WITH א, ה, ח OR ע: עָזַר "TO HELP", ETC.

EXAMPLES

1.	As I was with Moses, so will I be with you (Josh. 1:5).	כַּאֲשֶׁר הָיִיתִי עִם-מֹשֶׁה אֶהְיֶה עִמָּךְ׃	א.
2.	But a mist was rising from the earth and watering all the surface of the ground (Gen. 2:6).	וְאֵד יַעֲלֶה מִן־הָאָרֶץ וְהִשְׁקָה אֶת-כָּל־פְּנֵי הָאֲדָמָה׃	ב.
3.	I do not know who has done this thing (Gen. 21:26).	לֹא־יָדַעְתִּי מִי עָשָׂה אֶת־הַדָּבָר הַזֶּה׃	ג.
4.	And the woman said to the serpent, "Of the fruit of the trees of the garden we may eat"(Gen. 3:2).	וַתֹּאמֶר הָאִשָּׁה אֶל־הַנָּחָשׁ מִפְּרִי עֵץ הַגָּן נֹאכֵל׃	ד.
5.	Stand at the gate of the Lord's house, and say, "Hear the word of the Lord!" (Jer. 7:2).	עֲמֹד בְּשַׁעַר בֵּית יְהוָֹה וְאָמַרְתָּ שִׁמְעוּ אֶת-דְּבַר יְהוָֹה׃	ה.
6.	At that time Hazael, king of Syria went up and fought against Gath (II Kgs.12:18).	אָז יַעֲלֶה חֲזָאֵל מֶלֶךְ אֲרָם וַיִּלָּחֶם עַל־גַּת׃	ו.

ANALYSIS

1. כַּאֲשֶׁר "as" is a conjunction introducing a subordinate clause (XIX).

הָיִיתִי is *1s* of הָיָה "to be" and אֶהְיֶה is *1s* of the same verb. In verbless clauses הָיָה may indicate tense, aspect or mood: e.g.

הָאִישׁ גָּדוֹל מְאֹד	"the man is/was/will be very great"
הָיָה הָאִישׁ גָּדוֹל מְאוֹד	"the man was very great"

יִהְיֶה הָאִישׁ גָּדוֹל מְאֹד׃ "the man will be very great"
In all three examples the subject and predicate are the same: and הָיָה does not alter the structure of the sentence.

Tense. In traditional grammar, the English verb has three tenses, the past tense, the present tense and the future tense, corresponding respectively to past time, present time and future time. In practice, however, the situation is more complex. Examples like *The ship sails next week* and *If you found it tomorrow, would you use it*? make it clear that in some contexts the so-called "present tense" of the verb does not always point to present time, and the so-called "past tense" can also express hypotheticalness in the future. Because of this, it is not uncommon to find grammarians nowadays making only one distinction, namely, that between "past" and "non-past". In Hebrew, where the verb has only two tenses, the Suffix Conjugation (IV) and the Prefix Conjugation (VI), this kind of distinction between past and non-past, modal and non-modal, and the like is often helpful. In the present example, the opposition between the two Conjugations is between past and non-past: the SC form הָיִיתִי points to past time ["I was, i.e. up to (but not including) the present"], while the PC form אֶהְיֶה points to non-past (or present/future) time ("I shall be, i.e. from now on") (Joshua 1:5).

2. The sentence is divided into two clauses by the pause at הָאָרֶץ.

יַעֲלֶה is *3ms* PC of עָלָה "to go up". In this example the distinction between the two conjugations is one of *aspect*: the PC form יַעֲלֶה points to a continuous, repeated or habitual action or state of affairs, as opposed to a single, completed action or event:

e.g. וַיִּיצֶר "He formed... man" (V. 7) (-וַ + PC: cf. VI). The passage is a description of the state of affairs on the day when the Lord formed man from the dust of the earth, and there is no doubt what the tenses of the verbs refer to (Gen. 2:4b-9).

עָלָה "to go up" has two phonetic features which distinguish it from verbs of the type שָׁמַר (XI): (1) like עָזַר it begins with the guttural ע; (2) like רָאָה it has only two root-letters and ends in a vowel (ה is a vowel-letter: p.4). In verbs of the type עָזַר, the prefix-vowel is usually *-a-* (short vowel adjacent to a guttural: p.158). Verbs of the type רָאָה will be discussed below (XVIII). Three common verbs belong to both types: עָלָה "to go up", עָנָה "to answer" and עָשָׂה "to make, do".

וְהִשְׁקָה is *3ms* SC of the H-stem verb הִשְׁקָה "to water" (cf. the simple stem *שָׁקָה "to drink") with the prefix -וְ "and". -וְ + SC most often points to future time (cf. IV), but in this context, coming after a PC form expressing a continuous action in the past, -וְ + SC points to the same tense and aspect as the preceding verb.

3. The two clauses are separated by the pause at יָדָעְתִּי.

יָדַעְתִּי is *1s* SC of the verb יָדַע "to know". It is a *stative* verb, that is to say, a verb denoting a state of mind or disposition (knowing, learning, seeing, loving, hating, rejoicing, fearing, etc.) (XVI). The Suffix Conjugation of such verbs points to present time as often as to past: יָדַעְתִּי "I know"; יָכֹלְתָּ "you are able"; זָקְנָה "she is old".

עָשָׂה is *3ms* SC of the verb עָשָׂה "to do" (cf. עָלָה: 2). It is not a stative verb and points to past time (cf. 1), and is also distinguished from יָדַ֫עְתִּי "I know" in terms of aspect, since it expresses a single completed action.

4. This sentence is divided into two clauses at הַנָּחָשׁ.

וַתֹּ֫אמֶר is *3fs* PC of אָמַר "to say" with the prefix -וַ "and". -וַ + PC points to past time (p.41).

נֹאכֵל is *1pl* PC of the verb אָכַל "to eat". The third level of differentiation between SC and PC is in terms of *mood*: SC points to a fact (non-modal), PC to a conceptual idea not necessarily realized in fact (modal). In the present example, Eve is not saying that she and her husband are actually going to eat of the fruit of the trees in the garden (non-modal), but that they *may* eat (if they so desire) (modal), in contrast to the facts in a later verse of the same passage (Gen. 3:2-6). Mood or modality is expressed in English by the terms *can/may/should/would/could/must* (XIII).

In verbs of the type אָמַר, which begin with another of the gutturals (cf. 2), the PC prefix vowel is -ō- and the א silent: יֹאמַר "he will say"; תֹּאבַד "she will perish".

5. The pause in this sentence is at יְהוָֹה.

עֲמֹד is *ms* imperative of the verb עָמַד "to stand" (VI).

In וְאָמַרְתָּ֫, -וְ + SC points to future time. Whether it is thought of as a plain statement of fact (non-modal) or as a command (modal) must be determined by the context: coming after the imperative עֲמֹד, the construction probably expresses a command. On the stressed suffix in this construction, see p.27.

6. The sentence is divided into two clauses by the pause at אֲרָ֑ם.

יַעֲלֶה is *3ms* PC of עָלָה "to go up". The last construction to be dealt with in this chapter on tense and aspect involves an adverb: אָז "then" + PC points to past time. Without אָז (or (בְּ)טֶ֫רֶם "before") Prefix Conjugation forms pointing to a fact in past time are confined to poetry: e.g. צָרָה וְיָגוֹן אֶמְצָא "I met with distress and anguish (Ps. 116:3)".

SUMMARY

A. The distinction in meaning between the two Hebrew conjugations can be defined in terms of

(1) *tense* : SC points to past time; PC to non-past (present or future).

(2) *aspect*: SC points to a single completed action; PC to a habitual, continuous or repeated action.

(3) *mood* : SC expresses a fact (non-modal), PC a conceptual idea not necessarily realized in fact (modal).

In various contexts any one of these oppositions may receive the main emphasis, overshadowing or even eliminating the others. The context (passage, sentence, clause, adjacent particles) normally makes the meaning clear.

B. There are also the following general rules:

(1) -וַ + PC points to past time (VI)

(2) -וְ + PC is modal (XIII)

(3) -וְ + SC points to future time (statement or command) (IV)

(4) -וְ + SC expresses past continuous in some contexts

(5) אָז and (בְּ)טֶ֫רֶם with PC point to past time.

VERBS BEGINNING WITH א, ה, ח OR ע: עָזַר "TO HELP", ETC.

C. The commonest verbs of the type עָזַר, characterized by the initial guttural ה, ח, or ע, and the prefix vowel *-a-* (or *-e-*) are:

הָרַג "to kill"	עָבַד "to serve"	עָזַב "to leave"
הָפַךְ "to overthrow"	עָבַר "to pass, cross"	עָלָה "to go up"
חָשַׁב "to think"	עָזַר "to help"	עָנָה "to answer"
חָלַק "to divide"	עָמַד "to stand"	עָשָׂה "to make, do"

	Simple Stem עָזַר "to help"	 אָמַר "to say"	N-stem נֶעֱזַר "to be helped"	H-stem הֶעֱמִיד "to set up"
SUFFIX CONJUGATION				
1s "I"	עָזַ֫רְתִּי	אָמַ֫רְתִּי	נֶעֱזַ֫רְתִּי	הֶעֱמַ֫דְתִּי
2ms "you"	עָזַ֫רְתָּ	אָמַ֫רְתָּ	נֶעֱזַ֫רְתָּ	הֶעֱמַ֫דְתָּ
2fs "you"	עָזַרְתְּ	אָמַרְתְּ	נֶעֱזַרְתְּ	הֶעֱמַדְתְּ
3ms "he, it"	עָזַר	אָמַר	נֶעֱזַר	הֶעֱמִיד
3fs "she, it"	עָזְרָה	אָמְרָה	נֶעֶזְרָה	הֶעֱמִ֫ידָה
1pl "we"	עָזַ֫רְנוּ	אָמַ֫רְנוּ	נֶעֱזַ֫רְנוּ	הֶעֱמַ֫דְנוּ
2mpl "you"	עֲזַרְתֶּם	אֲמַרְתֶּם	נֶעֱזַרְתֶּם	הֶעֱמַדְתֶּם
2fpl "you"	עֲזַרְתֶּן	אֲמַרְתֶּן	נֶעֱזַרְתֶּן	הֶעֱמַדְתֶּן
3pl "they"	עָזְרוּ	אָמְרוּ	נֶעֶזְרוּ	הֶעֱמִ֫ידוּ
PREFIX CONJUGATION				
1s "I"	אֶעֱזֹר	אֹמַר	אֵעָזֵר	אַעֲמִיד
2ms "you"	תַּעֲזֹר	תֹּאמַר	תֵּעָזֵר	תַּעֲמִיד
2fs "you"	תַּעַזְרִי	תֹּאמְרִי	תֵּעָזְרִי	תַּעֲמִ֫ידִי
3ms "he, it"	יַעֲזֹר	יֹאמַר	יֵעָזֵר	יַעֲמִיד
3fs "she, it"	תַּעֲזֹר	תֹּאמַר	תֵּעָזֵר	תַּעֲמִיד
1pl "we"	נַעֲזֹר	נֹאמַר	נֵעָזֵר	נַעֲמִיד
2mpl "you"	תַּעַזְרוּ	תֹּאמְרוּ	תֵּעָזְרוּ	תַּעֲמִ֫ידוּ

2fpl "you"	תַּעֲזֹרְנָה	תֹּאמַ֫רְנָה	תֵּעָזַ֫רְנָה	תַּעֲמֵ֫דְנָה
3mpl "they"	יַעַזְרוּ	יֹאמְרוּ	יֵעָזְרוּ	יַעֲמִ֫ידוּ
3fpl "they"	תַּעֲזֹ֫רְנָה	תֹּאמַ֫רְנָה	תֵּעָזַ֫רְנָה	תַּעֲמֵ֫דְנָה
IMPERATIVE				
2ms	עֲזֹר	אֱמֹר	הֵעָזֵר	הַעֲמֵד
2fs	עִזְרִי	אִמְרִי	הֵעָזְרִי	הַעֲמִ֫ידִי
3mpl	עִזְרוּ	אִמְרוּ	הֵעָזְרוּ	הַעֲמִ֫ידוּ
3fpl	עֲזֹ֫רְנָה	אֱמֹ֫רְנָה	הֵעָזַ֫רְנָה	הַעֲמֵ֫דְנָה
וַ + PC				
3ms "and he..."	וַיַּעֲזֹר	וַיֹּ֫אמֶר	וַיֵּעָזֵר	וַיַּעֲמֵד
3mpl "and they."	וַיַּעַזְרוּ	וַיֹּאמְרוּ	וַיֵּעָזְרוּ	וַיַּעֲמִ֫ידוּ
ACTIVE PARTICIPLE				
ms ("-er")	עֹזֵר	אֹמֵר	נֶעֱזָר	מַעֲמִיד
mpl ("-ers")	עֹזְרִים	אֹמְרִים	נֶעֱזָרִים	מַעֲמִידִים
PASSIVE PARTICIPLE				
ms	עָזוּר	אָמוּר		מָעֳמָד
mpl	עֲזוּרִים	אֲמוּרִים		מָעֳמָדִים
VERBAL NOUN				
Basic form	עָזוֹר	אָמוֹר	הֵעָזֹר	הַעֲמֵד
Pregenitive	עֲזֹר	אֱמֹר	הֵעָזֵר	הַעֲמִיד
PG with *1s* suffix	עָזְרִי	אָמְרִי	הֵעָזְרִי	הַעֲמִידִי

D. The commonest verbs of the type אָמַר, characterized by the initial א and the PC prefix vowel *-ō-*, are:

אָבַד "to die, be lost"; H "to destroy"

אָכַל "to eat"; H "to feed"

אָמַר "to say"

VOCABULARY

אָבַד "to die, be lost"
H "to destroy"

אֱדוֹם "Edom"

אָז "then"

אִיּוֹב "Job"

הַיּוֹם "today"

זָקֵן "old, elder"

חָכָם "wise"

יוֹאָב "Joab"

כָּכָה "so, thus"

לֵוִי "Levite"

לֶחֶם "bread, food"

עָבַר "to pass over"

עָנָה "to answer"

עֵצָה f. "counsel"

שָׁר "to sing"

שִׁירָה f. "song, poem"

EXERCISE

Translate:

א. אָז יָשִׁיר־מֹשֶׁה וּבְנֵי יִשְׂרָאֵל אֶת־הַשִּׁירָה הַזֹּאת לַיהוָה:

ב. אַעֲלֶה אֶתְכֶם מִמִּצְרַיִם וְהֵבֵאתִי אֶתְכֶם לָאָרֶץ אֲשֶׁר אֶתֵּן לָכֶם:

ג. תּוֹרָה תֹּאבַד מִכֹּהֵן וְעֵצָה מִזְּקֵנִים:

ד. וַתַּעַן הָאִשָּׁה וַתֹּאמֶר לַמֶּלֶךְ עַבְדְּךָ יוֹאָב הוּא צִוָּנִי:

ה. אָבִיא חֶרֶב עַל־הָאָרֶץ הַהִיא וְאָמַרְתִּי חֶרֶב תַּעֲבֹר בָּאָרֶץ:

ו. יִרְאוּ אֶת־הַלֶּחֶם אֲשֶׁר הֶאֱכַלְתִּי אֶתְכֶם בַּמִּדְבָּר:

ז. כָּכָה יַעֲשֶׂה אִיּוֹב כָּל־הַיָּמִים:

ח. וְהֶאֱבַדְתִּי חֲכָמִים מֵאֱדוֹם בַּיּוֹם הַהוּא:

ט. בַּחֲרוּ לָכֶם הַיּוֹם אֶת־מִי תַּעֲבֹדוּ וְאָנֹכִי וּבֵיתִי נַעֲבֹד אֶת־יְהוָה:

י. וְהֶעֱמַדְתָּ אֶת־הַלְוִיִּם לִפְנֵי אַהֲרֹן וּבָנָיו:

CHAPTER XIII. MODAL AND NON-MODAL SENTENCES. VERBS ENDING WITH א, ה, ח OR ע : שָׁלַח "TO SEND", ETC.

EXAMPLES

1.	I will keep your law always (Ps. 119:44).	אֶשְׁמְרָה אֶת־תּוֹרָתְךָ תָמִיד׃	א.
2.	Arise and let us go back to our people (Jer. 46:16).	קוּמָה וְנָשׁוּבָה אֶל־עַמֵּנוּ׃	ב.
3.	Put forth your hand and strike everything that is his (Job. 1:11).	שְׁלַח־נָא יָדְךָ וְגַע בְּכָל־אֲשֶׁר־לוֹ׃	ג.
4.	Let all those who fear the Lord say, "His mercy (endures) for ever" (Ps. 118:4).	יֹאמְרוּ־נָא כָל־יִרְאֵי יְהוָה כִּי לְעוֹלָם חַסְדּוֹ׃	ד.
5.	May the Lord lift up his countenance upon you and give you peace (Num. 6:26).	יִשָּׂא יְהוָה פָּנָיו אֵלֶיךָ וְיָשֵׂם לְךָ שָׁלוֹם׃	ה.
6.	All the people need not go up (Josh. 7:3).	אַל־יַעַל כָּל־הָעָם׃	ו.

ANALYSIS

1. אֶשְׁמְרָה is *1s* PC of the verb שָׁמַר "to keep" with the *modal suffix* -*ā*. Distinguished in various ways from simple, declarative statements of fact are commands (Imperative: VI), questions (XI) and other sentences in which the speaker's intentions, demands, prayers and the like with respect to what he is saying are expressed. Modal sentences of this type are not always marked grammatically in Hebrew (cf. p. 71).

There are however five ways in which the Prefix Conjugation of the verb may be marked with respect to mood: the first of these is the suffix *-ā*. In the present example, in the context of a Psalmist's confession of faith (Ps. 119:44), it indicates the speaker's determination to fulfil his intentions as expressed in the verb. The *shall/will* opposition in English perhaps offers a rough parallel. On the overlap between tense and mood, see XII.

2. קוּמָה is the *ms* imperative of קָם "to arise" with the modal suffix *-ā*. There is no appreciable difference in meaning between this form and the normal imperative form (VI).

וְנָשׁוּבָה is *1pl* PC of שָׁב "to return" (XVII) with the modal suffix *-ā*. Here it distinguishes the clause from a statement of fact ("we shall return") and expresses what the speaker suggests or calls for (cf. Jer. 46:16), corresponding to the command in the previous clause.

3. The two clauses are separated by the pause marked at יָדְךָ.

שְׁלַח־נָא is the *ms* imperative of שָׁלַח "to send", with the modal particle נָא-. As the verb is here already marked as an imperative, the particle scarcely alters the meaning. Older translations used to represent it in English by phrases like "I beseech you", "please" and "I pray".

גַּע is *ms* imperative of the verb נָגַע "to touch". In verbs of this type, the initial root-letter נ is lost in the Prefix-Conjugation by assimilation (p. 161). On verbs of the type נָפַל, see Chapter XIV.

נָגַע also belongs to the verb type שָׁלַח in which the third root-letter is a guttural. In this type the second vowel in the Prefix Conjugation becomes *-a-* (unlike שָׁמַר : XI): יִקְרָא "he calls": נִשְׁמַע "we hear".

4. The major pause in this verse comes after יְהוָה.

יֹאמְרוּ is *3mpl* PC of אָמַר "to say" (XII) with the modal particle -נָא. Here the particle distinguishes between a statement of fact ("They will say"), and an exhortation ("Let them say").

In the genitive phrase יִרְאֵי יְהוָה the pregenitive term is the active participle of יָרֵא "to fear" (XV).

5. Two parts of the blessing are separated by the pause at אֵלֶיךָ.

יִשָּׂא is *3ms* PC of the verb נָשָׂא "to lift up". (On the verb-type, cf. 3 above). There are two indications that this sentence is not a simple statement of fact: (1) the context is a prayer (Num. 6:26); (2) the form of the second verb וְיָשֵׂם "and may he put, give", as opposed to the normal PC form יָשִׂים. Vowel-reduction (p. 161) in the Prefix Conjugation is a third grammatical mark of modality in the verb: e.g.

יָשִׂים "he will put"	יָשֵׂם "let him put"
יָשׁוּב "he will return"	יָשֹׁב "let him return"
יִהְיֶה "it will be"	יְהִי "let it be"
יֵלֵךְ "he will go"	יֵלֵךְ "let him go"
יַעֲלֶה "he will go up"	יַעַל "let him go up"

Unlike the suffix *-ā* (1, 2) and the particle -נָא (3, 4), vowel-reduction cannot be applied to every verb-type for phonetic reasons: thus in the present example modality is unmarked in יִשָּׂא but there is vowel-reduction in וְיָשֵׂם. The chief verb types in which vowel-reduction is a mark of modality are קָם, רָאָה, and יָשַׁב, together with the H-stem of all verb-types.

-וְ + PC is normally a modal form, not to be confused with -וַ + PC which regularly points to past time (XII).

6. -אַל is a negative particle which never occurs in simple declarative sentences. It is thus a fifth mark of modality.

יַעַל is *3ms* PC of the verb עָלָה "to go up" (XVIII) with vowel-reduction (יַעֲלֶה > יַעַל). Vowel-reduction is a second indication that the sentence is modal.

SUMMARY

A. In addition to the imperative forms (VI) mood in the verb is marked in five ways, all of them based on the Prefix Conjugation:

(1) the suffix $-\bar{a}$ is attached to *1st* person forms ("Cohortative") and also to imperatives.

(2) the particle -נָא is attached by a hyphen to the Prefix-Conjugation (also to imperatives).

(3) there is vowel-reduction in the third person forms in the verb-types קָם, רָאָה, and יָשַׁב, and in the H-stem ("Jussive").

(4) the construction -וְ + PC (with vowel-reduction) is used.

(5) the negative particle -אַל is used.

B. These five grammatical features indicate that the verb expresses among other things certainty, obligation, a command, a wish or a prayer (expressed in English by the auxiliaries *will*, *can*, *could*, *shall*, *should*, *must*, *may*, *might*, etc.). They do not define the mood any more closely. Like the tense-system (XII)

VERBS ENDING WITH א, הּ, ח OR ע: שָׁלַח "TO SEND", ETC.

modality is context-bound, and it is probably best to make only one basic distinction, namely, between *modal sentences* (e.g. commands, wishes, intentions) and *non-modal sentences* (i.e. statements of fact).

	Simple Stem שָׁלַח "to send"	מָצָא "to find"	N-stem נִשְׁכַּח "to be forgotten"	H-stem הִשְׁמִיעַ "to proclaim"	D-stem פִּתַּח "to free"
SUFFIX COUNJUGATION					
1s "I"	שָׁלַ֫חְתִּי	מָצָ֫אתִי	נִשְׁכַּ֫חְתִּי	הִשְׁמַ֫עְתִּי	פִּתַּ֫חְתִּי
2ms "you"	שָׁלַ֫חְתָּ	מָצָ֫אתָ	נִשְׁכַּ֫חְתָּ	הִשְׁמַ֫עְתָּ	פִּתַּ֫חְתָּ
2fs "you"	שָׁלַחַתְּ	מָצָאת	נִשְׁכַּחַתְּ	הִשְׁמַעַתְּ	פִּתַּחַתְּ
3ms "he, it"	שָׁלַח	מָצָא	נִשְׁכַּח	הִשְׁמִיעַ	פִּתַּח
3fs "she, it"	שָׁלְחָה	מָצְאָה	נִשְׁכְּחָה	הִשְׁמִ֫יעָה	פִּתְּחָה
1pl "we"	שָׁלַ֫חְנוּ	מָצָ֫אנוּ	נִשְׁכַּ֫חְנוּ	הִשְׁמַ֫עְנוּ	פִּתַּ֫חְנוּ
2mpl "you"	שְׁלַחְתֶּם	מְצָאתֶם	נִשְׁכַּחְתֶּם	הִשְׁמַעְתֶּם	פִּתַּחְתֶּם
2fpl "you"	שְׁלַחְתֶּן	מְצָאתֶן	נִשְׁכַּחְתֶּן	הִשְׁמַעְתֶּן	פִּתַּחְתֶּן
3pl "they"	שָׁלְחוּ	מָצְאוּ	נִשְׁכְּחוּ	הִשְׁמִ֫יעוּ	פִּתְּחוּ
PREFIX CONJUGATION					
1s "I"	אֶשְׁלַח	אֶמְצָא	אֶשָּׁכַח	אַשְׁמִיעַ	אֲפַתַּח
2ms "you"	תִּשְׁלַח	תִּמְצָא	תִּשָּׁכַח	תַּשְׁמִיעַ	תְּפַתַּח
2fs "you"	תִּשְׁלְחִי	תִּמְצְאִי	תִּשָּׁכְחִי	תַּשְׁמִ֫יעִי	תְּפַתְּחִי
3ms "he, it"	יִשְׁלַח	יִמְצָא	יִשָּׁכַח	יַשְׁמִיעַ	יְפַתַּח
3fs "she, it"	תִּשְׁלַח	תִּמְצָא	תִּשָּׁכַח	תַּשְׁמִיעַ	תְּפַתַּח
1pl "we"	נִשְׁלַח	נִמְצָא	נִשָּׁכַח	נַשְׁמִיעַ	נְפַתַּח
2mpl "you"	תִּשְׁלְחוּ	תִּמְצְאוּ	תִּשָּׁכְחוּ	תַּשְׁמִ֫יעוּ	תְּפַתְּחוּ
2fpl "you"	תִּשְׁלַ֫חְנָה	תִּמְצֶ֫אנָה	תִּשָּׁכַ֫חְנָה	תַּשְׁמַ֫עְנָה	תְּפַתַּ֫חְנָה
3mpl "they"	יִשְׁלְחוּ	יִמְצְאוּ	יִשָּׁכְחוּ	יַשְׁמִ֫יעוּ	יְפַתְּחוּ
3fpl "they"	תִּשְׁלַ֫חְנָה	תִּמְצֶ֫אנָה	תִּשָּׁכַ֫חְנָה	תַּשְׁמַ֫עְנָה	תְּפַתַּ֫חְנָה

VERBS ENDING WITH א, ה, ח OR ע: שָׁלַח "TO SEND", ETC.

IMPERATIVE					
2ms	שְׁלַח	מְצָא	הִשָּׁכַח	הַשְׁמַע	פַּתַּח
2fs	שִׁלְחִי	מִצְאִי	הִשָּׁכְחִי	הַשְׁמִיעִי	פַּתְּחִי
2mpl	שִׁלְחוּ	מִצְאוּ	הִשָּׁכְחוּ	הַשְׁמִיעוּ	פַּתְּחוּ
2fpl	שְׁלַחְנָה	מְצֶאנָה	הִשָּׁכַחְנָה	הַשְׁמַעְנָה	פַּתַּחְנָה
וַ + PC					
3ms "and he..."	וַיִּשְׁלַח	וַיִּמְצָא	וַיִּשָּׁכַח	וַיַּשְׁמַע	וַיְפַתַּח
3pl "and they..."	וַיִּשְׁלְחוּ	וַיִּמְצְאוּ	וַיִּשָּׁכְחוּ	וַיַּשְׁמִיעוּ	וַיְפַתְּחוּ
ACTIVE PARTICIPLE					
ms ("-er")	שֹׁלֵחַ	מֹצֵא	נִשְׁכָּח	מַשְׁמִיעַ	מְפַתֵּחַ
mpl ("-ers")	שֹׁלְחִים	מֹצְאִים	נִשְׁכָּחִים	מַשְׁמִיעִים	מְפַתְּחִים
PASSIVE PARTICIPLE					
ms	שָׁלוּחַ			מָשְׁמָע	מְפֻתָּח
mpl	שְׁלוּחִים			מָשְׁמָעִים	מְפֻתָּחִים
VERAL NOUN					
Basic form	שָׁלוֹחַ	מָצוֹא	הִשָּׁכֵחַ	הַשְׁמֵעַ	פַּתּוֹחַ
Pregenitive	שְׁלֹחַ	מְצֹא	הִשָּׁכַח	הַשְׁמִיעַ	פַּתַּח
PG with suffix.	שָׁלְחִי	מָצְאִי	הִשָּׁכְחִי	הַשְׁמִיעִי	פַּתְּחִי

C. In the verb-type שָׁלַח the third root-letter is a guttural, and the second vowel in PC forms is *-a-*. The commonest are:

בָּטַח "to trust"	זָרַע "to sow"	לָקַח "to take" (p.94)
בָּרָא "to create"	חָטָא "to sin"	מָצָא "to find"
זָבַח "to sacrifice"	יָדַע "to know"	מָשַׁח "to anoint"

VERBS ENDING WITH א, ה, ח OR ע: שָׁלַח "TO SEND", ETC.

נָגַע "to touch, arrive at"	נָשָׂא "to lift, carry, forgive"	שָׁכַח "to forget"
		שָׁלַח "to send"
נָטַע "to plant"	פָּתַח "to open"	שָׁמַע "to hear"
נָסַע "to pull out, march off"	קָרָא "to call"	

VOCABULARY

בֵּין...וּבֵין "between...and"	יֶ֫לֶד "child"	קָבַר "to bury"
בְּקֶ֫רֶב "inside" (prep.)	יֶשׁ־ "there is/are"	קֶ֫בֶר "grave, tomb"
בֵּרַךְ D. "to bless"	לְמַ֫עַן "in order that, for the sake of"	קֶ֫רֶב "inside, inner parts"
חָיָה "to live"	מָצָא "to find"	שָׁכַח "to forget"
חֵן "favour, grace"	פָּתַח "to open"	שַׁ֫עַר "gate"

EXERCISE

Translate:

א. יְהִי שֵׁם יְהוָה מְבוֹרָךְ מֵעַתָּה וְעַד־עוֹלָם׃

ב. שְׁמַע־נָא בְּקוֹל יְהוָה וּתְחִי נַפְשֶׁךָ׃

ג. וַיִּקְרָא יְהוָה לְמֹשֶׁה אֶל־רֹאשׁ הָהָר וַיַּעַל מֹשֶׁה׃

ד. הוֹדִיעֵנִי־נָא אֶת־דַּרְכְּךָ לְמַעַן אֶמְצָא חֵן בְּעֵינֶיךָ׃

ה. הֲיֶשׁ־נְבִיא יְהוָה בַּמָּקוֹם הַזֶּה וְנִשְׁמְעָה אֶת־דְּבָרָיו וְנִהְיֶה חֲכָמִים׃

ו. תָּשָׁב־נָא נֶפֶשׁ הַיֶּלֶד הַזֶּה עַל־קִרְבּוֹ׃

ז. פִּתְחוּ שְׁעָרִים וְיָבֹא גוֹי צַדִּיק׃

ח. לֹא־יִשְׁכַּח אֶת־בְּרִית אֲבוֹתֶיךָ אֲשֶׁר כָּרַת לָהֶם׃

ט. תְּנוּ לִי קֶבֶר וְאֶקְבְּרָה אֶת־מֵתִי׃

י. נִקְרְבָה־נָּא אֶל־יְהוָה וְיִשְׁפֹּט בֵּינִי וּבֵינֶךָ׃

CHAPTER XIV. NEGATIVE SENTENCES. VERBS BEGINNING WITH נ : נָפַל "TO FALL", ETC. לָקַח "TO TAKE"

EXAMPLES

1.	The Israelites remained where they were and did not move on. (Num. 9:22).	יַחֲנוּ בְנֵי־יִשְׂרָאֵל וְלֹא יִסָּעוּ׃	א.
2.	Let us fall into the hand of the Lord; but let me not fall into the hand of man (II Sam. 24:14).	נִפְּלָה־נָּא בְיַד יְהוָה וּבְיַד אָדָם אַל־אֶפֹּלָה׃	ב.
3.	You must not take a wife from among the Canaanite women (Gen. 28:1).	לֹא־תִקַּח אִשָּׁה מִבְּנוֹת כְּנָעַן׃	ג.
4.	But the hand of Ahikam was with Jeremiah, so that he was not given over to the people (Jer. 26:24).	אַךְ יַד אֲחִיקָם הָיְתָה אֶת־יִרְמְיָהוּ לְבִלְתִּי תֵּת־אֹתוֹ בְיַד־הָעָם׃	ד.
5.	There is nothing new under the sun (Eccl. 1:9).	אֵין כָּל־חָדָשׁ תַּחַת הַשָּׁמֶשׁ׃	ה.
6.	He will not obey the voice of his father (Deut. 21:18).	אֵינֶנּוּ שֹׁמֵעַ בְּקוֹל אָבִיו׃	ו.

ANALYSIS

1. יַחֲנוּ and יִסָּעוּ are *3mpl* PC forms pointing to a continuous action in the past (XII.2).

In the phrase בְּנֵי־יִשְׂרָאֵל "Isra elites", בֵּן denotes a member of a group, not literally "son" (IX.1).

לֹא is the normal negative word in non-modal verbal sentences, where it immediately precedes the verb.

VERBS BEGINNING WITH נ: נָפַל "TO FALL", ETC.

יִסָּעוּ is *3mpl* PC of the verb נָסַע "to pull out, march off" (pausal form). נָסַע belongs to the verb-type נָפַל. In these verbs the first root-letter is נ, and this is omitted by assimilation (p. 161) after most of the prefixes: e.g. יִפּוֹל/נָפַל "to fall"; הִגִּיד "to tell" (H-stem of *נָגַד). The assimilation is marked by the doubling of the second root-letter, unless it occurs at the beginning of a word as in the imperative and some verbal noun forms: e.g. סְעוּ (*2mpl* imp. of נָסַע "to journey"); שְׂאֵת (verbal noun of נָשָׂא "to carry") (cf.p.5).

2. נִפְּלָה־נָּא is *1pl* PC of נָפַל "to fall" with the modal suffix ־ָה (-*ā*) and the modal particle ־נָא (p. 87). The modality in the verb expresses David's reluctant choice of what he feels to be the least unpleasant of three evils (II Samuel 24:13-14).

־אַל in the second clause is a second negative word which is used only in modal sentences (XIII): cf. אַל־תִּירָא "do not fear" (Gen. 15.1), as opposed to לֹא־יָרֵאתָ "you are not afraid" (II Sam. 1:14).

אֶפֹּ֫לָה (*epṓlā*) is the pausal form of אֶפְּלָה (p. 157).

3. תִּקַּח is *2ms* PC of the verb לָקַח "to take". The first root-letter ל is omitted by assimilation after the prefixes in this verb, like the initial נ in verbs of the type נָפַל (1 above). There are also some verbs in which an initial י is assimilated (p.115).

The context (Gen. 28:1) makes it clear that this sentence is a command, not a plain statement of fact, and the use of לֹא instead of the normal modal word ־אַל (2 above) is to be explained as turning a normal request into an emphatic prohibition. Eight of the Ten Commandments (Ex. 20, Deut. 5) have the same construction. On emphasis, see Chapter XX.

בְּנוֹת, like בְּנֵי in 1, denotes members of an ethnic group.

4. A major pause in this sentence is marked at יִרְמְיָהוּ.

הָיְתָה is *3fs* SC of the verb הָיָה, pointing to past time (XII.1). It belongs to the verb-type רָאָה (XVIII).

לְבִלְתִּי is the normal negative word with verbal nouns: cf. לְבִלְתִּי שְׁמֹעַ "not to listen" (p.59). Related to this is the negative word בַּל, a poetic variant of לֹא (p. 115).

תֵּת is the verbal noun of נָתַן "to give" (IX. 5). In this form both the initial נ and the final ן of the root are omitted by assimilation. With the suffix pronouns, the form is -תִּת, in which doubling is marked.

5. אֵין is a common negative word in verbless sentences. Here it corresponds to English "there is no(t)"; but cf. אַבְנֵר אֵינֶ֫נּוּ בְּחֶבְרוֹן "Abner is not in Hebron".

In negative sentences כָּל- corresponds to English "any".

6. אֵינֶ֫נּוּ is the negative word אֵין with the *3ms* suffix pronoun ֶנּוּ (*énu*) (VIII. 6).

שֹׁמֵעַ is the *ms* active participle of שָׁמַע "to hear". Participles can function both as verbs and nouns (IX), and sentences like the present example may be considered as verbless, taking the normal negative word אֵין (cf. 5 above).

On the prepositional verb -שָׁמַע בְּ "to obey", see Chapter XV.

XIV

NEGATIVE SENTENCES

SUMMARY

A. Negation is marked by a set of negative words, which are normall placed (sometimes with a hyphen) immediately before the word they negate.

B. There are five negative words with the following distribution:

(1) לֹא in non-modal verbal sentences; less often in verbless and modal sentences, where it has a special function.

(2) אַל־ with the Prefix Conjugation in modal sentences (wishes, commands, exhortations).

(3) בַּל a poetic variant of לֹא (p. 115).

(4) לְבִלְתִּי with verbal nouns.

(5) אֵין in verbless sentences.

C. In verbs of the type נָפַל, the initial נ of the citation-form is omitted by assimilation after most prefixes. The following are the commonest verbs of this type:

לָקַח "to take"

נָגַע "to touch"
H "to arrive at"

נָגַשׁ "to approach"
H "to present"

נִחַם N "to repent"
D "to comfort"

נָטָה "to spread out"
H "to turn"

נִסָּה D "to test, try"

נָסַע "to set out"

נָפַל "to fall"

נָצַר "to keep"

נָשָׂא "to lift, carry, forgive"

נָתַן "to give"

An important sub-group of H-stem verbs with assimilated נ, like הִגִּיד "to tell", are listed in Chapter XIX.
There are some verbs in which the נ is not assimilated:
e.g. הִנְחִיל "to give as an inheritance"; הִנְחָה "to lead".

VERBS BEGINNING WITH נ : נָפַל "TO FALL", ETC. לָקַח "TO TAKE".

	Simple Stem נָפַל "to fall"	Simple Stem נָתַן "to give"	Simple Stem לָקַח "to take"	N-Stem נִשָּׂא "to be lifted up"
SUFFIX CONJUGATION				
1s "I"	נָפַלְתִּי	נָתַתִּי	לָקַחְתִּי	נִשֵּׂאתִי
2ms "you"	נָפַלְתָּ	נָתַתָּ	לָקַחְתָּ	נִשֵּׂאתָ
2fs "you"	נָפַלְתְּ	נָתַתְּ	לָקַחַתְּ	נִשֵּׂאת
3ms "he, it"	נָפַל	נָתַן	לָקַח	נִשָּׂא
3fs "she, it"	נָפְלָה	נָתְנָה	לָקְחָה	נִשְּׂאָה
1pl "we"	נָפַלְנוּ	נָתַנּוּ	לָקַחְנוּ	נִשֵּׂאנוּ
2mpl "you"	נְפַלְתֶּם	נְתַתֶּם	לְקַחְתֶּם	נִשֵּׂאתֶם
2fpl "you"	נְפַלְתֶּן	נְתַתֶּן	לְקַחְתֶּן	נִשֵּׂאתֶן
3pl "they"	נָפְלוּ	נָתְנוּ	לָקְחוּ	נִשְּׂאוּ
PREFIX CONJUGATION				
1s "I"	אֶפֹּל	אֶתֵּן	אֶקַּח	אֶנָּשֵׂא
2ms "you"	תִּפֹּל	תִּתֵּן	תִּקַּח	תִּנָּשֵׂא
2fs "you"	תִּפְּלִי	תִּתְּנִי	תִּקְחִי	תִּנָּשְׂאִי
3ms "he, it"	יִפֹּל	יִתֵּן	יִקַּח	יִנָּשֵׂא
3fs "she, it"	תִּפֹּל	תִּתֵּן	תִּקַּח	תִּנָּשֵׂא
1pl "we"	נִפֹּל	נִתֵּן	נִקַּח	נִנָּשֵׂא
2mpl "you"	תִּפְּלוּ	תִּתְּנוּ	תִּקְחוּ	תִּנָּשְׂאוּ
2fpl "you"	תִּפֹּלְנָה	תִּתֵּנָּה	תִּקַּחְנָה	תִּנָּשֶׂאנָה
3mpl "they"	יִפְּלוּ	יִתְּנוּ	יִקְחוּ	יִנָּשְׂאוּ
3fpl "they"	תִּפֹּלְנָה	תִּתֵּנָּה	תִּקַּחְנָה	תִּנָּשֶׂאנָה
IMPERATIVE				
2ms	נְפֹל	תֵּן	קַח	הִנָּשֵׂא
2fs	נִפְלִי	תְּנִי	קְחִי	הִנָּשְׂאִי
2mpl	נִפְלוּ	תְּנוּ	קְחוּ	הִנָּשְׂאוּ
2fpl	נְפֹלְנָה	תֵּנָּה	קַחְנָה	הִנָּשֶׂאנָה

VERBS BEGINNING WITH נ : נָפַל "TO FALL", ETC. לָקַח "TO TAKE".

וַ + PC				
3ms "and he..."	וַיִּפֹּל	וַיִּתֵּן	וַיִּקַּח	וַיִּנָּשֵׂא
3mpl "and they.."	וַיִּפְּלוּ	וַיִּתְּנוּ	וַיִּקְּחוּ	וַיִּנָּשְׂאוּ
ACTIVE PARTICIPLE				
ms ("-er)	נֹפֵל	נֹתֵן	לֹקֵחַ	
mpl ("-ers)	נֹפְלִים	נֹתְנִים	לֹקְחִים	
PASSIVE PARTICIPLE				
ms		נָתוּן	לָקוּחַ	נִשָּׂא
mpl		נְתוּנִים	לְקוּחִים	נִשָּׂאִים
VERBAL NOUN				
Basic form	נָפוֹל	נָתוֹן	לָקוֹחַ	הִנָּשֵׂא
Pregenitive	נְפֹל	תֵּת	קַחַת	הִנָּשֵׂא
PG with *1s* suffix	נָפְלִי	תִּתִּי	קַחְתִּי	הִנָּשְׂאִי

VOCABULARY

אֹהֶל "tent"

אֵין "not, there is/are not"

אַל־ "not (modal sentences)"

אַרְנוֹן "Arnon"

בַּל "not (poetic)"

כֵּן "so, thus"

מִלְחָמָה f. "battle, war"

מִשְׁפָּט "judgment"

נַחַל "wadi"

נִחַם N "repent"

נָסַע "to set out"

נִשְׁבַּע N "to swear an oath"

סָר "depart, turn away"

עוֹד "again, more"

תַּרְדֵּמָה f. "deep sleep"

VERBS BEGINNING WITH נ: נָפַל "TO FALL", ETC.

EXERCISE

Translate:

א. לֹא תַעֲלוּ וְלֹא תִלָּחֲמוּ כִּי אֵינֶנִּי בְּקִרְבְּכֶם:

ב. נִשְׁבַּע יְהוָה וַיֹּאמֶר לֹא־אֵצֵא עוֹד מִן־הַבַּיִת הַזֶּה:

ג. קוּמוּ סְעוּ וְעִבְרוּ אֶת־נַחַל אַרְנוֹן:

ד. לֹא עָשָׂה כֵן לְכָל־גּוֹי וּמִשְׁפָּטִים בַּל־יְדָעוּם:

ה. וַיִּנָּחֶם יְהוָה כִּי עָשָׂה אֶת־הָאָדָם עַל־הָאָרֶץ:

ו. סוּרוּ־נָא מֵעַל אָהֳלֵי הָאֲנָשִׁים הָאֵלֶּה וְאַל־תִּגְּעוּ בְּכָל־אֲשֶׁר לָהֶם:

ז. וְהוֹשַׁעְתִּים בַּיהוָה אֱלֹהֵיהֶם וְלֹא אוֹשִׁיעֵם בְּחֶרֶב וּבְמִלְחָמָה:

ח. וַיִּשָּׂא יָדוֹ לָהֶם לְהַפִּיל אֹתָם בַּמִּדְבָּר:

ט. כְּמַעֲשֵׂה יְדֵיהֶם תֵּן לָהֶם:

י. וְאֵין רֹאֶה וְאֵין יוֹדֵעַ כִּי תַּרְדֵּמַת יְהוָה נָפְלָה עֲלֵיהֶם:

CHAPTER XV. PREPOSITIONS. ADVERBIAL EXPRESSIONS. STATIVE VERBS: זָקֵן "TO BE OLD", ETC.

EXAMPLES

1. No man living can be righteous before you (Ps. 143:2).	א. לֹא־יִצְדַּק לְפָנֶיךָ כָל־חָי׃
2. So he went down to Egypt to dwell there because the famine was severe in the land (Gen. 12:10).	ב. וַיֵּרֶד מִצְרַיְמָה לָגוּר שָׁם כִּי־כָבֵד הָרָעָב בָּאָרֶץ׃
3. The Lord your God has chosen him from all your tribes (Deut. 18:5).	ג. בּוֹ בָּחַר יְהוָה אֱלֹהֶיךָ מִכָּל־שְׁבָטֶיךָ׃
4. Do not fear him because tomorrow I shall hand him over to you (Josh. 11:6).	ד. אַל־תִּירָא מִמֶּנּוּ כִּי מָחָר אָנֹכִי נֹתֵן אֹתוֹ בְּיָדֶךָ׃
5. And David rejoiced very greatly too (I Chr. 29:9).	ה. וְגַם דָּוִד שָׂמַח שִׂמְחָה גְדוֹלָה׃
6. Abraham spoke to him again (Gen 18:29).	ו. וַיּוֹסֶף עוֹד אַבְרָהָם לְדַבֵּר אֵלָיו׃

ANALYSIS

1. יִצְדַּק is *3ms* PC of the stative verb צָדַק "to be righteous". In this sentence PC points to a timeless idea or concept and may be represented in English by "can/could" (XII. 4).

Stative verbs denote a state of mind or disposition, rather than an action. They are characterized in the Prefix Conjugation by the vowel *-a-*: יִצְדַּק "he is righteous"; תֶּאֱהַב "she loves"; נִלְמַד "we shall learn".

ADVERBIAL EXPRESSIONS.

לְפָנֶ֫יךָ is made up of the preposition לִפְנֵי "before" and the *2ms* suffix pronoun ךָ- "you, your" (VIII). Like many Hebrew prepositions לִפְנֵי is itself made up of two elements: the prepositional prefix -לְ and the pregenitive form of the plural noun פָּנִים "face". Before all the singular and the first person plural suffixes, לִפְנֵי becomes -לְפָנ: לְפָנַי "before me"; לְפָנֵ֫ינוּ "before us" (*CəCVCV(C)* (p. 156).).

-כָּל in a negative sentence corresponds to English "any" (XIV.5)

2. וַיֵּ֫רֶד is *3ms* PC of יָרַד "to go down" (verb-type יָשַׁב: XVI) with -וַ "and, so"

מִצְרַ֫יְמָה "to Egypt" consists of the proper name מִצְרַיִם "Egypt" and the unstressed adverbial suffix ה- *(-ā)* which expresses direction. About thirty nouns and proper names occur in Biblical Hebrew with this suffix: e.g. יָ֫מָּה "towards the sea, westwards"; הַשָּׁמַ֫יְמָה "towards the sky"; בָּבֶ֫לָה "to Babylon". The suffix occurs also in the adverb שָׁ֫מָּה "to there, thither", and the question word אָ֫נָה "whither?". The syllable preceding this suffix is always stressed.

The preposition -לְ "to" with the verbal noun of verbs of the type יָשַׁב (XVI), קָם (XVII), נָתַן (XIV) and others is written -לָ *(lā-)*: לָשֶׁ֫בֶת "to dwell"; לָקוּם "to stand"; לָתֵת "to give".

שָׁם "there" is an *adverb*. In Hebrew there are relatively few pure adverbs, that is, single items which function primarily as verb-modifiers. A few are marked by special suffixes, notably ית- (*-īt*) in שֵׁנִית "a second time" and יְהוּדִית "in the Jewish language"; and ם- (*-ām*) in יוֹמָם "by day", אָמְנָם "truly" and רֵיקָם "in vain". The chief unmarked adverbs are:

אוּלַי "perhaps" מְעַט "a little" פֹּה "here"
אָז "then" מָחָר "tomorrow" רַק "only"
אֶתְמוֹל "yesterday" עוֹד "still, again" שָׁם "there"
כֹּה, כֵּן "so, thus" עַתָּה "now" תָּמִיד "always"

כָּבֵד is *3ms* SC of the stative verb כָּבֵד "to be severe, heavy". The suffix tense of stative verbs points to a state, attitude or condition in past time as well as present (XII.3)

Many stative verbs are distinguished from action verbs by the vowel -*ē*- in the citation-form (*3ms* SC). The *ms* participle of these verbs is identical with the citation-form and frequently functions as a pure adjective: e.g. כָּבֵד "heavy"; זָקֵן "old"; מָלֵא "full".

3. The phrase בָּחַר בּוֹ "he chose him" is made up of the prepositional verb- בָּחַר בְּ "to choose" and the *3ms* suffix pronoun וֹ-. *Prepositional verbs* are so-called because they consist of one item which on its own functions as a verb and another item which on its own functions as a preposition: cf. "I *took to* him at once".

On the distinctive word-order, probably expressing emphasis, see Chapter XX.

מִכָּל- "from all" is made up of the preposition מִן "from" and the pregenitive form of כָּל- "all, any". The final ן of the citation-form of this preposition is frequently omitted by assimilation (p.161). Before the gutturals and ר (pp.158f.), which are never doubled the vowel is -*ē*-: מִבֵּית לֶחֶם "from Bethlehem"; but מֵהָעִיר "from the city". Before definite nouns with הַ-, מִן is sometimes written in full, but often becomes -מֵ: e.g. מִן-הָעִיר or מֵהָעִיר "from the city".

4. -אַל is the negative word in modal sentences (p. 89).

תִּירָא is *2ms* PC of the stative verb יָרֵא "to fear". The second vowel is -*a*- because it is a stative verb (cf. 1 above) and also because it ends in a guttural like verbs of the type שָׁלַח (XIII).

מִמֶּנּוּ "from him" is made up of the preposition מִן and the *3ms* suffix pronoun ־ֶנּוּ (cf. VIII. 6). The prepositions מִן "from" and -כְּ "like, as" take -מ- before the singular suffixes and *1pl* suffix: e.g. מִמֶּנִּי "from me"; כָּמֹנִי "like me"; כָּמוֹךָ "like you".

מָחָר "tomorrow" is a pure adverb (cf. 2. above).

5. גַּם "also" is another pure adverb (cf. 2, 4 above)

שָׂמַח is *3ms* SC of the stative verb שָׂמַח "to rejoice" (cf.2 above), and linked to it like an adverb is the noun-phrase שִׂמְחָה גְדוֹלָה "great joy", in which the root of the verb is repeated in order to enrich its meaning (cf. XX. 2). It is best represented in English by an appropriate adverb: cf. וַיִּירְאוּ יִרְאָה גְדוֹלָה "they were *very* afraid"; וַיֵּרַע אֶל־יוֹנָה רָעָה גְדוֹלָה "and it displeased Jonah *exceedingly*" (p. 111).

6. וַיּוֹסֶף "and he added" is *3ms* PC of the H-stem verb הוֹסִיף "to add" (cf. יָשַׁב : XVI), with -וַ "and" pointing to past time. This verb and a number of others function adverbially in relation to another verb in the clause, and are best represented in English by adverbs:

הוֹסִיף H "again (to add)" | מִהַר D. "quickly (to hurry)"
הֵיטִיב H "well (to be good)" | שָׁב "again (to return)"
הִרְבָּה H "much (to multiply)"

In this example the verbal noun דַּבֵּר "to speak" (D-stem) is modified by the adverb עוֹד "again" as well as the verb הוֹסִיף "to add".

STATIVE VERBS: זָקֵן "TO BE OLD", ETC.

אֵלָיו "to him" is made up of the preposition אֶל־ and the *3ms* suffix pronoun (VIII). The following prepositions have a singular citation-form, but a plural form when the suffix pronouns are attached: (e.g. אֵלַי "to me"; עָלֶיהָ "on her"):

אֶל־ "to"	עַל־ "on concerning, against"
עַד־ "up to, until"	תַּחַת "under, instead of"

SUMMARY

A. Stative verbs like זָקֵן denote a state, attitude or condition, rather than an action, and are distinguished from action-verbs in three ways:

(1) The second vowel in Prefix Conjugation forms is *-a-*.

(2) The second vowel in the citation-form is often *-ē-* and occasionally *-ō-* (instead of *-a-*: IV. 1).

(3) Suffix Conjugation forms point to present time as often as past.

The commonest verbs of this type are:

אָהֵב "to love"	טָהֵר "to be clean"	לָמַד "to learn"
אוֹר "to shine"	טָמֵא "to be unclean"	מֵת "to die"
בּוֹשׁ "to be ashamed"	יָדַע "to know"	מָלֵא "to be full"
בָּחַר "to choose"	יָטַב "to be good"	צָדַק "to be just"
בָּטַח "to trust"	יָכֹל "to be able"	קָדַשׁ "to be holy"
גָּדַל "to be great"	יָרֵא "to fear"	קָטֹן "to be small"
זָקֵן "to be old"	כָּבֵד "to be heavy"	שָׂנֵא "to hate"
חָזַק "to be strong"		

STATIVE VERBS: זָקֵן "TO BE OLD", ETC.

	SIMPLE STEM			
	זָקֵן "to be old"	מֵת "to die"	לָמַד "to learn"	יָכֹל "to be able"
SUFFIX CONJUGATION				
1s "I"	זָקַ֫נְתִּי	מַ֫תִּי	לָמַ֫דְתִּי	יָכֹ֫לְתִּי
2ms "you"	זָקַ֫נְתָּ	מַ֫תָּ	לָמַ֫דְתָּ	יָכֹ֫לְתָּ
2fs "you"	זָקַנְתְּ	מַתְּ	לָמַדְתְּ	יָכֹלְתְּ
3ms "he, it"	זָקֵן	מֵת	לָמַד	יָכֹל
3fs "she, it"	זָקְנָה	מֵ֫תָה	לָמְדָה	יָכְלָה
1pl "we"	זָקַ֫נּוּ	מַ֫תְנוּ	לָמַ֫דְנוּ	יָכֹ֫לְנוּ
2mpl "you"	זְקַנְתֶּם	מַתֶּם	לְמַדְתֶּם	יְכָלְתֶּם
2fpl "you"	זְקַנְתֶּן	מַתֶּן	לְמַדְתֶּן	יְכָלְתֶּן
3pl "they"	זָקְנוּ	מֵ֫תוּ	לָמְדוּ	יָכְלוּ
PREFIX CONJUGATION				
1s "I"	אֶזְקַן	אָמוּת	אֶלְמַד	אוּכַל
2ms "you"	תִּזְקַן	תָּמוּת	תִּלְמַד	תּוּכַל
2fs "you"	תִּזְקְנִי	תָּמ֫וּתִי	תִּלְמְדִי	תּוּכְלִי
3ms "he, it"	יִזְקַן	יָמוּת	יִלְמַד	יוּכַל
3fs "she, it"	תִּזְקַן	תָּמוּת	תִּלְמַד	תּוּכַל
1pl "we"	נִזְקַן	נָמוּת	נִלְמַד	נוּכַל
2mpl "you"	תִּזְקְנוּ	תָּמ֫וּתוּ	תִּלְמְדוּ	תּוּכְלוּ
2fpl "you"	תִּזְקַ֫נָּה	תְּמוּתֶ֫נָה	תִּלְמַ֫דְנָה	תּוּכַ֫לְנָה
3mpl "they"	יִזְקְנוּ	יָמ֫וּתוּ	יִלְמְדוּ	יוּכְלוּ
3fpl "they"	תִּזְקַ֫נָּה	תְּמוּתֶ֫נָה	תִּלְמַ֫דְנָה	תּוּכַ֫לְנָה
וַ + PC				
3ms "and he..."	וַיִּזְקַן	וַיָּ֫מָת	וַיִּלְמַד	וַיּ֫כַל
3mpl "and they.."	וַיִּזְקְנוּ	וַיָּמֻתוּ	וַיִּלְמְדוּ	וַיּוּכְלוּ
PARTICIPLE				
ms ("-er")	זָקֵן	מֵת	לֹמֵד	יָכוֹל
mpl ("-ers")	זְקֵנִים	מֵתִים	לֹמְדִים	יְכוֹלִים

PREPOSITIONS

VERBAL NOUN				
Basic form	זָקוֹן	מוּת	לָמוֹד	יָכוֹל
Pregenitive	זְקַן	מוּת	לְמֹד	יְכֹלֶת
PG with *1s* suffix	זָקְנִי	מוּתִי	לָמְדִי	יְכָלְתִּי

B. There are four *preposition prefixes:*

-בְּ "in, by, with, against" -לְ "to, for, of"

-כְּ "like, as, about" -מִ "from, than"

The commonest *prepositions* are:

אַחַר, אַחֲרֵי "after, behind"	-מִן "from, than"
-אֶל "to, towards"	-מִסָּבִיב לְ "around"
-אֶת "with"	-מֵעַל "above"
בְּיַד "by"	מֵעִם "from"
בַּעֲבוּר "for the sake of"	מִפְּנֵי "because of"
בְּעֵבֶר "over, across"	-מִתַּחַת לְ "beneath, under"
בְּקֶרֶב "inside, among"	נֶגֶד "opposite"
בְּתוֹךְ "in the middle of"	סָבִיב "around"
בֵּין..וּבֵין "between, among"	-עַד "up to, until"
בְּלִי "without"	-עַל "on, concerning"
לְמַעַן "for the sake of"	עַל־יַד "besides"
לְפִי "according to"	-עִם "with"
לִפְנֵי "before"	תַּחַת "under"
לִקְרַאת "against"	

Some common *prepositional verbs* are:

-אָחַז בְּ "to grasp"	-מָשַׁל בְּ "to rule"	-שָׁאַל בְּ "to consult"
-בָּחַר בְּ "to choose"	-נָגַע בְּ "to touch"	-שָׁמַע בְּ "to obey"
-הוֹשִׁיעַ לְ "to save"	רָדַף אַחֲרֵי "to pursue"	-קָרָא לְ "to call"

C. In addition to pure *adverbs*, a verb may be modified by nouns or verbal nouns with an adverbial function, and by a small group of verbs like הוֹסִיף "to add".

STATIVE VERBS: זָקֵן "TO BE OLD", ETC.

VOCABULARY

אֲדָמָה	f. "ground, earth"	זָבַח	"to sacrifice"	לַ֫יְלָה	"night"
אֵם	f. "mother"	יוֹנָה	"Jonah"	מַ֫יִם	"water"
אַרְבָּעִים	"forty"	יָטַב	H. "to do well"	מִשְׁפָּחָה	f. "family"
אֶת־	"with"	יָרֵא	"to fear"	קִיקָיוֹן	"gourd"
הוֹסִיף	H. "to add"	כִּבֵּד	D. "to honour"	רַק	"only"

EXERCISE

Translate:

א. רַק אֶתְכֶם יָדַ֫עְתִּי מִכֹּל־מִשְׁפְּחוֹת הָאֲדָמָה:

ב. אַל־תִּירָא כִּי אִתְּךָ אָנִי:

ג. זָקֵן הָאִישׁ וְכָבֵד וְהוּא שָׁפַט אֶת־יִשְׂרָאֵל אַרְבָּעִים שָׁנָה:

ד. וַיִּקְרָא פַּרְעֹה אֶל־מֹשֶׁה וְאֶל־אַהֲרֹן וַיֹּאמֶר לְכוּ זִבְחוּ לֵאלֹהֵיכֶם בָּאָרֶץ:

ה. וַיִּשְׂמַח יוֹנָה עַל־הַקִּיקָיוֹן שִׂמְחָה גְדוֹלָה:

ו. אַחֲרֵי הַדְּבָרִים הָאֵלֶּה שָׁלַח הַמֶּלֶךְ אֶת־עֲבָדָיו יְרוּשָׁלַ֫יְמָה:

ז. כַּבֵּד אֶת־אָבִיךָ וְאֶת־אִמֶּךָ לְמַעַן יִיטַב לְךָ עַל־הָאֲדָמָה אֲשֶׁר יְהוָה נֹתֵן לָךְ:

ח. רְאִיתֶם אֶת־מִצְרַיִם הַיּוֹם וְלֹא־תוֹסִיפוּ לִרְאוֹתָם עוֹד עַד־עוֹלָם:

ט. וַיְהִי שָׁם עִם־יְהוָה אַרְבָּעִים יוֹם וְאַרְבָּעִים לַ֫יְלָה לֶחֶם לֹא־אָכַל וּמַיִם לֹא־שָׁתָה:

י. קְרַב אַתָּה וּשְׁמַע אֵת־כָּל־אֲשֶׁר יֹאמַר יְהוָה אֱלֹהֵינוּ:

CHAPTER XVI. ACTIVE AND PASSIVE. IMPERSONAL CONSTRUCTIONS. POETIC LANGUAGE. VERBS BEGINNING WITH י: יָשַׁב "TO SIT", ETC. הָלַךְ "TO GO".

EXAMPLES

1.	The Lord will be known to the Egyptians, and the Egyptians will know the Lord on that day (Isa. 19:21).	וְנוֹדַע יְהוָה לְמִצְרַיִם וְיָדְעוּ מִצְרַיִם אֶת־יְהוָה בַּיּוֹם הַהוּא׃	א.
2.	A child has been born to us; a son has been given to us (Isa. 9:5).	יֶלֶד יֻלַּד־לָנוּ בֵּן נִתַּן־לָנוּ׃	ב.
3.	Those blessed by him shall possess the land, but those cursed by him shall be cut off (Ps. 37:22).	מְבוֹרָכָיו יִירְשׁוּ אָרֶץ וּמְקֻלָּלָיו יִכָּרֵתוּ׃	ג.
4.	Has it not been told my lord what I did? (I Kgs. 18:13).	הֲלֹא־הֻגַּד לַאדוֹנִי אֶת־אֲשֶׁר־עָשִׂיתִי׃	ד.
5.	Jonah was exceedingly displeased and very angry (Jon. 4:1).	וַיֵּרַע אֶל־יוֹנָה רָעָה גְדוֹלָה וַיִּחַר לוֹ׃	ה.
6.	There will be no crying or shouting or calling out (for help) in the street (Isa. 42:2).	לֹא יִצְעַק וְלֹא יִשָּׂא וְלֹא־יַשְׁמִיעַ בַּחוּץ קוֹלוֹ׃	ו.

ANALYSIS

1. וְנוֹדַע is *3ms* SC of the N-stem of יָדַע "to know" with וְ- "and". One of the commonest functions of the N-stem is to express the passive of a simple stem verb (X. 4). A *passive sentence* is one in which the object of an active verb has become the subject: e.g. "David (subject) *killed* Goliath (object)" becomes "Goliath (subject) *was killed* (by David)". In English passive sentences always contain

the verb "to be". In the present example the same idea is expressed twice, first in a passive clause and then in an active one: the subject in the passive clause (יְהוָה "the Lord") is the object in the active clause (אֶת־יְהוָה). The verb in the first clause is passive, active in the second.

There are six common verbs of the type יָשַׁב. In these the initial semi-vowel of the root is omitted after most prefixes, and the prefix-vowel is -*ō*- in most N-stem and H-stem forms: e.g. נוֹלַד "to be born" (from יָלַד); הוֹצִיא "to take out (cause to go out)" (from יָצָא).

2. יֻלַּד is *3ms* SC of יָלַד "to be born". It is a rounded stem form and therefore passive (p.65), and in meaning is indistinguishable from the more common N-stem forms נוֹלַדְתִּי "I was born", נוֹלַדְתָּ "you were born", etc. יָלַד is one of the six verbs of the type יָשַׁב.

נִתַּן is also *3ms* SC of a passive stem, the N-stem of the verb נָתַן "to give" (cf. נָפַל: XIV). The first root-letter, which is also *n*, is omitted by assimilation after the prefix *ni*- (cf. p.161).).

In this short sentence from one of the great "messianic oracles" (Isaiah 9:5) the same thought is expressed twice: יֶלֶד "a child" is parallel to בֵּן "a son", and יֻלַּד־לָנוּ "is born to us" parallel to נִתַּן־לָנוּ "has been given to us". This *parallelism of synonyms* is one of the distinctive features of Hebrew poetic structure, in which units of similar meaning "rhyme", instead of units of similar sound.

3. מְבֹרָכָיו is *3mpl* of a passive participle of the D-stem verb בֵּרַךְ "to bless", with *3ms* suffix pronoun "him, his". The suffix refers to the subject of a corresponding active clause "those whom *he*

blesses", and stands for the agent-noun "by him" in a passive construction. The agent is expressed far more rarely in Hebrew than in English.

Similarly, מְקֻלָּלָיו is *3mpl* of the passive participle of the D-stem verb קִלֵּל "to curse" with the *3ms* suffix pronoun "by him".

בֵּרַךְ represents a type of verb in which the second root-letter is א or ר. These letters are never doubled (p.158), and the preceding vowel (which is always short before a doubled consonant: p.156) is lengthened instead. In Doubled-stem verbs, therefore, of the type בֵּרַךְ, the second root-letter is not doubled: e.g. בֵּרַךְ (*bēraχ*) "to bless" (cf. דִּבֶּר); מְבוֹרָךְ *məvōrāχ* "blessed" (cf. מְקֻלָּל).

יִירְשׁוּ is *3mpl* PC of the verb יָרַשׁ "to possess, inherit". In the PC of the simple stem, this verb is stative in form (second vowel -*a*-: XV) (see p.115 D).

יִכָּרֵתוּ "they shall be cut off" is *3mpl* PC of the N-stem of כָּרַת "to cut (off)"(pausal form). The characteristic נ of the N-stem is omitted by assimilation to the first letter of the root, which is then doubled (p.161).

The two parts of this verse from an acrostic psalm (Psalm 37:22) are linked by another type of parallelism, namely, *parallelism of opposites*: מְבוֹרָכָיו "blessed by him" is parallel to מְקֻלָּלָיו "cursed by him", and יִירְשׁוּ אָרֶץ "shall possess the land" to יִכָּרֵתוּ "shall be cut off".

Another factor in the structure of Hebrew poetry is the number and grouping of stressed units. The pattern in the present example 3:2, is a common one, and has been called the *qina*-metre because it seems to be frequent in laments (קִינָה "a lament"): cf. Lamentations 3.

Thirdly, the omission of the prefix -הַ "the" with אֶרֶץ "the earth" is likewise a characteristic feature of Hebrew Poetry.

4. הֻגַּד is *3ms* SC of another passive verb-form, the rounded stem of the H-stem verb הִגִּיד "to tell" (XIX).

This is an *impersonal passive construction*: that is, the subject of the corresponding active sentence is non-specific ("Has some-one not told my lord what I did?"). The subject of the passive sentence in this example is the clause אֲשֶׁר עָשִׂיתִי "what I did": "what I did (subject) has been told..." The object-marker -אֶת indicates that the active "version" (in which "what I did" is the object) is uppermost in the mind of the speaker, even although grammatically this is a passive construction.

אֲדֹנִי "my lord" is frequently substituted for the *2ms* pronouns in polite speech addressed to a superior: cf. עַבְדְּךָ "your servant" substituted for the *1ms* pronouns. On לַאדֹנִי, see p.159.

5. וַיֵּרַע is *3ms* PC of רָעַע "to be evil" with -וַ. In this comparatively rare type of verb, the third root-letter, which is identical with the second, is omitted in PC forms: cf. יָסֹב "he will come round" (סָבַב). The following are the commonest of this type:

אָרַר "to curse"	סָבַב "to go round"
חָנַן "to favour, be gracious"	רָנַן "to cry out"
מָדַד "to measure"	שָׁמֵם "to be desolate"

Only the *3rd* person forms of רָעַע occur in Biblical Hebrew, and *3ms* is usually impersonal. The root of the verb is repeated in the noun-phrase רָעָה גְדוֹלָה, which enriches the meaning of the verb and is translated by an appropriate adverb (cf. XV. 5).

וַיִּ֫חַר is similar to וַיֵּ֫רַע. The two impersonal constructions correspond to the English expressions "to be displeased" and "to be angry": cf. וַיִּ֫חַר לְקַ֫יִן "Cain was angry"; וַיֵּ֫רַע לְדָוִיד "and David was displeased".

	Verbs with identical 2nd and 3rd root-letters: סָבַב "to surround, etc."			Verbs with 2nd root-letter א or ר
	SIMPLE STEM סָבַב "to surround"	N-STEM נָסַב "to turn round"	H-STEM הֵרַע "to injure"	D-STEM בֵּרַךְ "to bless"
SUFFIX CONJUGATION				
1s "I"	סַבּ֫וֹתִי	נְסַבּ֫וֹתִי	הֲרֵע֫וֹתִי	בֵּרַ֫כְתִּי
2ms "you"	סַבּ֫וֹתָ	נְסַבּ֫וֹתָ	הֲרֵע֫וֹתָ	בֵּרַ֫כְתָּ
2fs "you"	סַבּוֹת	נְסַבּוֹת	הֲרֵעוֹת	בֵּרַכְתְּ
3ms "he, it"	סָבַב	נָסַב	הֵרַע	בֵּרַךְ
3fs "she, it"	סָבְבָה	נָסַ֫בָּה	הֵרֵ֫עָה	בֵּרְכָה
1pl "we"	סַבּ֫וֹנוּ	נְסַבּ֫וֹנוּ	הֲרֵע֫וֹנוּ	בֵּרַ֫כְנוּ
2mpl "you"	סַבּוֹתֶם	נְסַבּוֹתֶם	הֲרֵעוֹתֶם	בֵּרַכְתֶּם
2fpl "you"	סַבּוֹתֶן	נְסַבּוֹתֶן	הֲרֵעוֹתֶן	בֵּרַכְתֶּן
3pl "they"	סָבְבוּ	נָסַ֫בּוּ	הֵרֵ֫עוּ	בֵּרְכוּ
PREFIX CONJUGATION				
1s "I"	אָסֹב	אִסַּב	אָרַע	אֲבָרֵךְ
2ms "you"	תָּסֹב	תִּסַּב	תָּרַע	תְּבָרֵךְ
2fs "you"	תָּסֹבִּי	תִּסַּ֫בִּי	תָּרֵ֫עִי	תְּבָרְכִי
3ms "he, it"	יָסֹב	יִסַּב	יָרַע	יְבָרֵךְ
3fs "she, it"	תָּסֹב	תִּסַּב	תָּרַע	תְּבָרֵךְ

VERBS WITH SECOND ROOT-LETTER א OR ר: בֵּרַךְ "TO BLESS", ETC.

1pl "we"	נָסֹב	נִסַּב	נָרַע	נְבָרֵךְ
2mpl "you"	תָּסֹבּוּ	תִּסַּבּוּ	תָּרֵעוּ	תְּבָרְכוּ
2fpl "you"	תְּסֻבֶּינָה	תִּסַּבֶּנָה	תְּרֵעֶינָה	תְּבָרֵכְנָה
3mpl "they"	יָסֹבּוּ	יִסַּבּוּ	יָרֵעוּ	יְבָרְכוּ
3fpl "they"	תְּסֻבֶּינָה	תִּסַּבֶּנָה	תְּרֵעֶינָה	תְּבָרֵכְנָה
IMPERATIVE				
2ms	סֹב	הִסַּב	הָרַע	בָּרֵךְ
2fs	סֹבִּי	הִסַּבִּי	הָרֵעִי	בָּרְכִי
2mpl	סֹבּוּ	הִסַּבּוּ	הָרֵעוּ	בָּרְכוּ
2fpl	סֻבֶּינָה	הִסַּבֶּנָה	הֲרֵעֶינָה	בָּרֵכְנָה
וַ + PC				
3ms "and he.."	וַיָּסָב	וַיִּסַּב	וַיָּרַע	וַיְבָרֶךְ
3mpl "and they.."	וַיָּסֹבּוּ	וַיִּסַּבּוּ	וַיָּרֵעוּ	וַיְבָרְכוּ
ACTIVE PARTICIPLE				
ms ("-er")	סֹבֵב	נָסָב	מֵרַע	מְבָרֵךְ
mpl ("-ers")	סֹבְבִים	נְסַבִּים	מְרֵעִים	מְבָרְכִים
PASSIVE PARTICIPLE				
ms	סָבוּב			מְבוֹרָךְ
mpl	סְבוּבִים			מְבוֹרָכִים
VERBAL NOUN				
Basic form	סָבוֹב	הִסֹּב	הָרֵעַ	בָּרוֹךְ
Pregenitive	סֹב	הִסֵּב	הָרַע	בָּרֵךְ
PG with *1s* suff.	סֻבִּי	הִסַּבִּי	הֲרֵעִי	בָּרְכִי

6. The subject of the three verbs in this famous sentence is normally taken to be the servant of the Lord: "he will not cry or lift up his voice, or make it heard in the street" (Isaiah 42:2 RSV). But it has also been suggested, in view of the political and regal

aspects of the Servant's functions stressed in this poem, that the verbs are all impersonal: "there will be no crying..." the verse would then describe conditions of peace and social justice in a new age. In Biblical Hebrew, *3ms* and *3mpl* forms of the verb are frequently used impersonally: e.g. לֵילוֹת עָמָל מִנּוּ־לִי "nights of toil have been allotted to me"(lit. "they have allotted to me...") Job 7:3)"; אַף־יִצְעַק אֵלָיו וְלֹא יַעֲנֶה "if one cries to it, it will not answer" (Isaiah 46:7). Impersonal *2ms* forms also occur: לֹא־תָבוֹא שָׁמָּה "no-one will be able to get in there" (Isaiah 7:25).

יִשָּׂא is *3ms* PC of נָשָׂא "to lift up" (cf. נָפַל : XIV). The word קוֹלוֹ "his voice", part of the idiom נָשָׂא קוֹל "to lift up the voice, i.e. cry, shout", is omitted without affecting the meaning. The word is not omitted after יַשְׁמִיעַ "he will cause to be heard" (*3ms* PC of the H-stem of שָׁמַע "to hear").

The structure of this poem (Isaiah 42:1-4), the first "Servant Song", seems to consist of a symmetrical arrangement of 3- and 4-unit sections:

```
1.   ---:---
     ---:---
2.  ----:----
3.  ----:----
4.   ---:---
     ---:---
```

Short words like לֹא "not" are sometimes counted as a complete unit, apparently, sometimes hyphenated and counted as half a unit. In the present example (v.2) two 4-unit sections are linked by parallelism of synonyms (cf. 2. above).

SUMMARY

A. The passive forms of the verb are the N-stem, the two rounded stems (X. 6), and the simple passive participle (IX. 2).

B. Impersonal constructions include *3ms* passive forms, as well as *2ms*, *3ms* and *3mpl* active forms of the verb.

C. Biblical Hebrew poetry may be distinguished from prose as follows:

(1) parallelism of synonyms or opposites.

(2) symmetrical patterning of stressed units.

(3) frequent omission of הַ-, אֶת; אֲשֶׁר and וְ-.

(4) some distinctive forms (e.g. לָמוֹ for לָהֶם) and words (e.g. בַּל "not"; אֹרַח "way, path"; חָזָה "to see"; לְבָנָה "moon").

D. Verbs of the type יָשַׁב begin with the semi-vowel י which is not pronounced after prefixes. In the Simple Stem of six very common verbs the prefix vowel is *-ē-* in PC forms and the י is not written (הָלַךְ "to go" also belongs to this group):

הָלַךְ "to go"	יָלַד "to have a child"	יָרַד "to go down"
יָדַע "to know"	יָצָא "to go out"	יָשַׁב "to sit, dwell"

In the rest of the group the PC prefix-vowel is the normal *-i-* (XI), and the initial root-letter י may or may not be written: e.g. יָרַשׁ: יִירַשׁ or יִרַשׁ "to take possession of, inherit". In most N-stem and H-stem forms the prefix vowel is *-ō-* and the י is not written.

The commonest are:

הוֹדָה H "to praise, confess"	יָטַב "to be good"	יָרֵא "to fear"
הוֹשִׁיעַ H "to help, save"	יָסַף "to add" (H-stem has same meaning)	יָרַשׁ "to possess"
יָבֵשׁ "to be dry"	יָעַץ "to advise"	יָצַר "to form"

The stative verb יָכֹל "to be able" is irregular: יוּכַל "he will be able", and the H-stem of the verb יָטַב "to be good" is הֵיטִב.

There are a few verbs in which an initial י is assimilated as though it were a נ (p.96): cf. אֶצֹּק from יָצַק "to pour".

XVI

VERBS BEGINNING WITH י : יָשַׁב "TO DWELL", ETC. הָלַךְ "TO GO".

	Simple Stem		H-Stem	N-Stem
	יָשַׁב "to dwell"	הָלַךְ "to go"	הוֹצִיא "to take out"	נוֹלַד "to be born"
SUFFIX CONJUGATION				
1s "I"	יָשַׁבְתִּי	הָלַכְתִּי	הוֹצֵאתִי	נוֹלַדְתִּי
2ms "you"	יָשַׁבְתָּ	הָלַכְתָּ	הוֹצֵאתָ	נוֹלַדְתָּ
2fs "you"	יָשַׁבְתְּ	הָלַכְתְּ	הוֹצֵאת	נוֹלַדְתְּ
3ms "he, it"	יָשַׁב	הָלַךְ	הוֹצִיא	נוֹלַד
3fs "she, it"	יָשְׁבָה	הָלְכָה	הוֹצִיאָה	נוֹלְדָה
1pl "we"	יָשַׁבְנוּ	הָלַכְנוּ	הוֹצֵאנוּ	נוֹלַדְנוּ
2mpl "you"	יְשַׁבְתֶּם	הֲלַכְתֶּם	הוֹצֵאתֶם	נוֹלַדְתֶּם
2fpl "you"	יְשַׁבְתֶּן	הֲלַכְתֶּן	הוֹצֵאתֶן	נוֹלַדְתֶּן
3pl "they"	יָשְׁבוּ	הָלְכוּ	הוֹצִיאוּ	נוֹלְדוּ
PREFIX CONJUGATION				
1s "I"	אֵשֵׁב	אֵלֵךְ	אוֹצִיא	אִוָּלֵד
2ms "you"	תֵּשֵׁב	תֵּלֵךְ	תּוֹצִיא	תִּוָּלֵד
2fs "you"	תֵּשְׁבִי	תֵּלְכִי	תּוֹצִיאִי	תִּוָּלְדִי
3ms "he, it"	יֵשֵׁב	יֵלֵךְ	יוֹצִיא	יִוָּלֵד
3fs "she, it"	תֵּשֵׁב	תֵּלֵךְ	תּוֹצִיא	תִּוָּלֵד
1pl "we"	נֵשֵׁב	נֵלֵךְ	נוֹצִיא	נִוָּלֵד
2mpl "you"	תֵּשְׁבוּ	תֵּלְכוּ	תּוֹצִיאוּ	תִּוָּלְדוּ
2fpl "you"	תֵּשַׁבְנָה	תֵּלַכְנָה	תּוֹצֶאנָה	תִּוָּלַדְנָה
3mpl "they"	יֵשְׁבוּ	יֵלְכוּ	יוֹצִיאוּ	יִוָּלְדוּ
3fpl "they"	תֵּשַׁבְנָה	תֵּלַכְנָה	תּוֹצֶאנָה	תִּוָּלַדְנָה
IMPERATIVE				
2ms	שֵׁב	לֵךְ	הוֹצֵא	הִוָּלֵד
2fs	שְׁבִי	לְכִי	הוֹצִיאִי	הִוָּלְדִי
2mpl	שְׁבוּ	לְכוּ	הוֹצִיאוּ	הִוָּלְדוּ
2fpl	שֵׁבְנָה	לֵכְנָה	הוֹצֶאנָה	הִוָּלַדְנָה

VERBS BEGINNING WITH י : יָשַׁב "TO DWELL", ETC. הָלַךְ "TO GO".

וַ + PC				
3ms "and he.."	וַיֵּשֶׁב	וַיֵּלֶךְ	וַיּוֹצֵא	וַיִּוָּלֵד
3mpl "and they.."	וַיֵּשְׁבוּ	וַיֵּלְכוּ	וַיּוֹצִיאוּ	וַיִּוָּלְדוּ
ACTIVE PARTICIPLE				
ms ("-er")	ישֵׁב	הֹלֵךְ	מוֹצִיא	נוֹלָד
mpl ("-ers")	ישְׁבִים	הֹלְכִים	מוֹצִיאִים	נוֹלָדִים
VERBAL NOUN				
Basic form	יָשׁוֹב	הָלוֹךְ	הוֹצֵא	הִוָּלֵד
Pregenitive	שֶׁבֶת	לֶכֶת	הוֹצִיא	הִוָּלֵד
PG with *1s* suff.	שִׁבְתִּי	לֶכְתִּי	הוֹצִיאִי	הִוָּלְדִי

VOCABULARY

אֶבֶן	f. "stone"	יִצְחָק	"Isaac"	פֶּה	"mouth"
אַחֵר	"other"	יָרַד	"to go down"	צָבָא	"host"
זָעַק	"to cry"	יָרַשׁ	"to possess"	רָם	"high"
חָרָה לְ-	"to be angry" (impers)	כְּמֹשׁ	"Chemosh"	שְׁמוּאֵל	"Samuel"
יָלַד	N "to be born"	מוֹעֵד	"time, season"	שָׂרָה	f."Sarah"

EXERCISE

Translate

א. וָאֶרְאֶה אֶת־יְהוָה יוֹשֵׁב עַל־כִּסֵּא רָם וְנִשָּׂא׃

ב. הִנֵּה בֵן נוֹלָד לְבֵית דָּוִד וְזָבַח עָלֶיךָ אֶת־כֹּהֲנֵי הַבָּמוֹת׃

ג. לְזֹאת יִקָּרֵא אִשָּׁה כִּי מֵאִישׁ לֻקְחָה־זֹּאת׃

ד. וְאֶת־בְּרִיתִי אָקִים אֶת־יִצְחָק אֲשֶׁר תֵּלֵד לְךָ שָׂרָה לַמּוֹעֵד הַזֶּה בַּשָּׁנָה הָאַחֶרֶת׃

ה. בִּדְבַר יְהוָה שָׁמַיִם נַעֲשׂוּ וּבְרוּחַ פִּיו כָּל־צְבָאָם׃

ו. שָׁבוּ עַל־עֲוֹנֹת אֲבוֹתָם וַיֵּלְכוּ אַחֲרֵי אֱלֹהִים אֲחֵרִים לְעָבְדָם׃

ז. הֲלֹא אֵת־אֲשֶׁר יוֹרִישׁ לְךָ כְּמֹשׁ אֱלֹהֶיךָ אֹתוֹ תִּירָשׁ׃

ח. וְהַלְוִיִּם הוֹרִידוּ אֶת־אֲרוֹן יְהוָה וַיָּשִׂימוּ אֶל־הָאֶבֶן הַגְּדוֹלָה׃

ט. וַיִּחַר לִשְׁמוּאֵל וַיִּזְעַק כָּל־הַלָּיְלָה׃

י. וַיֵּרָא כְבוֹד יְהוָה בְּאֹהֶל מוֹעֵד אֶל־כָּל־בְּנֵי יִשְׂרָאֵל׃

CHAPTER XVII. CAUSATIVE CONSTRUCTIONS. NUMERALS. THE CALENDAR. MONOSYLLABIC VERBS: קָם "TO STAND", ETC.

EXAMPLES

1.	The Lord kills and brings to life; he brings down to Sheol and raises up (I Sam. 2:6).	יְהוָה מֵמִית וּמְחַיֶּה מוֹרִיד שְׁאוֹל וַיָּעַל׃	א.
2.	After two days he will revive us; on the third day he will raise us up that we may live in his presence (Hos. 6:2)	יְחַיֵּנוּ מִיֹּמָיִם בַּיּוֹם הַשְּׁלִישִׁי יְקִימֵנוּ וְנִחְיֶה לְפָנָיו׃	ב.
3.	Give him no rest until he establishes Jerusalem and makes it a praise in the earth (Isa. 62:7).	וְאַל־תִּתְּנוּ דֳמִי לוֹ עַד־יְכוֹנֵן וְעַד־יָשִׂים יְרוּשָׁלַםִ תְּהִלָּה בָּאָרֶץ׃	ג.
4.	So Moses, the servant of the Lord, died at the age of 120. (Deut. 34:5..7).	וַיָּמָת מֹשֶׁה עֶבֶד יְהוָה וְהוּא בֶּן מֵאָה וְעֶשְׂרִים שָׁנָה׃	ד.
5.	In the month of Abib the Lord your God brought you out of Egypt by night (Deut. 16:1).	בְּחֹדֶשׁ הָאָבִיב הוֹצִיאֲךָ יְהוָה אֱלֹהֶיךָ מִמִּצְרַיִם לָיְלָה׃	ה.
6.	In the second year of Darius the king, in the sixth month on the first day of the month the word of the Lord came to Haggai the prophet (Hagg. 1:1).	בִּשְׁנַת שְׁתַּיִם לְדָרְיָוֶשׁ הַמֶּלֶךְ בַּחֹדֶשׁ הַשִּׁשִּׁי בְּיוֹם אֶחָד לַחֹדֶשׁ הָיָה דְבַר יְהוָה אֶל־חַגַּי הַנָּבִיא׃	ו.

ANALYSIS

1. This verse of poetry is divided into parallel halves (XVI) by the major pause at וּמְחַיֶּה.

CAUSATIVE CONSTRUCTIONS.

The four verbs are *causative* in function : מֵמִית is *ms* active participle of the H-stem of מֵת "to die" (X. 3); מְחַיֶּה is *ms* active participle of the D-stem of חָיָה "to live" (XVIII); מוֹרִיד is *ms* active participle of the H-stem of יָרַד "to go down" (XVI); and וַיַּעַל is the reduced form of the *3ms* PC of the H-stem of עָלָה "to go up" (XVIII). D-stem and H-stem forms are very often causative in meaning (X), and correspond in many cases to English verb-forms with in *-en* ("deaden", "blacken"), *-ize* ("immortalize", "immunize"), *-ify* ("justify", "codify"), *en-* ("enliven", "enslave") and the like. Causative constructions, in which a common simple stem verb, such as מֵת "to die", חָיָה "to live" and יָרַד "to go down" occurs in a derived stem, however, are more productive in Hebrew than in English.

מֵת "to die" is a monosyllabic verb of the type קָם. These normally have *-ā-* in SC forms. On the vowels in the stative verbs מֵת and בּוֹשׁ "to be ashamed", see Chapter XV. In the PC of the Simple Stem the prefix vowel is always *-ā-* and the second vowel normally *-ū-*: e.g. יָקוּם "it will stand"; נָשׁוּב "we shall return". Some verbs have the vowel *-ō-* in the second syllable (e.g. יָבוֹא "he will come"), others *-ī-* (e.g. תָּבִין "you will understand").

שְׁאוֹל "Sheol" is the place where the dead lead a shadowy and colourless existence. Here it has an adverbial function: "to Sheol"; cf. אַשּׁוּר "to Assyria" (Gen.10:11).

2. יְחַיֵּנוּ is *3ms* PC of the D-stem of חָיָה "to live" with the *1pl* suffix pronoun ֵנוּ "us". In this clause a simple statement ("we shall live") is "embedded" in a causative construction in such a way as to make it the result of an action by a new subject (God: Hos. 6:2): "God will cause us to live". In Hebrew, the D-stem (חִיָּה)

is causative in relation to the Simple Stem (חָיָה).

מִן־ "after, from" is common with expressions of time: cf. מֵעוֹלָם "from of old"; מֵהַיּוֹם "after today"; מִקֵּץ יָמִים "after some days, at the end of some time".

As well as with objects normally found in pairs (p. 45) and numerals (see below, 6), the dual forms occur in expressions of time: יוֹמַיִם "two days"; שְׁנָתַיִם "two years"; פַּעֲמַיִם "two times".

הַשְּׁלִישִׁי "third" is an adjective agreeing with the noun הַיּוֹם "the day". Adjectives formed from the numerals 2-10 are marked by the suffix ִי (-*ī*) (feminine sing. -*īt*).

יְקִימֵנוּ is *3ms* PC of the H-stem of קָם "to stand up" with the *1pl* suffix pronoun ֵנוּ (cf. יְחַיֵּנוּ above): "he will cause *us* to stand". The suffix is stressed (p. 50), and the prefix-vowel accordingly reduced to shwa (p. 156).

In וְנִחְיֶה - וְ with PC expresses mood (XIII).

3. A major pause is marked after the imperatival clause "Give him no rest".

אַל־ is the negative word in modal sentences (XIV. 2). תִּתְּנוּ is *2mpl* PC of נָתַן "to give" (XIV). עַד־ "until" with verbs is a subordinating conjunction (X); with nouns it is a preposition (XV).

יְכוֹנֵן is *3ms* PC of the verb כּוֹנֵן "to establish". In this type of D-stem, chiefly reserved for monosyllabic verbs like קָם, the second root-letter is repeated in place of the normal doubling (X.1):

קָם "to stand"	קוֹמֵם "to establish"
רָם "to be high"	רוֹמֵם "to raise"
שָׁב "to return"	שׁוֹבֵב "to restore"

The Simple Stem of כּוֹנֵן does not occur: cf. עוֹרֵר "to waken".

יָשִׂים is *3ms* PC of שָׂם "to put" (on PC stem vowels in verbs like קָם, see above on 1.). This verb, along with נָתַן "to give" occurs frequently in a type of causative construction corresponding to English "to make X into Y": cf. וְנָתַתִּי אֶת־יְרוּשָׁלַםִ לְגַלִּים "I shall make Jerusalem into a heap of ruins". In the present example, the noun תְּהִלָּה "a praise", like גַּלִּים "ruins", has an adverbial function (cf. 1 above), but without the preposition -לְ.

תְּהִלָּה is a noun formed from the root ה-ל-ל (cf. הִלֵּל "to praise") by the prefix *t*-: cf. תְּפִלָּה "prayer" (הִתְפַּלֵּל "to pray"); תּוֹלֵדוֹת "generations" (יָלַד "to bear").

4. וַיָּמָת is the reduced form of the *3ms* PC of מֵת "to die" with -וַ "and". In the -וַ + PC construction (XII), vowel-reduction is normal in verbs of the type קָם (p. 161):

יָקוּם "he will stand"	וַיָּקָם "and he stood"
תָּמִית "you will kill"	וַתָּמֶת "and you killed"
יָשִׁיב "he will bring back"	וַיָּשֶׁב "he brought back"

On circumstantial clauses introduced by the conjunction -וְ, see Chapter XIX. 1.

-בֶּן "aged (lit. son of)" is normal idiomatic usage (cf. IX. 1). מֵאָה "100" has the plural מֵאוֹת (שָׁלֹשׁ מֵאוֹת "300") and the dual מָאתַיִם "200".

עֶשְׂרִים "20" is made up of the root *עשׂר (cf. עֶשֶׂר "10") and the suffix ִים (-*īm*) which corresponds to English -*ty* in "twen*ty*", "thir*ty*", etc. cf. שְׁלֹשִׁים "30"; אַרְבָּעִים "40".

Two digit numerals are normally connected by -וְ "and": cf.

שְׁלֹשִׁים וְשָׁלֹשׁ "33". The noun after numerals above 10 is normally in the singular: שְׁלֹשׁ מֵאוֹת הָאִישׁ "the 300 men" (Judg. 7:7).

5. אָבִיב "Abib" is the best-known of the five month names that have survived from the Old Hebrew calendar, employed in Israel before the Babylonian exile. It was the month of the Passover (Ex. 13:4; 23:15; 34:18; Deut. 16:1).

הוֹצִיאֲךָ is *3ms* SC of the H-stem of יָצָא "to go out" (XVI), with the *2ms* suffix pronoun: "he caused you to go out".

לָיְלָה "by night" has an adverbial function in this context (cf. שְׁאוֹל in 1).

6. The major pause, marked at לַחֹדֶשׁ, comes between the date ("in the second year...") and the main clause ("the word of the Lord came.."). Pauses are also marked between the three parts of the date.

בִּשְׁנַת שְׁתַּיִם is a genitive phrase in which שְׁנַת is the PG form of שָׁנָה "a year", and שְׁתַּיִם is the citation-form of the Hebrew word for "two". The citation-forms of the numerals "1-10" are feminine, characterized by ת in אַחַת (masc. אֶחָד) "one" and שְׁתַּיִם (masc. שְׁנַיִם) "two", but by the absence of any normal feminine suffix in "3-10" (see Table).

לְדָרְיָוֶשׁ "of Darius" illustrates how a genitive relationship may be expressed by the preposition -לְ where a normal PG form cannot be used.

In Biblical usage the year is normally defined in terms of the reign of a monarch. From the time of the Babylonian exile, Israel apparently adopted the Babylonian Calendar although they did not at first use the Babylonian names (probably for religious reasons), and numbered them instead from the first month [in the spring according to one system (e.g. Ex. 12:2); in the autumn according to another system (e.g. Ex. 23:16)] to the twelfth (e.g. Jer. 52:31).

הַשִּׁשִּׁי "sixth" is made up of the root *שׁשׁ (in שֵׁשׁ "6") and the adjectival suffix ִי (-ī).

בְּיוֹם אֶחָד "on the first day": there is no adjectival form in ִי for "first". The adjective רִאשׁוֹן (cf. רֹאשׁ "head") is normally used, or occasionally, as here, the plain numeral אַחַת "one" in a type of genitive phrase: cf. בִּשְׁנַת שְׁתַּיִם "in the second year" (above).

לַחֹדֶשׁ "of the month" is the second part of a genitive phrase of the type mentioned above.

SUMMARY

A. H-stem and D-stem forms of many verbs frequently have a causative function by means of which a simple non-causative verbal sentence ("Goliath died") is embedded in a more complex causative sentence ("David caused Goliath to die": i.e. "David killed Goliath"). Many verbs like "to kill" and "to bring", which need not be considered causative in English, correspond to Hebrew H-stem verbs (הֵמִית "to cause to die", הֶרְאָה "to cause to see", and הֵבִיא "to cause to come").

B. שָׂם "to put" and נָתַן "to give" are common in another type of causative construction ("to make X (into) Y").

C. The feminine forms of the numerals are simpler and constitute the citation-forms: ...אַחַת, שְׁתַּיִם, שָׁלֹשׁ "one, two, three..."

NUMERALS

Adjectives ("second, third...") are formed from the numerals 2-10 by the suffix ִי (-ī). "First" is רִאשׁוֹן; "last" is אַחֲרוֹן.

NUMERALS

No.	Citation-forms	Masc. forms	Position	Pregenitive forms
0	אֶפֶס			
1	אַחַת	אֶחָד	after noun in singular	אַחַד(m) אַחַת(f)
2	שְׁתַּיִם	שְׁנַיִם	usually after noun in plural	שְׁנֵי(m) שְׁתֵּי(f)
3	שָׁלֹשׁ	שְׁלֹשָׁה	before noun in plural	שְׁלֹשֶׁת
4	אַרְבַּע	אַרְבָּעָה		אַרְבַּעַת
5	חָמֵשׁ	חֲמִשָּׁה		חֲמֵשֶׁת
6	שֵׁשׁ	שִׁשָּׁה		שֵׁשֶׁת
7	שֶׁבַע	שִׁבְעָה		שִׁבְעַת
8	שְׁמֹנֶה	שְׁמֹנָה		שְׁמֹנַת
9	תֵּשַׁע	תִּשְׁעָה		תִּשְׁעַת
10	עֶשֶׂר	עֲשָׂרָה		עֲשֶׂרֶת
11	אַחַת עֶשְׂרֵה	אַחַד עָשָׂר	before noun in singular	
20	עֶשְׂרִים			
30	שְׁלֹשִׁים			
100	מֵאָה			
200	מָאתַיִם			
1000	אֶלֶף			

D. Monosyllabic verbs of the type קָם are characterized by long vowels, reduced (p.161) in certain forms of the SC and in the shortened forms of the PC (p.39). A special type of Doubled Stem (Polel)is characterized by the repeating of the second root-letter instead of the usual doubling. The commonest are (PC vowel of Simple Stem is given in brackets):

MONOSYLLABIC VERBS: קָם "TO STAND", ETC.

בָּא *(ō)* "to come, enter"

בּוֹשׁ *(ō)* "to be ashamed"

בִּין *(ī)* "to understand"

גָּר *(ū)* "to sojourn"

כּוֹנֵן D "to establish
H "to prepare"

מֵת *(ū)* "to die"
H "to kill"

נָח *(ū)* "to rest"
H "to set down"

נָס *(ū)* "to flee"

סָר *(ū)* "to turn aside"

עוֹרֵר D "to waken"

קָם *(ū)* "to get up, stand"
H,D "to set up, establish"

רָם *(ū)* "to be high"
H,D "to raise"

רָץ *(ū)* "to run"

רָב *(ī)* "to contend"

שָׁב *(ū)* "to return, turn"
H,D "to bring back"

שָׂם *(ū, ī)* "to put, set"

	Simple Stem			H-Stem	D-Stem
	קָם "to stand"	בָּא "to come"	שָׂם "to put"	הֵקִים "to set up"	קֹמֵם "to establish"
SUFFIX CONJUGATION					
1s "I"	קַמְתִּי	בָּאתִי	שַׂמְתִּי	הֲקִימוֹתִי	קֹמַמְתִּי
2ms "you"	קַמְתָּ	בָּאתָ	שַׂמְתָּ	הֲקִמֹתָ	קֹמַמְתָּ
2fs "you"	קַמְתְּ	בָּאת	שַׂמְתְּ	הֲקִמֹת	קֹמַמְתְּ
3ms "he, it"	קָם	בָּא	שָׂם	הֵקִים	קֹמֵם
3fs "she, it"	קָמָה	בָּאָה	שָׂמָה	הֵקִימָה	קֹמְמָה
1pl "we"	קַמְנוּ	בָּאנוּ	שַׂמְנוּ	הֲקִמֹנוּ	קֹמַמְנוּ
2mpl "you"	קַמְתֶּם	בָּאתֶם	שַׂמְתֶּם	הֲקִמֹתֶם	קֹמַמְתֶּם
2fpl "you"	קַמְתֶּן	בָּאתֶן	שַׂמְתֶּן	הֲקִמֹתֶן	קֹמַמְתֶּן
3pl "they"	קָמוּ	בָּאוּ	שָׂמוּ	הֵקִימוּ	קֹמְמוּ
PREFIX CONJUGATION					
1s "I"	אָקוּם	אָבוֹא	אָשִׂים	אָקִים	אֲקוֹמֵם
2ms "you"	תָּקוּם	תָּבוֹא	תָּשִׂים	תָּקִים	תְּקוֹמֵם
2fs "you"	תָּקוּמִי	תָּבוֹאִי	תָּשִׂימִי	תָּקִימִי	תְּקוֹמְמִי
3ms "he, it"	יָקוּם	יָבוֹא	יָשִׂים	יָקִים	יְקוֹמֵם

XVII

MONOSYLLABIC VERBS: קָם "TO STAND", ETC.

3fs "she, it"	תָּקוּם	תָּבוֹא	תָּשִׂים	תָּקִים	תְּקוֹמֵם
1pl "we"	נָקוּם	נָבוֹא	נָשִׂים	נָקִים	נְקוֹמֵם
2mpl "you"	תָּקוּמוּ	תָּבֹאוּ	תָּשִׂימוּ	תָּקִימוּ	תְּקוֹמְמוּ
2fpl "you"	תָּקֹמְנָה	תָּבֹאנָה	תָּשֵׂמְנָה	תְּקִימֶנָה	תְּקוֹמֵמְנָה
3mpl "they"	יָקוּמוּ	יָבֹאוּ	יָשִׂימוּ	יָקִימוּ	יְקוֹמְמוּ
3fpl "they"	תָּקֹמְנָה	תָּבֹאנָה	תָּשֵׂמְנָה	תְּקִימֶנָה	תְּקוֹמֵמְנָה
IMPERATIVE					
2ms	קוּם	בּוֹא	שִׂים	הָקֵם	קֹמֵם
2fs	קוּמִי	בּוֹאִי	שִׂימִי	הָקִימִי	קֹמְמִי
2mpl	קוּמוּ	בּוֹאוּ	שִׂימוּ	הָקִימוּ	קֹמְמוּ
2fpl	קֹמְנָה	בֹּאנָה	שֵׂמְנָה	הָקֵמְנָה	קֹמֵמְנָה
וַ + PC					
3ms "and he.."	וַיָּקָם	וַיָּבֹא	וַיָּשֶׂם	וַיָּקֶם	וַיְקֹמֵם
3mpl "and they.."	וַיָּקֻמוּ	וַיָּבֹאוּ	וַיָּשִׂמוּ	וַיָּקִמוּ	וַיְקֹמְמוּ
ACTIVE PARTICIPLE					
ms ("-er")	קָם	בָּא	שָׂם	מֵקִים	מְקוֹמֵם
mpl ("-ers")	קָמִים	בָּאִים	שָׂמִים	מְקִימִים	מְקֹמְמִים
PASSIVE PARTICIPLE					
ms				מוּקָם	
mpl				מוּקָמִים	
VERBAL NOUN					
Basic form	קוֹם	בּוֹא	שִׂים	הָקֵם	קוֹמֵם
Pregenitive	קוּם	בּוֹא	שִׂים	הָקִים	קוֹמֵם
PG with *1s* suff.	קוּמִי	בּוֹאִי	שִׂימִי	הֲקִימִי	קֹמְמִי

CAUSATIVE CONSTRUCTIONS

VOCABULARY

אַחַת	f. "one"	זְרֻבָּבֶל	"Zerubbabel"	קֹ֫דֶשׁ	"holiness"
אֶ֫לֶף	"thousand"	חֹ֫דֶשׁ	"month, new moon"	שָׁאוּל	"Saul"
אַרְבַּע	f. "four"	חָמֵשׁ	f. "five"	שָׁלֹשׁ	f. "three"
אֶתְמוֹל	"yesterday"	חוֹתָם	"signet-ring"	שְׁתַּ֫יִם	f. "two"
דּוֹר	"generation"	מֵאָה	f. "hundred"	תְּפִלָּה	f. "prayer"

EXERCISE

Translate:

א. וַיהוָה נִחַם כִּי הִמְלִיךְ אֶת־שָׁאוּל עַל־יִשְׂרָאֵל׃

ב. נָתַתִּי רוּחִי עָלָיו מִשְׁפָּט לַגּוֹיִם יוֹצִיא׃

ג. וְקִדַּשְׁתִּי אֹתָם וְיִהְיוּ לִי כֹּהֲנִים ׃

ד. וַיָּבֹא אֵלָיו וַיֹּאמֶר לוֹ שְׁנֵי אֲנָשִׁים הָיוּ בְּעִיר אֶחָת׃

ה. אֶקָּחֲךָ זְרֻבָּבֶל עַבְדִּי וְשַׂמְתִּיךָ כַּחוֹתָם כִּי בָחַרְתִּי בָךְ׃

ו. לֹא־אָכַל לֶחֶם וְלֹא־שָׁתָה מַיִם שְׁלֹשָׁה יָמִים וּשְׁלֹשָׁה לֵילוֹת׃

ז. וַהֲבִיאוֹתִים אֶל־הַר קָדְשִׁי וְשִׂמַּחְתִּים בְּבֵית תְּפִלָּתִי׃

ח. וַיְחִי אִיּוֹב אַחֲרֵי־זֹאת מֵאָה וְאַרְבָּעִים שָׁנָה וַיַּרְא אֶת־בָּנָיו וְאֶת־בְּנֵי בָנָיו
וְאֶת־בְּנֵיהֶם אַרְבָּעָה דֹּרוֹת׃

ט. בַּחֹדֶשׁ הַחֲמִישִׁי בְּאַרְבָּעָה לַחֹדֶשׁ בָּא עֶבֶד מֶלֶךְ בָּבֶל יְרוּשָׁלָ͏ִם׃

י. אֶלֶף שָׁנִים בְּעֵינֶיךָ כְּיוֹם אֶתְמוֹל כִּי יַעֲבוֹר׃

CHAPTER XVIII. REFLEXIVE CONSTRUCTIONS. COMPARISON. VERBS ENDING IN A VOWEL: רָאָה "TO SEE", ETC. NOUNS WITH PREFIX מ: מִקְדָּשׁ "SANCTUARY", ETC.

EXAMPLES

1. If they hide themselves at the bottom of the sea, I will command the serpent and it will bite them (Amos 9:3).

   א. אִם־יִסָּתְרוּ בְּקַרְקַע הַיָּם אֲצַוֶּה אֶת־הַנָּחָשׁ וּנְשָׁכָם׃

2. Then Amaziah sent to Jehoash king of Israel, saying, "Come let us look one another in the face (II Kgs. 14:8).

   ב. וַיִּשְׁלַח אֲמַצְיָה אֶל־יְהוֹאָשׁ מֶלֶךְ יִשְׂרָאֵל לֵאמֹר לְכָה נִתְרָאֶה פָנִים׃

3. Why do you bring a great disaster against yourselves (Jer. 44:7)?

   ג. לָמָּה אַתֶּם עֹשִׂים רָעָה גְדוֹלָה אֶל־נַפְשֹׁתֵכֶם׃

4. They will fight one another, neighbour against neighbour, city against city, kingdom against kingdom (Isa. 19:2).

   ד. וְנִלְחֲמוּ אִישׁ בְּאָחִיו וְאִישׁ בְּרֵעֵהוּ עִיר בְּעִיר מַמְלָכָה בְּמַמְלָכָה׃

5. I desire loyalty and not sacrifice, the knowledge of God more than holocausts. (Hos. 6:6).

   ה. חֶסֶד חָפַצְתִּי וְלֹא־זָבַח וְדַעַת אֱלֹהִים מֵעֹלוֹת׃

6. A(good)name is better than precious ointment, and the day of death than the the day of birth (Eccl. 7:1).

   ו. טוֹב שֵׁם מִשֶּׁמֶן טוֹב וְיוֹם הַמָּוֶת מִיּוֹם הִוָּלְדוֹ׃

ANALYSIS

1. אִם "if" is a subordinating conjunction which brings the clause "they hide themselves" into a conditional relationship with the main clause "I will command the serpent..." (XIX. 5).

REFLEXIVE CONSTRUCTIONS

יִסָּתְרוּ is *3mpl* PC of the N-stem verb נִסְתַּר "to hide". In this verb the N-stem has reflexive force and may be represented in English by "to hide oneself". A *reflexive* construction is one in which the subject and object refer to the same person or thing.

אֲצַוֶּה is *1s* PC of the D-stem verb צִוָּה "to command". This belongs to a large group of common verbs of the type *CāCā* (רָאָה "to see",etc). These have only two root-letters and end in the vowel-letter ה . All PC forms without suffixes (in the derived stems as well as the Simple Stem) end in ֶה (-*e*); all *3ms* SC forms (citation forms) end in ָה (-*ā*).

נְשָׁכָם is *3ms* SC of נָשַׁךְ "to bite" with stressed *3mpl* Suffix Pronoun ָם.

2. וַיִּשְׁלַח "and he sent" is *3ms* PC of שָׁלַח (XIII) with וַ- "and". For שָׁלַח "to send a message", cf. Gen. 38:25; Jer.29:28; etc.

לֵאמוֹר "saying" introduces direct speech. It is a verbal noun with לְ (p.159), used adverbially (p.58).

לְכָה is *ms* imperative of הָלַךְ (XVI) with the modal suffix -*ā* (XIII). Introducing a request, command or wish, it corresponds roughly to "Come, Come on" in English.

נִתְרָאֶה is *1pl* PC of the T-stem of רָאָה "to see". The T-stem is often reflexive in meaning: cf. הִתְאַזֵּר "to gird oneself; הִתְקַדֵּשׁ "to sanctify oneself".

The object of a plural verb in a reflexive construction is often best translated "each other, one another" (cf. 4 below).

פָּנִים "face" is not used in the singular, even when it refers to a single object. It has an adverbial function here (cf. XVII.1).

3. עֹשִׂים is *mpl* active participle of עָשָׂה "to do, make". In verbs of this type (רָאָה), the final vowel is omitted before vocalic suffixes: e.g. רָאוּ "they saw"; תַּעֲלִי "you (*fs*) will go up".

אֶל־נַפְשֹׁתֵכֶם "against yourselves" is the second element in another type of reflexive construction. With the Suffix Pronouns נֶ֫פֶשׁ "life, person" is the normal Hebrew term for "self": cf. לֹא־יַצִּ֫ילוּ אֶת־נַפְשָׁם "they cannot deliver themselves"; לֹא־יָדַ֫עְתִּי נַפְשִׁי "I did not know myself".

4. וְנִלְחֲמוּ is *3mpl* SC of the N-stem verb נִלְחַם "to fight" with -ְ‏ל. In the phrase אִישׁ בְּאָחִיו, the first term אִישׁ "a man" is the subject and the second אָחִיו "his brother" is the object of the verb but both refer to the same persons. This is a third type of reflexive construction, common with a plural subject, and corresponds to English constructions with "each other, one another".

מַמְלָכָה "kingdom" belongs to a common noun-type with the characteristic stem-formative מ (*ma-*, *mi-*, *mō-*) (cf. the prefix of some participles: X.2). This very productive type of word-formation greatly increases the general transparency of Hebrew vocabulary (p. 173): e.g.

קָדֹשׁ	"holy"	מִקְדָּשׁ	"sanctuary"
קָם	"to stand"	מָקוֹם	"place"
צִוָּה	D. "to command"	מִצְוָה	"commandment"
שָׁפַט	"to judge"	מִשְׁפָּט	"judgment"
מֶ֫לֶךְ	"king"	מַמְלָכָה	"kingdom"

5. This famous verse of poetry is divided into two parallel halves by the pause at זָבַח.

חָפַצְתִּי is *1s* SC of the stative verb חָפֵץ "to desire" (XV).

Comparison is drawn between spiritual and cultic values. This is expressed (1) by the negative word לֹא, which marks a straight positive/negative opposition between חֶסֶד "loyalty" and זֶבַח "sacrifice"; and (2) by the preposition מִן־ "from" which in comparisons functions like "than, more than" in English: דַּעַת אֱלֹהִים מֵעֹלוֹת "the knowledge of God more than holocausts".

זָבַח is the pausal form of זֶבַח (p.160).

6. The parallelism in this verse is also marked by a pause at טוֹב.

As in the previous example the preposition מִן־ "than" separating two nouns, indicates *comparison*. The adjective טוֹב therefore has comparative force and corresponds to the English comparative adjective "better". Adjectives have no special comparative or superlative forms in Biblical Hebrew: cf. רָעָה לְךָ זאת מִכָּל־הָרָעָה אֲשֶׁר.. "this will be worse for you than all the evil which ..." (II Sam. 19.8).

In the phrase מִשֶּׁמֶן טוֹב "than good (precious) ointment", טוֹב is not comparative, although formally identical with טוֹב in the previous phrase.

הִוָּלְדוֹ is a verbal noun from the N-stem of יָלַד "to bear" with the *3ms* Suffix Pronoun וֹ-. In verbs of this type (יָשַׁב: XVI), the initial semi-vowel י becomes וּ in all PC forms of the N-stem. In this context, parallel to מָוֶת "death", it functions as a noun. The suffix וֹ- "his" must be considered impersonal: "one's birth" (XVI).

NOUNS WITH PREFIX -מ: מִקְדָּשׁ "SANCTUARY", ETC.

SUMMARY

A. Reflexive constructions, that is, constructions in which subject and object refer to the same person or thing, normally contain one of the following elements:

(1) N-stem or T-stem forms.

(2) the word נֶ֫פֶשׁ "self" with Suffix Pronoun.

(3) when the subject is plural, phrases like אִישׁ...רֵעֵ֫הוּ "one another".

B. Comparison between two noun-like terms is normally expressed by the preposition מִן־ "than". Adjectives have no special comparative or superlative forms.

C. One of the commonest noun-types is characterized by the prefix מ. Twenty of the commonest are;

מָגֵן	"shield"	מִלְחָמָה	f. "battle, war"	מִקְדָּשׁ	"sanctuary"
מִדְבָּר	"wilderness"	מַמְלָכָה	f. "kingdom, reign"	מָקוֹם	"place"
מוּסָר	"chastisement, instruction"	מְנוּחָה	f. "rest, peace"	מַשָּׂא	"burden"
		מִנְחָה	f. "gift, offering"	מִשְׁכָּן	"tabernacle"
מוֹעֵד	"season, meeting"	מַעֲשֶׂה	"act, deed"	מִשְׁפָּחָה	f. "family"
מִזְבֵּחַ	"altar"	מַצֵּבָה	f. "pillar"	מִשְׁפָּט	"judgment, justice"
מַחֲשָׁבָה	f. "thought"	מִצְוָה	f. "commandment"		
מַטֶּה	"staff, rod, tribe"				

D. Verbs of the type רָאָה have two root-letters and end in a vowel. The final vowel is *-ā* in SC (all stems) and *-e* in PC (all stems), except before suffixes. Before vocalic suffixes the final vowel is omitted; before other suffixes it is *-ī-* in Simple Stem forms, and *-ē-* in H-stem and N-stem forms. The commonest are:

VERBS ENDING IN A VOWEL: רָאָה "TO SEE", ETC.

בָּכָה "to weep"

בָּנָה "to build"

גִּלָּה D. "to reveal"

הוֹדָה H. "to thank, confess"

הָיָה "to be"

הִכָּה H. "to strike, kill"

חָיָה "to live"

חָנָה "to encamp"

כָּלָה "to be finished"
D. "to complete"

כִּסָּה D. "to cover"

מָחָה "to destroy"

מָנָה "to count"

נָטָה "to spread, bend"

עָלָה "to go up"

עָנָה "to answer"

עָשָׂה "to make, do"

פָּדָה "to ransom"

פָּנָה "to turn, regard"

פָּרָה "to be fruitful"

צִוָּה D. "to command"

צָפָה "to watch"

קִוָּה D. "to hope, wait"

קָנָה "to acquire, create"

קָרָה "to meet, happen"

רָאָה "to see"
N. "to appear"
H. "to show"

רָבָה "to be much, many"

רָעָה "to feed, pasture"

רָצָה "to be pleased"

שָׁתָה "to drink"

תָּלָה "to hang"

	Simple Stem		D-Stem	H-stem	N-stem
	רָאָה "to see"	עָלָה "to go up"	צִוָּה "to command"	הִרְבָּה "to multiply"	נִגְלָה "to be revealed"
SUFFIX CONJUGATION					
1s "I"	רָאִיתִי	עָלִיתִי	צִוִּיתִי	הִרְבֵּיתִי	נִגְלֵיתִי
2ms "you"	רָאִיתָ	עָלִיתָ	צִוִּיתָ	הִרְבֵּיתָ	נִגְלֵיתָ
2fs "you"	רָאִית	עָלִית	צִוִּית	הִרְבֵּית	נִגְלֵית
3ms "he, it"	רָאָה	עָלָה	צִוָּה	הִרְבָּה	נִגְלָה
3fs "she, it"	רָאֲתָה	עָלְתָה	צִוְּתָה	הִרְבְּתָה	נִגְלְתָה
1pl "we"	רָאִינוּ	עָלִינוּ	צִוִּינוּ	הִרְבֵּינוּ	נִגְלֵינוּ
2mpl "you"	רְאִיתֶם	עֲלִיתֶם	צִוִּיתֶם	הִרְבֵּיתֶם	נִגְלֵיתֶם
2fpl "you"	רְאִיתֶן	עֲלִיתֶן	צִוִּיתֶן	הִרְבֵּיתֶן	נִגְלֵיתֶן
3pl "they"	רָאוּ	עָלוּ	צִוּוּ	הִרְבּוּ	נִגְלוּ

VERBS ENDING IN A VOWEL: רָאָה "TO SEE", ETC.

PREFIX CONJUGATION					
1s "I"	אֶרְאֶה	אַעֲלֶה	אֲצַוֶּה	אַרְבֶּה	אֶגָּלֶה
2ms "you"	תִּרְאֶה	תַּעֲלֶה	תְּצַוֶּה	תַּרְבֶּה	תִּגָּלֶה
2fs "you"	תִּרְאִי	תַּעֲלִי	תְּצַוִּי	תַּרְבִּי	תִּגָּלִי
3ms "he, it"	יִרְאֶה	יַעֲלֶה	יְצַוֶּה	יַרְבֶּה	יִגָּלֶה
3fs "she, it"	תִּרְאֶה	תַּעֲלֶה	תְּצַוֶּה	תַּרְבֶּה	תִּגָּלֶה
1pl "we"	נִרְאֶה	נַעֲלֶה	נְצַוֶּה	נַרְבֶּה	נִגָּלֶה
2mpl "you"	תִּרְאוּ	תַּעֲלוּ	תְּצַוּוּ	תַּרְבּוּ	תִּגָּלוּ
2fpl "you"	תִּרְאֶינָה	תַּעֲלֶינָה	תְּצַוֶּינָה	תַּרְבֶּינָה	תִּגָּלֶינָה
3mpl "they"	יִרְאוּ	יַעֲלוּ	יְצַוּוּ	יַרְבּוּ	יִגָּלוּ
3fpl "they"	תִּרְאֶינָה	תַּעֲלֶינָה	תְּצַוֶּינָה	תַּרְבֶּינָה	תִּגָּלֶינָה
IMPERATIVE					
2ms	רְאֵה	עֲלֵה	צַוֵּה	הַרְבֵּה	הִגָּלֵה
2fs	רְאִי	עֲלִי	צַוִּי	הַרְבִּי	הִגָּלִי
2mpl	רְאוּ	עֲלוּ	צַוּוּ	הַרְבּוּ	הִגָּלוּ
2fpl	רְאֶינָה	עֲלֶינָה	צַוֶּינָה	הַרְבֶּינָה	הִגָּלֶינָה
וַ- + PC					
3ms "and he.."	וַיַּרְא	וַיַּעַל	וַיְצַו	וַיֶּרֶב	וַיִּגָּל
3mpl "and they.."	וַיִּרְאוּ	וַיַּעֲלוּ	וַיְצַוּוּ	וַיַּרְבּוּ	וַיִּגָּלוּ
ACTIVE PARTICIPLE					
ms ("-er")	רֹאֶה	עֹלֶה	מְצַוֶּה	מַרְבֶּה	
mpl ("-ers")	רֹאִים	עֹלִים	מְצַוִּים	מַרְבִּים	
PASSIVE PARTICIPLE					
ms	רָאוּי		מְצֻוֶּה		נִגְלֶה
mpl	רְאוּיִם		מְצֻוִּים		נִגְלִים
VERBAL NOUN					
Basic form	רָאוֹ	עָלוֹ	צַוּוֹ	הַרְבֵּה	נִגְלוֹ
Pregenitive	רְאוֹת	עֲלוֹת	צַוּוֹת	הַרְבּוֹת	הִגָּלוֹת
PG with *1s* suff.	רְאוֹתִי	עֲלוֹתִי	צַוּוֹתִי	הַרְבּוֹתִי	הִגָּלוֹתִי

REFLEXIVE CONSTRUCTIONS

VOCABULARY

בִּין "to perceive"

בָּכָה "to weep"

בָּשָׂר "flesh"

גָּלָה "to reveal"

חַג "festival"

חֹק "rule"

יָהּ "the Lord (Yah)"

יַחְדָּו "together"

עֵת f. "time, occasion"

כָּלָה "to end, fail"
D. "to complete"

לָמַד "to learn"
D. "to teach"

מָלֵא "to fill"

נַחֲלָה f. "inheritance"

רָבָה "to be many"

פָּרָה "to be fruitful"

EXERCISE

Translate:

א. וַיֹּאמֶר יַעֲקֹב לְבָנָיו לָמָּה תִּתְרָאוּ׃

ב. לֹא־יִשָּׂא גוֹי אֶל־גּוֹי חֶרֶב וְלֹא יִלְמְדוּ עוֹד מִלְחָמָה׃

ג. וַיֹּאמְרוּ לֹא יִרְאֶה־יָּהּ וְלֹא יָבִין אֱלֹהֵי יַעֲקֹב׃

ד. וַיַּעַשׂ שְׁלֹמֹה בָעֵת־הַהִיא אֶת־הֶחָג וְכָל־יִשְׂרָאֵל עִמּוֹ׃

ה. וַיִּירְשׁוּ בְּנֵי יִשְׂרָאֵל אִישׁ נַחֲלַת אֲבוֹתָיו׃

ו. וַיִּבֶן שְׁלֹמֹה אֶת־הַבַּיִת וַיְכַלֵּהוּ׃

ז. וַיִּשְׂאוּ הָעָם אֶת־קוֹלָם וַיִּבְכּוּ וַיִּקְרְאוּ שֵׁם הַמָּקוֹם הַהוּא בֹּכִים׃

ח. עֲשֵׂה עִם־עַבְדְּךָ כְחַסְדֶּךָ וְחֻקֶּיךָ לַמְּדֵנִי׃

ט. וַיְבָרֶךְ אֹתָם אֱלֹהִים וַיֹּאמֶר פְּרוּ וּרְבוּ וּמִלְאוּ אֶת־הָאָרֶץ׃

י. וְנִגְלָה כְּבוֹד יְהוָה וְרָאוּ כָל־בָּשָׂר יַחְדָּו כִּי פִּי יְהוָה דִּבֵּר׃

CHAPTER XIX. SUBORDINATION IN COMPLEX SENTENCES. CONJUNCTIONS. H-STEM VERBS WITH ASSIMILATED נ : הִגִּיד "TO TELL", ETC.

EXAMPLES

1.	Elisha came to Damascus at a time when Ben Hadad king of Aram was ill. So they told him that the man of God had come (II Kings 8:7).	וַיָּבֹא אֱלִישָׁע דַּמֶּשֶׂק וּבֶן־הֲדַד מֶלֶךְ־אֲרָם חֹלֶה וַיַּגִּדוּ לוֹ לֵאמֹר בָּא אִישׁ הָאֱלֹהִים:	א.
2.	She replied, "Wait, my daughter, until you know how the matter turns out,	וַתֹּאמֶר שְׁבִי בִתִּי עַד אֲשֶׁר תֵּדְעִין אֵיךְ יִפֹּל דָּבָר	ב.
3.	because the man will not rest unless he settles it today"(Ruth 3:18).	כִּי לֹא יִשְׁקֹט הָאִישׁ כִּי־אִם־כִּלָּה הַדָּבָר הַיּוֹם:	ג.
4.	Obey all these words which I command you so that it may go well with you and with your children after you for ever (Deut. 12:28).	וְשָׁמַרְתָּ אֶת־כָּל־הַדְּבָרִים הָאֵלֶּה אֲשֶׁר אָנֹכִי מְצַוֶּךָּ לְמַעַן יִיטַב לְךָ וּלְבָנֶיךָ אַחֲרֶיךָ עַד־עוֹלָם:	ד.
5.	If men quarrel, and one strikes the other and the man is not killed, then, if he recovers, the one who struck him is not liable (Ex. 21:18).	וְכִי־יְרִיבוּן אֲנָשִׁים וְהִכָּה אִישׁ אֶת־רֵעֵהוּ וְלֹא יָמוּת וְאִם־יָקוּם וְנִקָּה הַמַּכֶּה:	ה.

ANALYSIS

1. The main pause marked at חֹלֶה divides this sentence into two parts, the first introduced by וַיָּבֹא "and he came..." (-וַ + PC), and the second by וַיַּגִּדוּ "and they told him" (-וַ + PC). The conjunction -וְ is much commoner in Biblical Hebrew than "and" is in literary

English. At the beginning of a sentence, as in the present example, it is often best left untranslated, and a long string of clauses connected by וְ- can normally as here be divided up into two or more separate sentences, and וְ- translated "then, so, but" or the like.

The first part is further subdivided into two clauses by the pause at דַּמָּ֫שֶׂק. On the adverbial use of the proper name דַּמֶּ֫שֶׂק "to Damascus", see XVII.1.

The second clause, beginning וּבֶן־הֲדַד "and Ben Hadad...", is a *circumstantial clause*, that is, a clause which gives the circumstances surrounding the state of affairs described in the main clause. Such clauses are frequently linked by the conjunction וְ- and again this must be represented in English by a conjunction like "while, when, as" or the like: "Elisha came... at a time when Ben Hadad was ill..." וְ- may be said to have a subordinating function in this type of sentence; that is to say, it links a subordinate clause (such as the present circumstantial one) to the main clause. The subject in the circumstantial clause, which is often different from that in the main clause, comes first: cf. הַשֶּׁ֫מֶשׁ יָצָא עַל־הָאָ֫רֶץ וְלוֹט בָּא צֹעֲרָה "the sun had risen on the earth when Lot came to Zoar" (Gen. 19:23); וַיֵּלְכוּ סְדֹ֫מָה וְאַבְרָהָם עוֹדֶ֫נּוּ עוֹמֵד לִפְנֵי יְהוָה "they went to Sodom, but Abraham still stood before the Lord" (Gen. 18:22).

חֹלֶה is the *ms* participle of the verb חָלָה "to be ill" (cf. רָאָה : XVIII).

וַיַּגִּ֫דוּ "and they told" is *3mpl* PC of הִגִּיד with prefix וַ-. Besides הִגִּיד there are six other common verbs of this type: H-stem verbs in which the first root-letter, being נ, is usually omitted by assimilation (p. 161). Thus הִגִּיד "to tell" comes from the root *נגד

הִצִּיל "to rescue" form the root *נצל, and הִכָּה "to strike" from the root *נכה. The only forms in which the initial נ of the root appears are PC forms of the N-stem: e.g. תִּנָּצֵל "you will be rescued". But these forms are rare in Biblical Hebrew.

On the impersonal use of the *3mpl* ("they told him"="it was told to him"="he was told"), see Chapter XVI.

לֵאמֹר "saying" is a verbal noun from אָמַר "to say" with the prefix לְ (*lē-* before א : p. 159). It is used adverbially here after וַיַּגִּדוּ לוֹ "and they told him" to introduce *direct speech*: "The man of God has come". Reported speech ("that the man of God had come") is less common in Hebrew than in English.

2. וַתֹּאמֶר "and she said": direct speech is normally introduced by some form of אָמַר "to say" even when it consists of an answer, as here, a question or the like. English prefers more precise introductory formulae (e.g. "he replied..."; "he asked...").

שְׁבִי is *fs* imperative of יָשַׁב "to sit" (XVI). The noun בַּת "daughter" with Suffix Pronouns has the form -בִּתּ: בִּתִּי "my daughter"; בִּתּוֹ "his daughter". These two words, שְׁבִי בִתִּי, make up the main clause of the sentence.

עַד־אֲשֶׁר תֵּדְעִין "until you know" is a subordinate clause linked to the main clause by the *subordinating conjunction* עַד־אֲשֶׁר "until". A number of subordinating conjunctions have the form preposition + אֲשֶׁר: cf. אחר־אֲשֶׁר "after"; כַּאֲשֶׁר "as". אֲשֶׁר is often omitted (cf. XX.4).

תֵּדְעִין is *2fs* PC of יָדַע "to know" with suffix ין- (p. 45). This common suffix on *2fs* and *mpl* forms with PC does not apparently affect the meaning in any way. PC in this context points to a hope or idea not necessarily realized in fact (XIII).

The question word אֵיךְ "how?" introduces a question, which here functions as a noun-like subordinate clause, object of the verb "you know". The PC form יִפֹּל points to future time and expresses the speaker's uncertainty with respect to the action of the verb (XIII).

Sentences 2 and 3 are divided by a major pause marked at דָּבָר.

3. The conjunction כִּי has a wide range of meaning and a variety of functions. Here it links the subordinate clause לֹא יִשְׁקֹט הָאִישׁ "the man will not rest" to the main clause שְׁבִי בִתִּי "wait, my daughter" (see above). It expresses a causal relationship between the two clauses, like English "because, since, as" (cf. p.165).

כִּי־אִם is another subordinating conjunction, expressing a conditional relationship between clauses: it corresponds to English "unless, except that, if..not", and often follows a negative clause: cf. וְשָׁמָּה לֹא־יָשׁוּב כִּי־אִם הִרְוָה אֶת־הָאָרֶץ׃ "(the rain) does not return there without watering the earth" (Isa. 55:10).

The SC form כִּלָּה expresses a single completed action in future time (XII).

4. אֲשֶׁר אָנֹכִי מְצַוֶּה is a subordinate clause linked to the main clause by the relative word אֲשֶׁר. This points back to an antecedent term in the previous clause, in this case כָּל־הַדְּבָרִים הָאֵלֶּה "all these words". In its own clause אֲשֶׁר is like a pronoun and is the object of the verb מְצַוֶּה "command" (cf. V.4; XX.4).

מְצַוֶּה is *ms* active participle of the D-stem verb צִוָּה (XVIII) with a *2ms* suffix pronoun.

לְמַ֫עַן is a subordinating conjunction introducing clauses which express a purpose or result of the activities or state of affairs described in the main clause, like English "in order that, so that, so as". Like עַד־ "until" לְמַ֫עַן also functions as a preposition "for the sake of" (XV).

יִיטַב is *3ms* PC of the stative verb יָטַב "to be well" (XV). PC again expresses a hope or promise not necessarily realized in fact (XIII).

5. In legal formulations, such as the "Book of the Covenant" (Ex. 20:22-23:33) or the "Holiness Code" (Lev. 17-26) eventualities or attested cases are normally introduced by the subordinating conjunction כִּי, which corresponds to English "if, supposing that, whereas". In the present example, three subordinate clauses introduced by כִּי, are separated from the main clause by the pause marked at יָמֻֽת. The short conditional clause אִם־יָקוּם is then taken with the main clause.

יְרִיבוּן is *3mpl* PC of רָב "to quarrel" (XVII) with the suffix ן- (see 2. above). (Prefix-vowel is reduced to shwa before stressed suffix: p. 156).

The PC forms יְרִיבוּן, יָמוּת, and יָקוּם express possibilities not necessarily realized in fact (XIII). וְ + SC in וְהִכָּה and וְנִקָּה points to future time.

וְהִכָּה is *3ms* SC of the H-stem verb הִכָּה (cf. הִצִּיל), and the clause וְהִכָּה אִישׁ אֶת־רֵעֵ֫הוּ is a reflexive construction (XVIII.4).

נִקָּה is *3ms* SC of the N-stem of נָקָה "to be innocent".

In complex sentences of this type the main clause is often introduced by וְ־, although in such cases "and" would be impossible in English: thus אִם אִישׁ יָבוֹא וְאָמַר הֲיֵשׁ־פֹּה אִישׁ וְאָמַרְתְּ אָיִן "if anyone comes and says, 'Is there anyone here?' then (וְ־) you will say, 'There is not'." (Judg. 4:20).

SUMMARY

A. In complex sentences one clause may be subordinated to another by a set of *subordinating conjunctions*, which indicate, with varying degrees of precision, the nature of the relationship between clauses. In addition to וְ־ "and" (which may in some contexts function as a subordinating conjunction), the following are among the commonest:

אַחֲרֵי (אֲשֶׁר) "after"
אַךְ "but, only"
אִם "if, whether"
אִם־לֹא "unless"
אֲשֶׁר "which, that, where, etc."
בַּעֲבוּר (אֲשֶׁר) "so that, in order to"
טֶרֶם, בְּטֶרֶם "before"
בַּאֲשֶׁר "because"
כַּאֲשֶׁר "as, when, while"
כִּי "that, if, because"
כִּי־אִם "unless, except that"
לוּ "if"
לוּלֵא "if not, unless"
לְמַעַן (אֲשֶׁר) "so that, in order to"
מֵאָז "since, from the time when"
עַד (אֲשֶׁר) "until, while"
עַל (אֲשֶׁר) "although, because"
עֵקֶב (אֲשֶׁר) "because"
פֶּן־ "lest, so that... not"

B. Verbs of the type הִצִּיל are H-stem verbs in which the first root-letter נ, is always omitted by assimilation. The seven commonest are:

H-STEM VERBS WITH ASSIMILATED נ : הִגִּיד "TO TELL", ETC.

הִבִּיט "to look at" הִצִּיב "to set up, establish"

הִגִּיד "to tell" הִצִּיל "to rescue, deliver"

הִכָּה "to strike, kill" הִשִּׂיג "to reach, overtake"

הִכִּיר "to recognize"

	no other peculiarity (XI)	ending in ע,ח,ה,א (XIII)	ending in a vowel (XVIII)
	הִגִּיד "to tell"	הִגִּיעַ "to reach"	הִכָּה "to strike"
SUFFIX CONJUGATION			
1s "I"	הִגַּדְתִּי	הִגַּעְתִּי	הִכֵּיתִי
2ms "you"	הִגַּדְתָּ	הִגַּעְתָּ	הִכֵּיתָ
2fs "you"	הִגַּדְתְּ	הִגַּעַתְּ	הִכֵּית
3ms "he, it"	הִגִּיד	הִגִּיעַ	הִכָּה
3fs "she, it"	הִגִּידָה	הִגִּיעָה	הִכְּתָה
1pl "we"	הִגַּדְנוּ	הִגַּעְנוּ	הִכֵּינוּ
2mpl "you"	הִגַּדְתֶּם	הִגַּעְתֶּם	הִכֵּיתֶם
2fpl "you"	הִגַּדְתֶּן	הִגַּעְתֶּן	הִכֵּיתֶן
3pl "they"	הִגִּידוּ	הִגִּיעוּ	הִכּוּ
PREFIX CONJUGATION			
1s "I"	אַגִּיד	אַגִּיעַ	אַכֶּה
2ms "you"	תַּגִּיד	תַּגִּיעַ	תַּכֶּה
2fs "you"	תַּגִּידִי	תַּגִּיעִי	תַּכִּי
3ms "he, it"	יַגִּיד	יַגִּיעַ	יַכֶּה
3fs "she, it"	תַּגִּיד	תַּגִּיעַ	תַּכֶּה
1pl "we"	נַגִּיד	נַגִּיעַ	נַכֶּה
2mpl "you"	תַּגִּידוּ	תַּגִּיעוּ	תַּכּוּ
2fpl "you"	תַּגֵּדְנָה	תַּגַּעְנָה	תַּכֶּינָה
3mpl "they"	יַגִּידוּ	יַגִּיעוּ	יַכּוּ
3fpl "they"	תַּגֵּדְנָה	תַּגַּעְנָה	תַּכֶּינָה

H-STEM VERBS WITH ASSIMILATED נ : הִגִּיד "TO TELL", ETC.

IMPERATIVE			
2ms	הַגֵּד	הַגַּע	הַכֵּה
2fs	הַגִּידִי	הַגִּיעִי	הַכִּי
2mpl	הַגִּידוּ	הַגִּיעוּ	הַכּוּ
2fpl	הַגֵּדְנָה	הַגַּעְנָה	הַכֶּינָה
וַ + PC			
3ms "and he.."	וַיַּגֵּד	וַיַּגַּע	וַיַּךְ
3mpl "and they.."	וַיַּגִּידוּ	וַיַּגִּיעוּ	וַיַּכּוּ
ACTIVE PARTICIPLE			
ms ("-er")	מַגִּיד	מַגִּיעַ	מַכֶּה
mpl ("-ers")	מַגִּידִים	מַגִּיעִים	מַכִּים
PASSIVE PARTICIPLE			
ms	מֻגָּד	מֻגָּע	מֻכֶּה
mpl	מֻגָּדִים	מֻגָּעִים	מֻכִּים
VERBAL NOUN			
Basic form	הַגֵּד	הַגֵּעַ	הַכֵּה
Pregenitive	הַגִּיד	הַגִּיעַ	הַכּוֹת
PG with *1s* suff.	הַגִּידִי	הַגִּיעִי	הַכּוֹתִי

VOCABULARY

אוֹיֵב "enemy"
אָסַף "to assemble"
גִּבּוֹר "mighty man, hero"
גֵּר "sojourner, alien"
גַּת f. "Gath"

הִכָּה H "to strike, kill"
הִצִּיל H "to deliver"
חָזַק "to be strong"
יַבָּשָׁה f. "dry land"
יָכֹל "to be able"

יָם "sea"
יַרְדֵּן "Jordan"
כֹּחַ "strength"
כִּי־אִם "unless"
פֶּן־ "lest"

CONJUNCTIONS

EXERCISE

Translate:

א. וַיִּשָּׂא דָוִד וְהָעָם אֲשֶׁר־אִתּוֹ אֶת־קוֹלָם וַיִּבְכּוּ עַד־אֲשֶׁר אֵין־בָּהֶם כֹּחַ לִבְכּוֹת:

ב. וַיְהִי כַּאֲשֶׁר חָזְקָה הַמַּמְלָכָה בְּיָדוֹ וַיַּךְ אֶת־עֲבָדָיו הַמַּכִּים אֶת־הַמֶּלֶךְ אָבִיו:

ג. וְלֹא זָכְרוּ בְּנֵי יִשְׂרָאֵל אֶת־יְהוָה אֱלֹהֵיהֶם הַמַּצִּיל אֹתָם מִיַּד כָּל־אוֹיְבֵיהֶם:

ד. וַיֻּגַּד לְדָוִד וַיֶּאֱסֹף אֶת־כָּל־יִשְׂרָאֵל וַיַּעֲבֹר אֶת־הַיַּרְדֵּן:

ה. לֹא אֲשַׁלֵּחֲךָ כִּי אִם־בֵּרַכְתָּנִי:

ו. וַיָּשֶׁב יְהוָה עֲלֵיהֶם אֶת־מֵי הַיָּם וּבְנֵי יִשְׂרָאֵל הָלְכוּ בַיַּבָּשָׁה בְּתוֹךְ הַיָּם:

ז. הַצִּילֵנִי כִּי אֵלִי אָתָּה:

ח. לָמָּה תִהְיֶה כְּגֵר בָּאָרֶץ כְּגִבּוֹר לֹא־יוּכַל לְהוֹשִׁיעַ:

ט. וַיַּכֵּהוּ כִּי אִישׁ מִלְחָמוֹת הָיָה:

י. אַל־תַּגִּידוּ בְגַת פֶּן־תִּשְׂמַחְנָה בְּנוֹת פְּלִשְׁתִּים:

CHAPTER XX. EMPHASIS. OATHS AND EXCLAMATIONS.

1.	Joseph said to his brothers, "I am about to die, but God will be sure to remember you " (Gen. 50:24)	וַיֹּאמֶר יוֹסֵף אֶל־אֶחָיו אָנֹכִי מֵת וֵאלֹהִים פָּקֹד יִפְקֹד אֶתְכֶם:	א.
2.	Then Jacob awoke from his sleep, and said, "The Lord is certainly in this place, and I did not know it " (Gen 28:16).	וַיִּיקַץ יַעֲקֹב מִשְּׁנָתוֹ וַיֹּאמֶר אָכֵן יֵשׁ יְהוָה בַּמָּקוֹם הַזֶּה וְאָנֹכִי לֹא יָדָעְתִּי:	ב.
3.	Then he was afraid and said, "How awesome is this place! This is none other than a house of God. It is the gate of heaven " (Gen. 28:17).	וַיִּירָא וַיֹּאמַר מַה־נּוֹרָא הַמָּקוֹם הַזֶּה אֵין זֶה כִּי אִם־בֵּית אֱלֹהִים וְזֶה שַׁעַר הַשָּׁמָיִם:	ג.
4.	On that day Moses swore this oath, "The land your foot has trodden shall be an inheritance for you and your children for ever " (Josh. 14:9).	וַיִּשָּׁבַע מֹשֶׁה בַּיּוֹם הַהוּא לֵאמֹר אִם־לֹא הָאָרֶץ אֲשֶׁר דָּרְכָה רַגְלְךָ בָּהּ לְךָ תִהְיֶה לְנַחֲלָה וּלְבָנֶיךָ עַד־עוֹלָם:	ד.
5.	But Elisha said, "As the Lord lives, and as you yourself live, I will not leave you " (II Kgs. 2:4).	וַיֹּאמֶר אֱלִישָׁע חַי־יְהוָה וְחֵי־נַפְשְׁךָ אִם־אֶעֶזְבֶךָּ:	ה.
6.	Would I had died in your place! Absalom, my son, my son! (II Sam. 19:1)	מִי־יִתֵּן מוּתִי אֲנִי תַחְתֶּיךָ אַבְשָׁלוֹם בְּנִי בְנִי:	ו.
7.	Alas! What a day! The day of the Lord is near! (Joel 1:15)	אֲהָהּ לַיּוֹם כִּי קָרוֹב יוֹם יְהוָה:	ז.

EMPHASIS

ANALYSIS

1. מֵת is *ms* participle of the stative verb מֵת "to die" (XV), and points to present or future time in this context.

In the second clause of Joseph's death-bed speech, there are two indications that he is laying particular *emphasis* on what he is saying:
(1) the normal word-order in verbal sentences is reversed so that the subject אֱלֹהִים comes first in the clause. The contrast between the subject of the first clause (the dying Joseph) and the subject of the second clause (the omnipotent God of Israel), linked to the first by -וְ "but", is thus emphasised. In v.25 the same statement is repeated, but this time the word-order is normal and the particular emphasis in v.24 is not repeated.
(2) in the phrase פָּקֹד יִפְקֹד the verb פָּקַד "to visit, bring kindness (or punishment) to" is repeated for emphasis. The verbal noun, which has an adverbial function in this construction, normally comes before the other verb-form. It is represented in English by an appropriate adverb (e.g. "certainly, truly"), or verb-phrase (e.g. "to be sure to, determined to") (cf. XVI. 5).

2. וַיִּיקַץ is *3ms* PC of the stative verb (יָקַץ) "to awaken" (cf. יָטַב: XV; XVI), with -וַ "and". מִשְּׁנָתוֹ is made up of the preposition -מִן "from", the PG form of the noun שֵׁנָה "sleep" and the *3ms* pronoun suffix וֹ-.

In Jacob's excited utterance on awaking after his dream at Bethel (Gen.28:16), emphasis is marked in three ways: (1) by the adverb אָכֵן "surely, certainly, indeed"; (2) by the quasi-verbal יֵשׁ. This term could be removed without affecting the grammatical wholeness of the sentence, and its emphatic force (in this context at any rate) is confirmed by (1) and (3). cf. אִם־יֶשְׁךָ מוֹשִׁיעַ "If you *really* mean to deliver.." (Judg. 6:36).

(3) the first person pronoun אָנֹכִי "I" at the beginning of a verbal clause, coming after the main pause at הַזֶּה, apparently also indicates that the speaker wishes to emphasise his own part in what he is describing (cf. 1 above). The form of the verb (*1s* SC) already makes it clear who the subject of the clause is, and, particularly in utterances involving indignation, penitence, boasting, the narration of unusual experiences (e.g. Jacob's dream), and the like, on the part of the speaker, the addition of an independent personal pronoun expresses emphasis. Cf. וְאַתֶּם עֲזַבְתֶּם אוֹתִי "yet you have forsaken me" (Judg. 10:13); וַאֲנִי הָיִיתִי עַל־אוּבַל אוּלָי "and I was at the river Ulai (scene of Daniel's vision of the four beasts)" (Dan. 8.2).

3. וַיִּירָא is *3ms* PC of the stative verb יָרֵא "to fear" (cf. XV,XVI) with -וַ "and".

Jacob's second utterance is an *exclamation* introduced by the word מָה "what, how!" The question words מָה, אֵיךְ and אֵיכָה distinguish plain statements of fact from exclamations: e.g. אֵיךְ נָפְלוּ גִבּוֹרִים "How are the mighty fallen!" (II Sam. 1:27); הִנֵּה מַה־טּוֹב וּמַה־נָּעִים "behold how good and pleasant it is ..." (Ps 133:1).

נוֹרָא is the *ms* N-stem participle of יָרֵא "to fear" (cf. נוֹדָע: XVI).

מָקוֹם is a noun of the same type as מַמְלָכָה (XVIII).

אֵין is a common negative word in verbless sentences (XIV). כִּי־אִם "except, unless" functions both as a subordinating conjunction and as a preposition. The phrase אֵין זֶה כִּי אִם.. "this is nothing other than.." is an emphatic form of the simple statement ...זֶה. Cf. לֹא תִּלָּחֲמוּ אֶת־קָטֹן וְאֶת־גָּדוֹל כִּי אִם־אֶת־מֶלֶךְ יִשְׂרָאֵל "Fight with neither small nor great but only with the King of Israel" (I Kings 22:31).

4. וַיִּשָּׁבַע is *3ms* PC of the N-stem verb נִשְׁבַּע "to swear an oath" (XIII) with וַ־ "and". On the verbal noun לֵאמֹר "saying", used adverbially to introduce direct speech, see XIX.1.

The actual words of an *oath* are normally introduced by the subordinating conjunctions אִם and אִם־לֹא : אִם introduces negative statements in an oath (cf. 5 below), and אִם־לֹא positive statements. In this surprising construction, probably אִם "if" introduces the conditional clause of an unexpressed prayer: thus "(May God punish me) *if* I go!" (i.e. "I swear an oath that I *will not* go"); but (May God punish me) *if* I do *not* go!" (i.e. I swear an oath that I *will* go"). By leaving out the main clause the threatening effect is heightened: cf. "Don't move, or else..."

The subordinate clause אֲשֶׁר דָּרְכָה רַגְלְךָ בָּהּ "which your foot has trodden" is related to הָאָרֶץ "the land" by the relative word אֲשֶׁר. A phrase like בָּהּ "in it, on it" is necessary in such a relative clause where the verb does not take a direct object: cf. כְּלֵי מִלְחָמָה אֲשֶׁר אַתֶּם נִלְחָמִים בָּם "the weapons with which you fight" (Jer 21:4); הַמָּקוֹם אֲשֶׁר יִהְיֶה־שָּׁם "the place where it would be" (I Kings 5:8). אֲשֶׁר is often omitted: e.g. הֵן עַבְדִּי אֶתְמָךְ־בּוֹ "this is my servant whom I uphold" (Isa. 42:1).

לְךָ "to you, yours" is in an emphatic position before the verb (cf. 1 above).

5. חַי־יְהוָה וְחֵי־נַפְשְׁךָ is one of several formulae introducing oaths

promises, threats, emphatic declarations, and the like. It may be followed by the same conjunctions as the verb נִשְׁבַּע "to swear an oath": in this case אִם introduces an emphatic negative declaration.

The form of the suffix pronoun ךָ- in אֶעֱזָבְךָ is normal in most modal (PC) forms of the verb. The n-forms (VIII.6) do not normally occur, however, in וַ- + PC constructions (VI), or in negative constructions with אַל- (XIII.6): e.g. לֹא-יַעֲנֶנּוּ "he could not answer him" (Job 9:3), as opposed to וַיַּעֲנֵהוּ "and he answered him" (I Sam. 7:9); יַכֶּנּוּ "he may strike him" (Deut. 25:3), as opposed to וַיַּכֵּהוּ "and he struck him" (Num. 21:24).

6. מִי-יִתֵּן (lit. "who will grant that...?") is an idiomatic formula used to introduce an exclamation of the type "Oh that I had..!" or "Would I were..!" Here it is followed by a verbal noun מוּתִי "my dying", and word for word corresponds to "who would grant my death?" But it may also be followed by a verb: e.g. מִי-יִתֵּן יָדַעְתִּי "would that I knew!" (Job 23:3).

The independent personal pronoun אֲנִי is grammatically in apposition to the *1s* Suffix Pronoun in מוּתִי "*my* dying", and emphasises the contrast between it and the *2ms* suffix in the prepositional phrase תַּחְתֶּיךָ "in *your* place, instead of *you*".

The repetition in בְּנִי בְנִי "my son, my son!" is a natural way of expressing the intensity of David's feelings for his son Absalom (II Sam. 19:1). Emphasis by repetition is common (cf. 1 above). A noun, verb, adjective, or adverb is repeated in the same or a different form: e.g. וַיִּירְאוּ מְאוֹד מְאוֹד: "they were exceedingly afraid" (II Kings 10:4); הֲבֵל הֲבָלִים "vanity of vanities, utter emptiness" (Eccl. 1:2; 12:8); אָכֹל תֹּאכֵל "you may certainly eat" (Gen. 2:16).

7. אֲהָהּ "alas!" is an interjection. In exclamations normal sentence structure often breaks down: cf. אוֹי לָנוּ "Woe unto us! We are lost!" (I Sam. 4:8); לְאֹהָלֶיךָ יִשְׂרָאֵל "to your tents, O Israel!" (I Kings 12:16).

כִּי, in this context, is probably an emphasis word introducing a second, separate exclamation. This emphatic usage is common in oaths: cf. חֵי פַרְעֹה כִּי מְרַגְּלִים אַתֶּם "by the life of Pharaoh, you must be spies!" (Gen. 42:16).

SUMMARY

A. Emphasis is expressed in the following ways:

(1) a term (or a root) is repeated in the same or a different form.

(2) (in verbal clauses) the word-order is changed so that the word emphasised comes before the verb.

(3) an independent personal pronoun is inserted alongside verb forms and suffix pronouns.

(4) there are several common terms which often correspond to English "certainly, really, indeed", and the like: אַךְ, אָכֵן, כִּי, הִנֵּה/הֵן, גַּם, אָמְנָם.

B. After verbs of swearing an oath (especially נִשְׁבַּע) and some other expressions (e.g. חַי־יְהוָה "as the Lord liveth"), the actual words of the speaker are normally introduced by the conjunctions אִם (negative) and אִם־לֹא (positive).

C. Exclamations may be distinguished from plain statements of fact in two ways:

(1) they are introduced by question-words like מָה, אֵיךְ, אֵיכָה, מִי־יִתֵּן or interjections like הוֹי, אוֹי and אֲהָהּ.

(2) they are incomplete sentences.

VOCABULARY

אֵיךְ	"how!"	זָהָב	"gold"	כֶּסֶף	"silver"
גַּם	"even, also"	זֶרַע	"seed,descendants"	מִי־יִתֵּן	"would that"
הֶבֶל	"Abel"	חַי	"living"	מִנְחָה	f. "offering
הֵיכָל	"palace, temple"	יִרְאָה	f. "fear"	מָשִׁיחַ	"anointed"
הֵכִין	H. "to establish"	כְּלִי	"weapon"	שְׁאוֹל	"Sheol"

EXERCISE

Translate:

א. אֵיךְ נָפְלוּ גִבּוֹרִים וַיֹּאבְדוּ כְּלֵי מִלְחָמָה׃

ב. וְהֶבֶל הֵבִיא גַם הוּא מִנְחָה לַיהוָה׃

ג. עַד־עוֹלָם אָכִין זַרְעֶךָ וּבָנִיתִי לְדוֹר־וָדוֹר כִּסְאֲךָ׃

ד. מִי־יִתֵּן וְהָיָה לְבָבָם זֶה לָהֶם לְיִרְאָה אֹתִי וְלִשְׁמֹר אֶת־כָּל־מִצְוֹתַי כָּל־הַיָּמִים׃

ה. חַי־יְהוָה כִּי בְנֵי מָוֶת אַתֶּם אֲשֶׁר לֹא־שְׁמַרְתֶּם עַל־אֲדֹנֵיכֶם עַל־מְשִׁיחַ יְהוָה׃

ו. כָּל־אֲשֶׁר תִּמְצָא יָדְךָ לַעֲשׂוֹת בְּכֹחֲךָ עֲשֵׂה כִּי אֵין מַעֲשֶׂה וְחָכְמָה בִּשְׁאוֹל אֲשֶׁר אַתָּה הֹלֵךְ שָׁמָּה׃
דוד

ז. וַתָּבוֹא אֵלֶיךָ תְּפִלָּתִי אֶל־הֵיכַל קָדְשֶׁךָ׃

ח. אִם־יְכֻפַּר הֶעָוֹן הַזֶּה לָכֶם עַד־תְּמֻתוּן אָמַר יְהוָה צְבָאוֹת׃

ט. טוֹב־לִי תוֹרַת־פִּיךָ מֵאַלְפֵי זָהָב וָכָסֶף׃

י. וְהָיָה בִּמְקוֹם אֲשֶׁר־יֵאָמֵר לָהֶם לֹא־עַמִּי אַתֶּם יֵאָמֵר לָהֶם בְּנֵי אֵל־חָי׃

APPENDIX A. PHONOLOGY

CONSONANTS

	Labial	Dento-alveolar	Palato-velar	Glottal
Stops	*p b*	*t d*	*k g*	'
Fricatives	*f v*	*s z* *sh*	χ	*h*
Affricate		*t͜s*		
Nasals	*m*	*n*		
Lateral		*l*		
Trill		*r*		
Semi-vowel			*y*	

The five *labials* (i.e. sounds produced with the lips) represented by פ ,ב ,ו and מ, are pronounced as in English. *p* and *b* do not occur at the end of a word; *f* does not normally occur at the beginning of a word (p.157).

Nine of the Hebrew consonants (represented by ד ,ז ,ט ,ל ,נ ,ס, צ ,ר ,ש ,ת) are *dento-alveolar* (i.e. sounds produced when the tongue touches the teeth or the ridge behind the teeth). They are all pronounced more or less as in English, except *r*, which is clearly articulated, as in most Scots dialects, with at least one tap or trill with the tip of the tongue on the teeth-ridge. The affricate *t͜s* is pronounced like *ts* in *cats and dogs* or *tsetse.*

There are four *palato-velar* sounds (i.e. sounds produced when the point of articulation is farther back in the mouth than the dento-alveolar): *k* and *g* are pronounced as in English *keg*; the semi-vowel *y* as in *yet*; and χ is the sound at the end of Scots *loch*, Irish *lough* and German *Johann Sebastian Bach*. They are represented by ג,גּ,ח,י,כ,כּ,ק.

In the two *glottal* sounds (represented by א,ה,ע) the point of articulation is as far back as is natural for an English speaker. *h* is pronounced as in English *hat*. The glottal stop ' is the sound substituted in some English dialects for intervocalic *t* in *metal*, *butter*, or the like, but commonly occurring also, although less noticeably, before the emphatically stressed syllable beginning with a vowel (e.g. "idiot!").

VOWELS

	Front	Central	Back	Diphthongs
Closed	*ī*		*u* (rounded)	*i͜a* *ū͜i*
	i	*ə*	*ō* (rounded)	*ē͜a*
	ē		*o* (rounded)	*ū͜a* *ō͜i*
Open	*e*		*ā*, *a* unrounded	*ō͜a* *ā͜i*

The four *front vowels* (i.e. vowels produced towards the front of the mouth) are represented in the script by the three vowel-signs ִ , ֵ , and ֶ , the first two often with the vowel letter

י after them. The four sounds are similar to the corresponding vowels in *grand prix*, *pig*, *café* and *bed*. The line over the letters *ī* and *ē*, in addition to distinguishing them from *i* and *e*, also marks lengthening (pp.160f.).

The *back vowels* (i.e. vowels produced towards the back of the mouth) are divided into two groups, according as to whether the lips are rounded or unrounded. Of the *rounded vowels* (represented by וּ, וֹ, ֹ , and ָ) *ū* and *o* are like the vowels in *soon* and *not*. *ō* comes between the vowels in *more* and *yawn*. The *unrounded* back vowel *a* (represented by ַ and ָ) is like the English long vowel in *calm*, but in Hebrew it also occurs as a short vowel as in French *pas* and German *Mann* (almost *u* in *shut*).

The central vowel ə is frequent both in English and in Hebrew although neither script has a specific sign for it. It is the vowel in the four unstressed syllables of *William the Conqueror*, where it is represented by the letters *a*, *e*, and *o*. In Hebrew it occurs in certain types of consonant cluster, in particular at the beginning of a word (*lədavid* "to Dāvīd"), and is always represented by the vowel sign ְ (shwa), which elsewhere stands for zero (p.4).

There are seven *diphthongs* (sequences of two vowels in the same syllable). In three of them the second element is *i* (represented by י): *ū͜i*, *ō͜i*, *a͜i* as in the final syllables of *chop-suey*, *joy* and *tie*. The other four diphthongs occur only in final syllables before one of the three gutturals, הּ, ח, ע (cf. p.159), and in them the second element is *a* (represented by the vowel-sign ַ under the guttural: p.5): *ī͜a*, *ē͜a*, *ū͜a*, *ō͜a*.

The sounds of Hebrew, as they have been recorded in the Hebrew Bible, are controlled by a system of rules and regularities. These were formalized before the tenth century A.D. and frequently depend on features which no longer exist in the modern pronunciation. A knowledge of these rules and regularities, however, can be valuable both for reading and writing Hebrew, although it is unnecessary and possibly ill-advised to study them in detail before acquiring some general familiarity with the sound and structure of the language.

They may conveniently be divided into three groups according as they are concerned with (a) word stress, (b) the peculiarities of certain sounds, and (c) types of sound-change.

(a) *Word Stress*. As in English every independent word has a main stress, which is clearly perceptible in pronunciation. The main stress is indicated by the punctuation marks and signs of musical notation. Secondary stress is also sometimes indicated (p.6). Except in the cases listed below, *the stress in Hebrew is on the last syllable*: e.g. בְּרֵאשִׁית בָּרָא אֱלֹהִים *bərēshī́t bārā́ elōhī́m* (Gen.1:1). Most suffixes are stressed: e.g. אֵלִי *ēlī́* "my God"; תּוֹרָתוֹ *tōrātṓ* "his law". On וְיָשַׁבְתִּי "I shall dwell" (וְ + SC), see p.27).

(1) *The penultimate syllable is stressed* in the following:

(i) verb-forms -

- *1s,2ms,1pl* SC	יָשַׁבְתִּי	*yasháv-ti*	"I sat" (IV)
- *2fpl,3fpl* PC	תֹּאמַרְנָה	*tōmárnā*	"you say" (VI)
- *fs,fpl,mpl* imperat. of קָם	קוּמִי	*kū́mī*	"arise" (VI)
- some forms of PC with וַ-	וַיֹּאמֶר	*va-yṓmer*	"and he said"(VI)

(ii) noun forms -

- citation-form of מֶלֶךְ	מֶלֶךְ	*méleχ*	"king" (I)
- citation-form of בַּיִת	בַּיִת	*báyit*	"house" (V)
- forms with suffix *-éCet*	קֹהֶלֶת	*kōhélet*	"Ecclesiastes"(IX)

- forms with suffix -*áyim* שָׁמַיִם *shāmáyim* "heaven"
- plural with *2s,3fs,1pl* suff.pron. דְּבָרֶיךָ *dəvāréχā* "your words"(VIII)
- forms with suffix ־ָה (p.101) אַרְצָה *ártsā* "to the ground" (XV)

(iii) a few other words: e.g. לָמָה *lā́mā* "why?" לַיְלָה *láylā* "night"

(2) When two stressed syllables occur together, at the end of one word and the beginning of the next, the stress in the first word is often moved back to the penultimate syllable: e.g. קָרָא לָיְלָה *kā́rā lā́ylā* (Gen. 1:5). In groups of words connected by a hyphen (p.5), there is only one stressed syllable: e.g. אֶת־כָּל־עֵשֶׂב *et-kol-ésev* (Gen. 1:29).

(3) Stressed vowels may be either long or short, but *vowel-length in unstressed syllables* is controlled by the following rules:
1. An unstressed vowel before two consonants or a doubled consonant is short: e.g. מִשְׁפָּט *mishpāt*; גִּבּוֹר *gibbōr*; חָכְמָה *χoχmā*.
2. The vowel in a syllable immediately before the stress is long (unless 1. applies): e.g. דָּבָר *dāvā́r*; תּוֹרָה *tōrā́*; מִשְׁפָּחָה *mishpāχā́*.
3. The vowel in a syllable two places before the stress is shwa or compound shwa (unless 1. applies): e.g. מְלָכִים *məlāχī́m*; אֲמַרְתֶּם *amartém*.
4. The vowel in a syllable after the stress is long in words ending in a vowel, short in words ending in a consonant: e.g. קוּמִי *kū́mī*; יָקָם *yā́kom*.

In many pregenitive forms (V) vowel-length is controlled by the same rules as those for unstressed syllables, since the last term in a genitive construction carries the main stress: e.g. דְּבַר הַמֶּלֶךְ *dəvar hamélex*.

(4) At the end of every verse, and often also at the end of a

sentence, clause or phrase within a verse, a *major pause* is marked (p. 6), which affects the vowels of the word immediately preceding it. *Pausal forms* are distinguished from the normal forms by changes in stress and vowel-length: e.g.

NORMAL FORMS		PAUSAL FORMS
יִשְׁמְרוּ *yishmərū*	*ə* > *ō*	יִשְׁמֹ֫רוּ *yishmṓrū*
דְּבָרְךָ *dəvārχā*	*ϕ* > *e*	דְּבָרֶ֫ךָ *dəvāréχ*
אַתָּה *atā*	*a* > *ā*	אָ֫תָּה *ā́tā*

(b) *The peculiarities of certain sounds*. In the ancient pronunciation ten consonants and the vowel represented by shwa exhibited peculiarities of pronunciation or phonetic behaviour which have been regularized as follows.

(1) In a *post-vocalic position* the consonants *b*, *k*, *p* (בּ, כּ, פּ) of citation forms become *v*, *χ*, *f* (ב, כ, פ): e.g. בֵּן *bēn* "a son", but כְּבֵן *kəvēn* "like a son"; כֵּן *ken* "so", but לָכֵן *lāχēn* "therefore"; פַּרְעֹה *par'ō* "Pharaoh", but לְפַרְעֹה *ləfar'ō* "to Pharaoh". Conversely, in a *post-consonantal* position *v*, *χ*, *f* in citation forms become *b*, *k*, *p*: e.g. שָׁבַר *shāvar* "to break" but יִשְׁבֹּר *yishbōr* "he breaks"; זָכַר *zāχar* "to remember", but יִזְכֹּר *yizkōr* "he remembers"; כֶּסֶף *kesef* "silver", but כַּסְפִּי *kaspi* "my silver". When two words are taken together as one phrase, with or without a hyphen, a final vowel in the first word may have the same effect on an initial *b*, *k*, *p* in the second word: e.g. וַיְהִי־כֵן *va-yəhī χēn* "and it was so". The inner dot (p. 5) distinguishes the stops בּ, כּ, פּ from the corresponding fricatives ב, כ, פ. Since the same dot indicates doubling, the three fricatives cannot be doubled. The distinction between גּ, דּ, תּ (with the dot) and ג, ד, ת (without the dot) is not realized in the modern pronunciation, but the same rules apply as to the other three "Beghadhkephath" letters (p.5).

(2) The four letters א, ה, ח and ע are traditionally called *gutturals*. In ancient times these stood for the "post-velars", i.e. sounds made (like English *h* in *hog*) farther back in the mouth than the velars *k*, *g*, χ (p.177). Although one of these letters, ח, no longer represents a post-velar sound, all four are grouped together in the massoretic vocalization system. In certain respects the letter ר was grouped with the four gutturals, although, like ח, it does not represent a post-velar sound.

(i) The gutturals and ר are never doubled, and where doubling was required for phonological or grammatical reasons (p.5), the short vowel preceding the guttural was often lengthened instead. This type of vowel-lengthening normally occurs before א, ע and ר, less often before ה and ח. For example, the vowel of הַ- "the" (p.17) is lengthened before א, ע (except unstressed עָ) and ר: e.g. הָאֶבֶן "the stone"; הָעֶבֶד "the servant" (but הֶעָוֹן "the sin"); הָראשׁ "the head". Before ה (except הָ) the vowel of הַ- "the" is unaffected: e.g. הַהוּא "that"; הַהֵיכָל "the temple" [but הָהָר (stressed הָ) "the mountain" and הֶהָרִים (unstressed הָ) "the mountains"]. Before ח (except חָ) the vowel is often unaffected: e.g. הַחָכְמָה "the wisdom" (but הֶחָכָם "the wise man"). The preposition מִ- (assimilated form of מִן- "from") becomes מֵ- *mē-* before the gutturals as a rule: e.g. מֵהָעִיר "from the city"; מֵעָוֹן "from sin" (but מִחוּץ "from outside").

(ii) Immediately before ה, ח and ע (always at the end of a word and often also within a word), a short vowel or an unstressed long vowel becomes *a*: e.g. מֶלֶךְ "king" but זֶרַע "seed"; יִשְׁמֹר "he keeps" but יִשְׁמַע "he hears", יַעֲשֶׂה "he makes"; יָנוּחַ "he rests" but וַיָּנַח *va-yánaχ* "and he rested". In many verb-forms, in particular the PC of stative verbs (XV) and the SC of N-stem and H-stem verbs, the prefix-vowel is *e* (not *i*) before the gutturals: e.g. יֶאֱהַב "he loves"; נֶחְמָד "desirable" (N-stem); הֶאֱבִיד "to destroy" (H-stem).

(iii) At the end of a word, the sound *a* was identified between a long vowel (except of course *ā*) and הּ, ח or ע, and the resulting diphthong was represented thus: גָּבוֹהַּ *gāvōa* "high"; רוּחַ *rūaχ* "wind, spirit"; מוֹשִׁיעַ *mōshīa* "saviour" (pp.4-5). At the end of a word א, ה and ע are not pronounced: e.g. בָּרָא *bārā* "he created"; תּוֹרָה *tōrā* "law"; יָדַע *yāda* "to know". Before another consonant, א is often not pronounced and the preceding vowel lengthened: e.g. בָּרָאתִי *bārātī* "I created"; יֹאמַר *yōmar* "he says".

(iv) After the prepositions -בְּ, -כְּ, and -לְ the guttural ה in the prefix -הַ "the" was not pronounced or written: הַתּוֹרָה "the law" but בַּתּוֹרָה "in the law"; הַמֶּלֶךְ "the king" but לַמֶּלֶךְ "to the king". After -וְ "and" this ה is unaffected: וְהַתּוֹרָה "and the law"; וְהַמֶּלֶךְ "and the king".

(3) Two *central vowels* (represented by *shwa*) cannot occur in adjacent syllables. The first normally becomes *i*: e.g. -לְ *lə*- -לִ *li*- in לִדְבוֹרָה *lidəvōrā* "to Deborah". But -וְ *və*- "and" becomes *ū*-: e.g. וּדְבוֹרָה *ūdəvōrā* "and Deborah"; וּלְדָוִד *ūlədāvīd* "and to David". Before -יְ *yə*- it becomes *ī* and י loses its consonantal value: e.g. בִּירוּשָׁלַיִם *bīrūshāláyim* "in Jerusalem"; לִיהוּדָה *līhūdā* "to Judah". When two shwas occur under adjacent letters in the text, the first denotes the absence of a vowel: e.g. יִמְלְכוּ *yimləχū* "they rule".

Before gutturals with ֱ , ֳ , and ֲ , a central vowel becomes *e*, *o*, and *a* respectively, by a type of vowel harmony: e.g. בֶּאֱדֹם *be'edōm* "in Edom"; וָחֳלִי *voχolī* "and sickness"; כַּעֲבָדִים *ka'avādīm* "like servants". Before אֱ and אֲ it often becomes *ē* and *a* and א is not pronounced: e.g. לֵאלֹהִים *lēlōhīm* "to God"; לַאדֹנִי *ladōnī* "to my lord". The same vowel harmony rules operate when an unstressed short vowel and a compound shwa occur in adjacent syllables: e.g. הֶאֱמִין *he'emīn* (prefix *hi-*) "to believe"; פָּעֳלוֹ *po'olō* "his work"; יַעֲלֶה *ya'ale* "he goes up".

(4) The *semi-vowel y* loses its consonantal nature in many contexts. Initial יְ *yə-* becomes *ī* after the prepositions -בְּ, -כְּ, -לְ and -מִ, and also after the conjunction -וְ "and": e.g. בִּיהוּדָה *bīhūdā* "in Judah"; מִירוּשָׁלַיִם *mīrūshālayim* "from Jerusalem"; וִיהוּדָה *vīhūdā* "and Judah". The middle root-letter of nouns of the type בַּיִת (V) is vocalic in the PG forms: e.g. בֵּית אֱלֹהִים *bēt elōhīm* "the house of God". The first root-letter in verbs of the type יָשַׁב (XVI) is vocalic and often omitted in the script, after the prefixes: e.g. תֵּשֵׁב *tēshēv* "you dwell"; תִּירָא *tīrā* "you fear" (יָרֵא). Similarly in Simple stem imperatives and verbal nouns the semi-vowel is often not written or pronounced: e.g. שֵׁב *shēv* "sit"; דַּעַת *dá'at* "knowledge".

In ancient times ו stood for a semi-vowel too (*w*), and in the PG form of nouns of the type מָוֶת (V) the middle root-letter is vocalic: e.g. מוֹת מֹשֶׁה *mōt mōshe* "the death of Moses". Before the labials *f*, *v*, *m*, -וְ "and" becomes *ū*-: e.g. וּפַרְעֹה *ūfar'ō* "and Pharaoh"; וּמַיִם *umayim* "and water". -וְ is also vocalic before another consonant with shwa (see above 3.)

(c) *Types of Sound-change*. (1) *Vowel-lengthening* occurs in pause (p.157) and, under certain conditions, before gutturals (pp.158f.). It involves the following sound-changes:

a > *ā*	מַיִם	*mayim*	>	מָיִם	*máyim*	(in pause)
e > *ā*	אֶרֶץ	*erets*	>	אָרֶץ	*árets*	(in pause)
i > *ē*	דִּבֵּר	*dibber*	but	בֵּרַךְ	*bēraχ*	(Doubled Stem : X)
u > *ō*	יְדֻבַּר	*yədubbar*	but	יְבֹרַךְ	*yəvōraχ*	(D-stem passive)
ø > *e*	דְּבָרְךָ	*dəvārχā*	>	דְּבָרֶךָ	*dəvāréχā*	(in pause)

ə is lengthened to *ā*, *ē* or *ō* in pausal verb forms: e.g. יִסְעוּ *yisə'ū* > יִסָּעוּ *yisā'ū*; יִמְלְכוּ *yimləχū* > יִמְלֹכוּ *yimlōχū*.

(2) *Vowel-reduction* occurs both for phonological and grammatical reasons. According to the stress rules (p.156), the vowels *ā*, *ē*, *e* and *ō* may be reduced to shwa in certain circumstances: e.g. with stressed suffixes

דָּבָר *dāvār*	דְּבָרִים *dəvārīm*
סֵפֶר *sēfer*	סְפָרִים *səfārīm*
מֶלֶךְ *meleχ*	מְלָכִים *məlāχīm*
יִשְׁמֹר *yishmōr*	יִשְׁמְרֵהוּ *yishmərēhū*

With gutturals, the same vowels are reduced to short-vowels, written with the compound shwas. The remaining vowels *ī*, *i* and *ū* are not reduced to shwa by a change in stress.

In PG forms, the reduced PC forms, and hyphenated phrases, the following are the regular vowel-reductions:

ī > *e* (*ē*)	יָקִים *yāqīm* > יָקֶם *yáqem*; תַּסְתִּיר *tastīr* > תַּסְתֵּר *tastēr*
ē > *e*	בֵּן *bēn* > בֶּן־ *ben* in בֶּן־מָוֶת
e > ∅ (final)	יַעֲלֶה *ya'ale* > יַעַל *yá'al*
ō > *o*	כֹּל *kōl* > כָּל־ *kol* in כָּל־הָאָרֶץ
ū > *o*	יָקוּם *yāqūm* > יָקָם *yáqom*
ā > *a*	יָד *yād* > יַד *yad* in יַד אֱלֹהִים

(3) *Assimilation* is the term used to describe a type of sound-change in which one sound becomes similar to or identical with another sound in close proximity to it. In Hebrew it is marked by doubling (p. 5). There are three common examples of this:

1. *n* and the consonant immediately following it: e.g. in verbs of the type נָפַל (יִפֹּל *yipōl* "he falls") (XIV); in nouns after -מִ "from" (מִדָּוִד *midāvīd* "from David"). There are also a few verbs in which an initial י is assimilated as though it were נ (p.115).

2. *l* and *k* in the verb לָקַח "to take": e.g. יִקַּח *yikaχ* "he takes".
3. *t* and *d* in the T-stem of verbs beginning with *d*:
e.g. מִדַּבֵּר "conversing" (T-stem of דִּבֶּר "to speak"). In verbs beginning with ט or צ, the infix ת of the T-stem becomes ט by assimilation: e.g. הִטָּהֵר "to purify oneself" (T-stem of טָהוֹר "to be clean"); הִצְטַדֵּק "to justify oneself" (T-stem of צָדַק "to be righteous"). In the ancient pronunciation the sounds represented by these two letters were both pharyngealized (ṭ and ṣ), and in these few instances an adjacent *t* was pharyngealized by assimilation (p. 177).

(4) There is one common example of *dissimilation*: the prefix -הַ "the" becomes -הֶ (*he-*) before unstressed הָ, חָ and עָ, and stressed חָ: e.g. הֶהָרִים *he-hārī́m* "the mountains"; הֶחָכָם *he-χāχā́m* "the wise man"; הֶעָוֹן *he-'āvōn* "the sin" (p. 158); הֶחָג *heχāg* "the feast".

(5) *Metathesis* occurs in the T-stem of verbs beginning with *s*, *š* or *ts*: e.g. הִסְתַּתֵּר "to hide oneself" (not *הִתְסַתֵּר : T-stem of *סָתַר); הִשְׁתַּחֲוָה "to worship"; הִצְטַדֵּק "to justify oneself" (see above).

(6) There are sporadic cases of *interchangeability*: e.g. *ts* interchanges with *z* in זָעַק/צָעַק "to cry aloud", and with *s* in צָחַק/שָׂחַק "to laugh".

APPENDIX B. SEMANTICS

Semantics is concerned with the history of the meaning of words and roots (etymology), methods of defining meaning, the arrangement of vocabulary in "fields" (sets of terms of related meaning), the analysis of meaning-relations such as synonymy and opposition, and all the other lexical (as opposed to phonological and grammatical) phenomena observable in a language. But the essential first stage in any semantic investigation is a precise definition of the context of the data, since the meaning of a term is to a large extent dependent on the context in which it occurs.

(1) CONTEXT

A. *The immediate linguistic environment* of a term is perhaps how "context" is most commonly understood. The word כִּי "that, because, indeed" provides a good example: with verbs of "saying, knowing, seeing, etc.", כִּי introduces a noun-clause (cf. English "that"), while at the beginning of an independent sentence it is emphatic ("certainly, indeed"), and in other contexts it is causal ("because"). Similarly דָּבָר must be defined one way in the idiom דְּבַר יְהוָֹה "the word of the Lord", and in another way after verbs of "doing" or "making" (מִי עָשָׂה אֶת־הַדָּבָר הַזֶּה "Who did this thing?")

B. *The wider, literary context* (passage, chapter, book, literary form, style, etc.) must also be taken into account. In the context of a legal formulation in the Deuteronomic law-code (22:27), for example, the word מוֹשִׁיעַ must be defined differently ("anyone to rescue her" JB) from its occurrence in the soteriological language of a sixth century prophet ("saviour": Isaiah 49:26). אֱלֹהִים in the highly charged, theological language of Genesis 1:2 is less likely to function as an intensive marker (cf. NEB "a mighty wind") than in the Book of Jonah: עִיר גְּדוֹלָה לֵאלֹהִים "an exceedingly great city" (3:3).

C. The whole *Hebrew Bible* is also a context in which the meaning of a term can be defined: what does it mean in Biblical Hebrew (as opposed to Mishnaic or Modern Hebrew)? The final texture of the massoretic text, in other words, has an overall unity, the result of centuries of liturgical use and editorial levelling, which makes it possible (and rewarding) to discuss the meaning of terms in that context too, without distinguishing separate styles or literary units within it. The AV is a superb example of semantics at this level. Whereas NEB translates צַלְמָוֶת "dark as death" in one passage (Psalm 23:4), but in other passages "darkness" (Amos 5:8; Job 3:5), AV consistently has "shadow of death". In Biblical Hebrew, followed by later Hebrew, אַל־מָוֶת denotes "immortality" (cf. AV "no death"; Prov. 12:28), although in most English versions the text is emended.

D. Finally, there is the *non-verbal context*, that is to say, the historical situation(s) in which a term has been understood. For Biblical Hebrew, clearly a bewildering variety of situational contexts of this type must be taken into account, from the reconstructed original context of particular literary units [e.g. the Enthronement of Yahweh Festival in which יְהוָה מָלָךְ (Ps. 93:1; 96:10; 97:1, etc.) was used], to the liturgical, theological and intellectual atmosphere of all the numerous religious communities that have read, sung, listened to or studied it up to the present. The verb קָנָה in some passages denotes "to create" (e.g. Gen. 14:19; cf. Ugaritic *qny*), and in others "to get", acquire" (e.g. Gen.47:20,

22; cf. Modern Hebrew). In Gen. 4:1 the term is applied to the begetting of a child, and in Proverbs 8:22 it is used of the creation (or the begetting) of wisdom at creation. The meaning of this verse in the context of the Arian controversy which split Christendom in the 3rd and 4th centuries A.D., depended on the theological doctrine of its readers or exegetes: Wisdom had been identified with Christ, "begotten not made", and in orthodox doctrine קָנָה here denoted "to beget", but for the Arian heretics it denoted "to create". The decision on what קָנָה in Prov. 8:22 means depends on non-verbal, or extra-lingual factors in the context where the passage was understood, and the decision on what is the correct or true meaning is an arbitrary one, outside the realm of scientific investigation.

It is often assumed that the "original meaning" in an "original context" is necessarily the right one: but this is unscientific and confusing. In the first place, "original meaning" is an ambiguous term: it may refer to the original meaning of separate literary units, each in its own situational context in ancient Israel, or to the original meaning of the final form of the text. For example the original meaning of the word שֵׁנָא in Psalm 127.2 is "sleep", probably referring to the dream of Solomon (cf.v.1) at Gibeon; but its "original meaning", when the heading is emended to omit any reference to Solomon, is "unintelligible" (NEB). A refreshing new trend in biblical research, however, is now observable: later interpretations, later historical contexts, and even textual "corruptions" are now being examined with the same objectivity and enthusiasm as the "original". The omission of the Psalm-headings from NEB, partly because "they are certainly not original", is a throwback to the days when chronological priority was considered to be some guarantee of historical importance or authenticity. Even if the Psalm-headings in their present form belong to the age of the Chronicler, let us say, about 4th century B.C., they are no less "authentic" than the Book of Chronicles itself.

The Biblical text is the result of a cumulative process, each historical context adding its own layer of tradition. The semanticist (translator, commentator, theologian or lexicographer) can "freeze" the process and describe the meaning of the text in 9th century B.C. Jerusalem, 6th century B.C. Babylon, 3rd century B.C. Alexandria, the Early Church or Mediaeval Europe, according to his particular interests and skills. The essential thing is that he makes it clear at the outset exactly what he is doing.

(2) SEMANTIC FIELDS

The meaning of a word can also be examined against the background of its "associative field". The "associative field" of a word theoretically includes all the terms associated with it in any way, for example, synonyms, opposites, terms that rhyme with it or look like it, terms which often occur in the same context, and so on, and may contain several hundred terms. Within this very large field there is a smaller, precisely defined "lexical group" of very closely related terms. The vocabulary of Biblical Hebrew has already been arranged into such lexical groups, based mainly on synonymy, by several scholars (cf. Roget's *Thesaurus* for English), and some interesting phenomena can be observed here which do not emerge so clearly either from examination of the text or from the alphabetically arranged dictionaries. Semantic "interference" (a type of analogy) occurs when a term is modified in some way as a result of frequent association with another. The verb עָנָה "to answer, testify", for example, by frequent association with verbs for "to rescue, save, deliver (a person from a thing)", particularly in the language of the Psalms, has almost come to denote "to defend (to testify on behalf of)" (Ps. 22:21f). From an investigation of the lexical group אֱמֶת ,אֱמוּנָה etc. ("true, truth") it emerged that the three roots of the main words אֱמֶת ,יַצִּיב and נָכוֹן also occur in words for "pillar" and "establish", suggesting a common "stability-component" in Hebrew words for "true, truth" not so evident in, for example, the corresponding Greek words. Concept-studies ("memory in the Old Testament", "the meaning of sacrifice", and the like) based on a semantic field are more promising than those which take as their starting-point a single "theological key-word", which inevitably does not occur in all the relevant passages.

But most important of all is the fact that within a semantic field the meaning of a term can be investigated without being translated into another language ("אֱמֶת means truth"), in terms of the meaning-relations which it contracts with associated terms. An investigation of the meaning of הוֹשִׁיעַ, for instance, against the background of its associative field, resulted in the following definition: הוֹשִׁיעַ is closer to עָזַר than הִצִּיל in not being followed so frequently by -מִן "from" or associated with physical terms like הוֹצִיא "to bring out" and רוֹמֵם "to lift up", but with medical or psychological terms (רָפָא "to heal", שָׁמַע "to hear") and colourful metaphorical expressions (קֶרֶן יִשְׁעִי "horn of my salvation"; מַעַיְנֵי הַיְשׁוּעָה "wells of salvation"); it is distinguished from עָזַר in being reserved almost exclusively for religious contexts and becoming unproductive in post-biblical and modern Hebrew (outside biblical expressions). In such a definition, meaning-relations can be carefully analysed and the distinctive semantic characteristics of a term, in opposition to the other terms most closely related to it, defined. The most important meaning-relations between terms are opposition, synonymy, collocation and association. Reference is the relation between a term and its non-verbal context. The structure of Biblical Hebrew poetry indicates the existence of a meaning-relation between two or more terms, without defining precisely what that meaning-relation is, and dictionaries often give poetic parallels (XVI).

Meaning-relations also exist between words in different languages, and simple definitions involving translation are of great practical value as a kind of shorthand, (עָזַר means "help" in many contexts rather than "save"). But the "monolingual" approach attains a higher degree of precision on a term's peculiar associations and overtones.

(3) ETYMOLOGY

In Hebrew the root of a word (p. 12) is usually more conspicuous than in English or other European languages, partly because of the nature of the script and partly because of its simple consonantal form. For centuries Hebrew vocabulary has been arranged in most dictionaries alphabetically by roots, עֵת under עָנָה for example, מִדְבָּר under (דָּבַר) and the like. This procedure inevitably focuses attention on the etymology of a word, as opposed to its use in particular contexts, and it has long been the custom to begin word-studies and dictionary-entries with a comparative survey tracing the root as far as possible over the Semitic or Hamito-Semitic language group from the earliest sources right up to modern times. The difficulty is that, although clearly it is probable that all words containing the same root have at one time had a semantic element in common, how important that element is varies so widely from one word to another and from one context to another, that the "root-meaning" as a starting-point for semantic description is at best inadequate, at worst totally misleading. Frequently the connection between a word as it is used in Biblical Hebrew and the meaning of its root, as far as we can reconstruct it, has virtually snapped [cf. מְחֹקֵק "commander" (Isa.33:22) from the root *חקק in חָקַק "to cut"], and can be dispensed with in the definition, however fascinating from a historical point of view. The etymology of a word is a necessary part of semantic description only in exceptional circumstances, for example, in the case of an unknown hapax legomenon (word attested only once: e.g. עָשִׁיר "refuse"? [Isa. 53:9 (NEB); cf. Arabic], or suspected textual corruption (*עֲמָלֵץ "shark" Ps. 74:14 NEB). On the etymological "transparency" of many Hebrew words, however, see below, pp.172f.

(4) SEMANTIC WORD-TYPES.

At the phonological and grammatical level noun-types and verb-types are distinguished in most grammars; but it is also useful to distinguish word-types at the semantic level.

1. *Taboo words* are words avoided, in certain contexts, for reasons of delicacy, decency or religious fear. In the sophisticated theological language of Genesis 1, for example, the words שֶׁמֶשׁ "sun" and יָרֵחַ "moon" are avoided because of their pagan, polytheistic overtones, and "greater light" and "a lesser light" respectively are euphemistic substitutions for them. The term בַּעַל "Baal" is a taboo-term in certain contexts, and the substitution of בֹּשֶׁת "shame" is well-known (p.73). The name of Israel's God was also a taboo word in spoken Hebrew, but for different reasons (p.12). Terms

for certain bodily functions and parts of the body were also taboo and various euphemisms occur: e.g. רַגְלַיִם "private parts (lit. feet)" (e.g. Isa. 6:3).

2. *Loan words* are words originally borrowed from another language. Biblical Hebrew examples of "lexical borrowing" from non-Semitic languages are הֵיכָל (Sumerian via Akkadian) "palace , temple", סוּס (Indo-Aryan) "horse", כּוֹבַע (Hittite) "helmet", פַּרְדֵּס (Persian) "park", and אַפִּרְיוֹן (Greek) "litter". Hamito-Semitic examples include מַבּוּל (Akkadian) "flood", זְמַן (Aramaic) "time", and גֹּמֶא (Egyptian) "papyrus". "Semantic borrowing" (calque) is the borrowing of a foreign meaning for a word already in the borrower language. This may produce a type of polysemy (see below): e.g. פָּרַק I. "to tear apart", II. "to rescue". II. is borrowed from Aramaic.

3. The distinction between *general* and *particular* terms is a valuable one, particularly as between one language and another, where it is a basic consideration for the translator. It arises from the fact that the "range of meaning" or "semantic spread" of a term in one language normally differs from its closest parallel in another language. In contrast to the general term "to put on" in English, for example, the semantic spread of Hebrew לָבַשׁ "to put on (clothes)" is limited by נָעַל "to put on (sandals)", עָטָה "to put on (a cloak)", שִׂים "to put on (ornaments)" and other related terms.

4. *Extension* and *restriction* of meaning are important historical processes which, like borrowing, have resulted in distinctive word-types. Hebrew participial forms like מַזְכִּיר and שׁוֹמֵר are examples of restriction of meaning from "one who reminds" and "one who keeps" (IX) to the technical sense of "secretary of state" (II Sam. 8:16)

and "watchman". נָסַע originally "to pull up a tent-peg" and later "to set out, journey" is an example of extension of meaning. Both the restricted and the extended meanings often occur, as in these examples, side by side in one language, and the connection between them may become so tenuous that two distinct words of identical form may be distinguished (polysemy).

5. *Polysemy* refers to the phenomenon of one word which has developed two or more entirely distinct meanings. The two most frequently quoted examples are English "pupil (of the eye)" alongside "pupil (at school)" and French *voler* "to fly" beside *voler* "to steal". There is enough historical evidence to prove that in each case the two words have undergone a separate semantic development from a single term. *Homonymy* on the other hand is the result of phonetic developments which have made two originally quite distinct lexical items converge. The disappearance of certain Proto-Semitic sounds in Hebrew (p.182) has produced many homonyms like I. צָלַל "to sink" (cf. Arabic *ṣalla*) beside II. צָלַל "to grow dark" (cf. Arabic *ẓalla*), and חָרַשׁ "to plough" (cf. Arabic *ḥaraṯa*) beside חָרֵשׁ "to be deaf" (cf. Arabic *ḫariša*). Comparative philologists have often tended to postulate homonyms rather than emend the massoretic text: e.g. I. עָשִׁיר "rich" beside II. עָשִׁיר "refuse"? [Isaiah 53:9: cf.(NEB): see above]; I. יָדַע "to know" beside II. יָדַע "to humble" (Isa. 53:3 : cf. NEB).

In an unpointed consonantal text a type of visual polysemy or homonymy is common and could be exploited by the writers or interpreters of Biblical Hebrew: e.g. the noun מכתם in the Psalm-headings was interpreted in LXX as two words, מך "humble" and תם "perfect", epithets of David (Pss.58 and 59); and ערש "bed" in Amos 3:12, being apparently out of place in the context, suggested the Greek word ἱερεῖς "priests", which made very good sense.

6. The distinction between *transparent* and *opaque* words can be useful in differentiating synonyms or detecting subtle overtones. The meaning of transparent words can be deduced from their structure, the meaning of opaque words cannot. Thus onomatopaeic words like *zoom* and *bang* are said to be transparent, being phonetically "motivated", as opposed to *voice* and *sound* which are opaque. Transparent compounds like *windscreen-wiper* and *underpass* are said to be morphologically motivated as opposed to *carburettor* and *derrick*. In Hebrew and other Semitic languages, the conspicuous relationship between words of the same root and the relatively simple system of word-formation (p.179) have produced a type of morphological or etymological motivation which greatly increases the transparency of Hebrew vocabulary. Examples from Genesis 1 would include רֵאשִׁית "beginning" (cf. רֹאשׁ "head" + abstract noun suffix ־ִית) and מִקְוֶה "gathering together" (cf.*קוה "to collect" with noun-prefix מ). צֶלֶם, however, in the phrase צֶלֶם אֱלֹהִים "the image of God" (Gen. 1:26f) is opaque as opposed to other words for "likeness, image, etc.", and was possibly selected intentionally to avoid anthropomorphism.

Transparency is often a historical matter: words originally transparent often become opaque as a result of phonetic developments. For example, English "lord" was once transparent (*hlaf-weard*: cf. "bread-winner") but is no longer so. There is also a subjective element in this transparent/opaque distinction. Modern scientific terms like "hypodermic" and "thixotropic" are transparent to someone who knows enough Greek but opaque (although, of course, not necessarily unintelligible) to everyone else. Similarly a knowledge of Aramaic (and an interest in folk-etymology) made the name Japheth transparent in Genesis 9:27: יַפְתְּ אֱלֹהִים לְיֶפֶת "May God enlarge Japheth('s land)!" הִפְתָּה is not attested elsewhere in Hebrew, but אַפְתִּי is a common Aramaic word for "to extend, widen".

APPENDIX C. HISTORY OF THE HEBREW LANGUAGE

The *Hamito-Semitic* (or "Afro-asiatic")languages divide into a *northern group* consisting of ancient Egyptian, Coptic, the Semitic languages and the Berber languages of North Africa, and a *southern group*, consisting of the Cushitic languages of modern Ethiopia and Somalia, and the Chadic languages of Central West Africa, the best known of which is Hausa. The Semitic languages, so-called because of similarities between the languages spoken by some of the "sons of Shem" (Gen. 10:21-31), are grouped as follows:

(a) *West Semitic* is first attested in *Amorite* proper names from the beginning of the Second Millennium B.C. and in particular in the Mari texts (18th century B.C.). It also includes *Ugaritic*, known to us chiefly from the Ras Shamra texts (c. 1450-1200 B.C.), and "Canaanite glosses" in the Amarna letters (14th century B.C.). From c. 1200 B.C. West Semitic divides into (1) the *Canaanite* languages of Palestine (Hebrew and Moabite) and Phoenicia. The Phoenician traders and colonists took their language (and alphabet: pp. 188f.) to many parts of the Mediterranean sea-board, such as Carthage in North Africa where Punic, a Phoenician dialect, was the language of Hannibal (247-183 B.C.); and (2) *Aramaic* which developed from a fairly circumscribed regional status in 9th and 8th century B.C. Syria ("Aram") into virtually the lingua franca of many parts of the ancient near east under Assyrian (II Kings 18:26), Babylonian and Persian imperial rule (7th to 4th centuries B.C.). Imperial Aramaic is the language of the Elephantine Papyri (5th century B.C.) and the Aramaic sections of the Old Testament (Gen. 31:47; Jer. 10:11; Ezra 4:8-6:18; 7:12-26; Dan.2:4-7:28). From the

1st century B.C. two dialect-groups can be distinguished: (i) *Western Aramaic* includes *Nabataean* and *Palmyrene*, spoken by two Arab states based on Petra and Palmyra c. 100 B.C. to 200 A.D., the *Jewish Palestinian Aramaic* of some of the Qumran texts (c. 150 B.C. to 70 A.D.), the Targums and the Jerusalem Talmud (1st to 4th centuries A.D.), the language of the *Samaritan* Targum (c. 4th century A.D.), the *Christian Palestinian Aramaic* of some religious texts from 5th to 8th centuries A.D., and the spoken dialects of several modern Syrian villages; (ii) *Eastern Aramaic* includes *Syriac*, in which the vast religious literature of Eastern Christendom was written from the 3rd to 13th centuries A.D., the Aramaic of the Babylonian Talmud (4th to 5th centuries A.D.), the language of the *Mandaean* sect in southern Mesopotamia (3rd to 8th centuries), and the dialects still spoken by communities of Christians and Jews in various parts of Iraq, Iran and the Soviet Union.

(b) *East Semitic* is confined to the languages of ancient Mesopotamia: *Akkadian*, the language of Sargon of Akkad who conquered the Sumerians c. 2300 B.C., *Old Babylonian*, in which, for example, the Law code of Hammurabi (c. 1728-1686 B.C.) is written, the *New Babylonian* of the time of Nebuchadnezzar (605-562 B.C.) and his successors, and *Assyrian*, the language of Northern Mesopotamia attested from c. 2000 B.C. down to the fall of Nineveh, capital of the Assyrian Empire, in 612 B.C.

(c) *South Semitic* comprises *Arabic*, from the pre-classical language of North Arabian inscriptions, and classical Arabic which includes the language of the Quran (7th century A.D.), to the many modern dialects such as Moroccan, Egyptian, Syrian, Arabian, and Iraqi; *Epigraphic South Arabian* which refers to the language of ancient

South West Arabian city-states from the 8th century B.C. to the 6th century A.D. (Sabaean, Minaean, etc.); and *Ethiopic* which includes both ancient Ethiopic (Gə'əz), attested from the beginning of the Christian era to modern times mainly in religious literature, and Amharic, with the other Semitic languages of modern Ethiopia (Tigre, Gurage, etc.).

a) *West Semitic*

Amorite
Ugaritic
Canaanite

Hebrew	Aramaic	
Moabite	Nabataean	Syriac
Phoenician	Palmyrene	Mandaean
Punic	Samaritan	

b) *East Semitic*

Akkadian
Babylonian
Assyrian

c) *South Semitic*

Arabic
Epigraphic South Arabian
Ethiopic
Gə'əz
Amharic, etc.

(i) PROTO-SEMITIC

If we could speak of a Hamito-Semitic "family", it would be theoretically possible to reconstruct a common "ancestor" comparable to Indo-European. In practice the historical and geographical diversities involved are so vast, our earliest sources for many of the languages so inadequate, and the influence of non-Hamito-Semitic languages in many cases so profound, that it has not so far proved possible to reconstruct more than a fraction of such a common source-language. The Semitic languages, however, exhibit enough shared characteristics, in phonology, grammar and vocabulary, to make the artificial reconstruction of "Proto-Semitic" (P-S) not only practical and convincing, but an essential working hypothesis for Semitic historical and comparative linguistics. Such a reconstruction is based on the evidence of all attested Semitic languages, but it is clear that these have not all developed at the same rate or in the same directions: for example, Classical Arabic appears to have been exceptionally conservative in its phonology and in some grammatical features (e.g. case-endings), while in many other respects (particularly at the semantic level) it has diverged very far from P-S. The following is a brief summary of the kind of information on P-S so far available.

(a) PHONOLOGY

The most distinctive features of P-S phonology are the five post-velar sounds, that is, the two glottal sounds (p.153), the uvular *q* in *Iraq*, and the two pharyngeals heard in Arabic *Aḥmed* and *ʿAbdullah* together with the "pharyngealization" of four other sounds (the "emphatics"). Most of these nine sounds are represented in the chief Semitic scripts, but do not always retain their original pronunciation.

There are 29 consonants in the P-S system, and the three vowel-sounds, *a*, *i* and *u*(lengthened *ā*, *ī* and *ū*).

TABLE OF CORRESPONDENCES*

		West Semitic			East Semitic	South Semitic		
	Proto-Semitic	Hebrew	Ugaritic	Aramaic	Akkadian	Arabic	Epigraphic South Arabian	Ethiopic
Labials	*p*	*p*	*p*	*p*	*p*	*f*	*f*	*f*
	b	*b*	*b*	*b*	*b*	*b*	*b*	*b*
	m	*m*	*m*	*m*	*m*	*m*	*m*	*m*
Dento-alveolars	*t*	*t*	*t*	*t*	*t*	*t*	*t*	*t*
	d	*d*	*d*	*d*	*d*	*d*	*d*	*d*
	ṯ(θ)	*š*	*ṯ*	*t*	*š*	*ṯ*	*ṯ*	*s*
	ḏ(ð)	*z*	*d*(*ḏ* ?)	*d*	*z*	*ḏ*	*ḏ*	*z*
	n	*n*	*n*	*n*	*n*	*n*	*n*	*n*
	l	*l*	*l*	*l*	*l*	*l*	*l*	*l*
	r	*r*	*r*	*r*	*r*	*r*	*r*	*r*
	s	*s*	*s*	*s*	*s*	*s*	*s*	*s*
	z	*z*	*z*	*z*	*z*	*z*	*z*	*z*
	š(ʃ)	*š*	*š*	*š*	*š*	*s*	*s*¹	*s*
	ś	*ś*	*š*	*s*	*š*	*š*	*s*²	*š*
Palato-velars	*k*	*k*	*k*	*k*	*k*	*k*	*k*	*k*
	g	*g*	*g*	*g*	*g*	*g*	*g*	*g*
	ḫ(χ)	*ḥ*	*ḫ*	*ḥ*	*ḫ*	*ḫ*	*ḫ*	*ḫ*
	ğ(γ)	ʿ	*ġ*	ʿ	ʾ	*ġ*	*ġ*	ʿ
Post-velars	ʾ(ʔ)	ʾ	ʾ	ʾ	ʾ	ʾ	ʾ	ʾ
	h	*h*	*h*	*h*	ʾ	*h*	*h*	*h*
	q	*q*	*q*	*q*	*q*	*q*	*q*	*q*
	ʿ(ʕ)	ʿ	ʿ	ʿ	ʾ	ʿ	ʿ	ʿ
	ḥ(ħ)	*ḥ*	*ḥ*	*ḥ*	ʾ	*ḥ*	*ḥ*	*ḥ*
Emphatics	*ṭ*(ŧ)	*ṭ*	*ṭ*	*ṭ*	*ṭ*	*ṭ*	*ṭ*	*ṭ*
	ḏ̣(ð̶)	*ṣ*	*ṣ*	ʿ	*ṣ*	*ḍ*	*ḍ*	*ḍ*
	ṯ̣(θ̶)	*ṣ*	*ṯ̣*	*ṭ*	*ṣ*	*ẓ*	*ẓ*	*ṣ*
	ṣ(s̶)	*ṣ*	*ṣ*	*ṣ*	*ṣ*	*ṣ*	*ṣ*	*ṣ*
Semi-vowels	*w*	*w*	*w*	*w*	*w*	*w*	*w*	*w*
	y(*j*)	*y*	*y*	*y*	*y*	*y*	*y*	*y*

*The International Phonetic Association symbols are given in brackets where they differ from the conventional transliteration system used by Semitists.

(b) GRAMMAR

The most distinctive characteristic of P-S grammar and word-formation is the consonantal root: most nouns and verbs are made up of a *root* consisting of one, two or, very frequently, three consonants, and various types of *formative* consisting of vowel-patterns, prefixes, suffixes and the like. For example, the basic P-S noun-types are *CVCC-*, *CVCVC-*, *CVCCVC-* and types with prefixes (especially *ʾ-*, *m-*, *t-*) and suffixes (*-ān*, *-ūt/īt*, *-ī*). There are two genders, masculine and feminine, and special dual forms as well as plural. There are three cases, Nominative, Genitive and Accusative, and a distinctive type of Genitive phrase in which the main stress falls on the last term and pregenitive terms take a special form (cf. V).

P-S has two types of pronoun, independent pronouns (cf. III) and suffix pronouns (cf. VIII). P-S prefixes also include three prepositions and the commonest conjunction.

In the P-S verbal system a Suffix Conjugation expresses a completed state or condition (cf. IV), and, on the evidence of Akkadian, Ugaritic and Hebrew (and also some of the Hamito-Semitic languages of Africa), there are two distinct Prefix Conjugations whose precise function in expressing tense, aspect and modality, however, is unclear. The function of most of the Derived Stems, formed by doubling, lengthening, the addition of prefixes or infixes and various combinations of these (cf. X), is also obscure. Participles with prefix *m* and verbal nouns are also postulated (IX).

(c) VOCABULARY

The vocabulary of a common source-language could theoretically throw light upon the ecological and cultural background of its speakers. Recent studies have noted, for example, the absence from P-S of common words for "mountain" and "desert", and the prominence of agricultural and horticultural terminology. Wild animals represented in P-S vocabulary include lions, wolves, hyenas, deer, gazelles, elephants and bears, while among domestic animals are sheep, goats, pigs, cattle and the ass, but not the horse. A start has also been made on terms for natural phenomena and religious terminology. Conclusions on the "original home" of an actual people speaking this artificially reconstructed language, however, must be treated with caution.

(2) HEBREW

The presence of Canaanites in Egypt and in particular the worship of Canaanite deities there (e.g. Baal, Baalat, Anat, and Astarte) from 15th century B.C. make it probable that the language of Moses would have been a Canaanite dialect akin to Ugaritic. "The language of the Jews" (II Kings 18:26), however, distinguished from Aramaic and eventually described as Hebrew by c. 180 B.C. (Ecclesiasticus, Prol.) cannot be profitably investigated much before the time of David (c. 1000 B.C.). Our chief source for Classical Hebrew, the Hebrew Bible, is written in a variety of Hebrew, which, although distinguishable from Mishnaic, Mediaeval and Modern Hebrew, is certainly not identical with the language spoken and written in ancient Israel during the "Classical period" (c. 1000-500 B.C.). "Biblical Hebrew" is the language of the Hebrew Bible as fixed by a Jewish scholar named Aaron ben Asher by c.900 A.D. It is the result of centuries of meticulous editorial activity on the part of the "*massoretes*" or "preservers of tradition (*masora*)" who devised numerous methods, including systems of vocalization and punctuation (p.192), to ensure that the text of the Hebrew Bible was preserved unchanged. That they were not entirely successful is *a priori* probable and proved by the occurrence of deviant forms [e.g. ין for BH יַיִן "wine"; שת (**šattu)* for BH שָׁנָה "year"] in contemporary inscriptions, ostraka, seals and coins. But enough of the original Hebrew forms have been faithfully recorded to make it possible to distinguish from standard BH an early northern variety in the Song of Deborah (Judges 5) and late Biblical Hebrew in the Books of Chronicles, Ezra-Nehemiah, Daniel, Song of Songs, Ecclesiastes and Esther.

(a) CLASSICAL HEBREW

Distinctive characteristics of Hebrew phonology which can confidently be traced back to the classical period are the assimilation of post-vocalic *n* to the consonant immediately following it (e.g. P-S * *antā* > *attā* "you"), and the reduction of the four emphatics to two: ט goes back to P-S *ṭ*, but צ may go back to P-S *ṣ*, *ṯ̣* or *ḍ* (cf. p. 171 on homonyms). Other developments include *ṯ* > *š* (e.g P-S **ṯalāṯū* > שָׁלשׁ "three": cf. Ugaritic *ṯlṯ*), *ḏ* > *z*(e.g. P-S * *ʾaḫaḏa* > אָחַז "to hold": cf. Ugaritic *ʾḫd*), and *á* > *ó* (e.g. P-S **šālāmu* > שָׁלוֹם "peace": cf. Arabic *sālāmu*).

The semi-vowel *w* becomes *y* in initial position (except in -וְ "and"), but reappears in verb-forms after some prefixes as the related rounded vowel *ō* : e.g. יָלַד "to have a child" (cf. Arabic *walad* "a child") but N-stem נוֹלַד "to be born". Final *-y* is lost in verbs like רָאָה "to see" but reappears as the related vowel *-ī-* before consonantal suffixes (e.g. רָאִיתִי "I saw": XVIII). Semi-vowels are reduced to vowels also in the pregenitive of nouns like בֵּית (V). Nouns of the type *CVCC-* (e.g. **malk-* "king", **sifr-* "book", **ʾuzn-* "ear") have developed into the "segholate nouns" in Hebrew, characterized by the pattern *CVCVC* in the citation-form but the original *CVCC-* form before most suffixes: מֶלֶךְ beside מַלְכִּי; סֵפֶר beside סִפְרִי; אֹזֶן beside אָזְנִי (VIII).

A conspicuous feature of BH which had not fully developed by the end of the classical period, but is represented in massoretic pointing (p.5), is the pronunciation of the six consonants *p/b, t/d* and *k/g* (the "Beghadhkephath" letters) in post-vocalic positions: in בָּבֶל "Babylon", for example, the first בּ (dotted) is a stop (b), the second ב (undotted) is a fricative (v) and in תּוֹרָתוֹ "his law" the first ת (dotted) is a stop (t), the second a fricative (θ).

The most remarkable feature of Classical Hebrew grammar is undoubtedly the complex verbal system in which opposition between The Suffix Conjugation and the various Prefix Conjugation forms cannot be defined simply in terms of tense, mood or aspect. Case-endings have for the most part disappeared in Hebrew although the adverbial suffix *-ām* (XV) may represent a relic of the accusative case.

BH vocabulary has the following peculiar, although not unexpected characteristics: many common terms are accidentally missing (e.g. words for "comb, "needle", and "spoon") and many more (over 2,000), some of them quite common in Mishnaic Hebrew, occur by chance only once (e.g. סֻלָּם "ladder", כַּדּוּר "ball", זְכוּכִית "glass", עֲטִישָׁה "sneezing"). These and the extraordinary size of certain semantic fields (pp.166f.) (e.g. the הוֹשִׁיעַ - field) illustrate the artificial nature of Biblical Hebrew and the discrepancy between it and the language actually spoken in ancient Israel. There are also many word-pairs occurring in parallel (XVI) in both Biblical and Ugaritic poetry, which include words not attested elsewhere in Hebrew [e.g. שָׁתַע "to be afraid" (Isa. 41:10); חָרוּץ "gold";] and point to some degree of dependence upon Ugaritic literary tradition.

(b) MISHNAIC HEBREW

Already in the late Biblical period a number of features characteristic of Mishnaic Hebrew can be observed: for example, vowel-letters (p.191), the relative prefix -שֶׁ (for BH אֲשֶׁר), and noun-formations with the suffixes -וֹן, ןָ and -וּת are more frequent. Borrowing from Aramaic, Persian and Greek (p.170) also occurs. Although by c. 400 B.C. it was being superseded by Aramaic (p.174), Hebrew was probably still spoken in many Jewish communities. Evidence for this continuity has now been found in Hebrew manuscripts from Qumran (c. 150 B.C. to 70 A.D.), a fragment of the Hebrew text of Ecclesiasticus from Massada (c. 70 A.D.) and several of Bar Kokhba's letters (131-134 A.D.) which appear to be written in varieties of Mishnaic Hebrew. This is the language in which the Mishnah and other early Jewish religious works were written between c.200 and 500 A.D.

In addition to an increase in every day vocabulary, in contrast to Biblical Hebrew (see above), and the characteristics of late Biblical Hebrew already mentioned, the following are some of the more obvious developments in Mishnaic Hebrew: the loss of the pronoun אָנֹכִי "I" (p.24), the passive D-stem forms [except the participle, e.g. מְדֻבָּר "spoken" (cf.X)], and -וַ + PC forms of the verb (VI); the active participle frequently points to present time (as opposed to SC for past and PC for future), and continuous action in the past may be expressed by הָיָה with an active participle (cf. English "I was going"). The genitive relationship is normally expressed by שֶׁל(-שֶׁ + -לְ "(lit.) which belongs to"), the BH system being mainly confined to fossilized expressions derived from the Hebrew Bible.

(c) MEDIAEVAL HEBREW

Mediaeval Hebrew is the language which continued to be written (but probably not spoken) by Jewish scholars and writers in the Arab countries and Europe after the end of the Mishnaic period. There is a vast body of mediaeval Jewish literature which includes religious poetry (Piyyuṭ), translations of Arabic scientific and philosophical works, and, best-known in the field of biblical research, the commentaries and treatises of great mediaeval scholars like Rashi of Troyes (1040-1105), Ibn Ezra of Cordova (1092-1167) and David Kimhi of Narbonne (1160-1235). Widespread borrowing from Arabic, mainly calque (p. 170), distinguishes Mediaeval from Mishnaic Hebrew.

(d) MODERN HEBREW

The modernization of Hebrew can be traced back to the sixteenth century; but it is not until the eighteenth century that the first Hebrew newspapers appeared and not until the nineteenth century that *Modern Hebrew*, a mixture of Biblical and Mishnaic elements, can be said to have emerged. Thanks partly to the legendary work of Eliezer Ben Yehuda, Hebrew was adopted by Jewish agricultural and urban settlements in Palestine from 1881 onwards, and in 1948 became the official language of the State of Israel. The development of the language has been recorded, investigated, and to a large extent controlled by scholars and writers, and in 1953 the Hebrew Language Academy was established.

Pronunciation varies considerably according to speech variety. In standard colloquial Hebrew the depharyngealization which began in

Classical Hebrew (p.182) is almost complete, in spite of official support for the orientalizing pronunciation of ח, ע, and ק. The glottals א and ה are not normally pronounced. ט is not distinguished from ת, צ stands for *t͜s*, and ו stands for *v*. In post-vocalic positions (p.157) only ב, כ and פ stand for fricatives the other three ג, ד and ת always stand for stops (p.152). Vowel-letters are written for short vowels as well as long (דִּיבֵּר "he spoke"; שׁוּלְחָן "table"), the massoretic system being reserved mainly for poetry and books for children.

In some European and American religious communities Ashkenazi pronunciations are still current (cf. אַשְׁכְּנַז "Europe" Gen. 10:3), in addition to the Sephardi varieties spoken in Israel. Distinctive features of these include the pronunciation of undotted ת as *s* and various vowel-sounds and stress-patterns influenced by European languages: e.g. שָׁלוֹם is pronounced *shólem*.

Some elements already observable in Mishnaic Hebrew grammar (e.g. the use of שֶׁל in genitive phrases and a verbal system using three tenses and the auxiliary הָיָה: p.184) have become standard, influenced no doubt to some extent by the European languages of immigrants. Vocabulary has been enormously enriched, not only by words gleaned from Biblical, Mishnaic and Mediaeval sources as well as Aramaic literature, but also by new words created from Hebrew or Aramaic roots[e.g. מַצְנֵחַ "parachute" from צָנַח "to alight" (Judg. 1:14): צַנְחָן "paratrooper", etc.], widespread borrowing from Yiddish and modern European languages (e.g. תַּפּוּחַ אֲדָמָה "potato": cf. French *pomme de terre*), and by coining new roots: e.g. *פסטר in מְפוּסְטָר "pasteurized"; דִּיוֵּחַ "to make a report" from דו"ח, the initial letters of דִּין וְחֶשְׁבּוֹן "report (lit. case and reckoning)". A loan-word and an indigenous Hebrew coinage may exist for a time side by side: e.g. אֶסְקָלָצְיָה (*eskālā́tsiā*) beside אַסְלָמָה (from סֻולָם "ladder") "escalation".

(3) HEBREW WRITING

Our earliest documents, such as the Moabite stone, the Gezer Calendar and the Siloam Inscription (9th to 8th centuries B.C.) are written in a lapidary form of the "Canaanite" or "Old Hebrew" script (*Col.1*). This is an alphabetical script, (neither hieroglyphic like the ancient Egyptian, nor syllabic like the cuneiform script of Mesopotamia), which can probably be traced back as far as "Proto-Sinaitic" inscriptions of about 1500 B.C. From it most of the alphabets of the world, including, thanks to Phoenician trading contacts, the Greek and Latin ones, are ultimately derived. Examples of a cursive form of this early Hebrew script are provided by the Lachish Letters (c. 590 B.C.) (*Col.2*).

Coins issued by the Hasmonaeans (2nd. to 1st. century B.C.) and the leaders of the First and Second Jewish Revolts (66-73 A.D., and 132-135 A.D.) bore inscriptions in this Old Hebrew script and the Samaritan community have retained it up to the present day. But, apart from such isolated instances of political and religious conservatism, it was completely superseded by the "Aramaic" or "Square Script" soon after the Babylonian Exile (586-538 B.C.). From that time Aramaic became the *lingua franca* from the Nile to the Indus, and the Aramaic script, a distinctive development of the Old Hebrew script, spread with the language. The next important set of Hebrew documents, namely the Dead Sea Scrolls (2nd. century B.C. to 1st century A.D.), are written in varieties of the Square Script called "Hasmonaean" and "Herodian" (*Col.3*).

Jewish tradition officially sanctioned this change of script by attributing it to the fifth century B.C. religious reformer Ezra, who was said to have brought it back with him to Jerusalem from

THE ALPHABET

	1	2	3	4	5	6	7	8	9
Aleph	𐤀	𐤀	א	א	א	א	א	1	ʾ
Beth	𐤁	𐤁	ב	ב	ב	ב	ב	2	*b,bh*
Gimel	𐤂	𐤂	ג	ג	ג	ג	ג	3	*g,gh*
Daleth	𐤃	𐤃	ד	ד	ד	ד	ד	4	*d,dh*
He	𐤄	𐤄	ה	ה	ה	ה	ה	5	*h*
Waw	𐤅	𐤅	ו	ו	ו	ו	ו	6	*w*
Zayin	𐤆	𐤆	ז	ז	ז	ז	ז	7	*z*
Ḥeth	𐤇	𐤇	ח	ח	ח	ח	ח	8	*ḥ*
Ṭeth	𐤈	𐤈	ט	ט	ט	ט	ט	9	*ṭ*
Yodh	𐤉	𐤉	י	י	י	י	י	10	*y*
Kaph	𐤊	𐤊	ך כ	כ ך	כ ך	כ ך	ך כ	20	*k,kh*
Lamedh	𐤋	𐤋	ל	ל	ל	ל	ל	30	*l*
Mem	𐤌	𐤌	ם מ	מ ם	מ ם	מ ם	ם מ	40	*m*
Nun	𐤍	𐤍	ן נ	נ ן	נ ן	נ ן	ן נ	50	*n*
Samekh	𐤎	𐤎	ס	ס	ס	ס	ס	60	*s*
Ayin	𐤏	𐤏	ע	ע	ע	ע	ע	70	ʿ
Pe	𐤐	𐤐	ף פ	פ ף	פ ף	פ ף	ף פ	80	*p,ph*
Ṣadhē	𐤑	𐤑	ץ צ	צ ץ	צ ץ	צ ץ	צ ץ	90	*ṣ*
Qoph	𐤒	𐤒	ק	ק	ק	ק	ק	100	*q*
Resh	𐤓	𐤓	ר	ר	ר	ר	ר	200	*r*
Shin,Sin	𐤔	𐤔	ש	ש	ש	ש	ש	300	*š, ś*
Tau	𐤕	𐤕	ת	ת	ת	ת	ת	400	*t,th*

Babylon. All subsequent developments can therefore be traced back to the Square Script: the massoretic manuscripts from Tiberias (10th century A.D.) (*Col.4*); the Rashi script, called after the eleventh century Jewish scholar (see p. 185) and still used in editions of the Talmud (*Col.5*); and the cursive script of modern times (*Col.6*).

Modern printed editions of the Hebrew Bible as a rule follow the massoretes very closely not only textually, but also typographically (*Col.7*), and this is naturally the script used in most BH grammars. Attempts to reproduce this printed type in manuscript have led to the evolution, particularly in British universities, of various other semi-cursive forms of the printed script. But it is becoming common practice in many parts of the world to use the cursive script for writing even Biblical Hebrew. Finally, since the boom in Hebrew printed books, periodicals and newspapers in the present century, not to mention the spread of shop-signs, advertising, and other areas of experiment in Israel, a large variety of new Hebrew type-faces and lettering, including the beautiful IBM "Shalom" type used in the present volume, has been designed.

Each letter of the alphabet has a numerical value as shown in *Column 8*. 11, 12, 13, etc. are represented thus: יא, יב, יג etc. 15 and 16 however are denoted by טו and טז, because יה and יו stand for Yahweh, especially in proper names (p.71). 500, 600, etc. are תק, תר, etc; 900 is תתק; and 1000, 2000, etc. are א׳, ב׳, etc. The numerical value of a word or phrase can then be worked out by totalling up the values of its letters, and equations such as נרון קסר "Nero Caesar"= 666 (the number of the beast in Revelation 13:18) established. Apart from this popular exegetical arithmetic, called "gematria" by the rabbis, the system is mainly confined to dates, the pages of the Talmud, and the numbering of chapters in most editions of the Hebrew Bible.

The transliteration system used in most Biblical studies and other works on Hebrew language and literature (*Col.9*) is designed to represent accurately each sign in the Massoretic script: for example, the "Beghadhkephath" letters (p.5) have two forms, *b* , *g*, *d*, etc. for the dotted forms and *bh*, *gh*, *dh* (or ḇ, ḡ, ḏ) for the undotted, post-vocalic forms, and *k* (Kaph) is distinguished from *q* (or ḳ) (Qoph), whether or not these distinctions are maintained in pronunciation. Although intended to be autonomous, unlike the system used in the present grammar which is purely an aid to pronouncing the Hebrew script, the conventional system can cause confusion since the value of some of the letters (e.g. *bh*, *ḥ*, *q*, *ṣ*) may not be the same as in other branches of linguistics, for example, Sanskrit and Phonetics.

None of the alphabetical scripts just described had any special forms to represent vowels. From the 10th century B.C., however, various systems of "vowel-letters" were introduced, the back vowel *ā* could be represented by one of the two gutturals א or ה, the front vowels *ē* and *ī* by the semi-vowel י, and the rounded vowels *ō* and *ū* by the semi-vowel ו. The Greek alphabet also used the pharyngeals, ח and ע (which were not required to represent consonants) as vowel-letters. The three most widely used vowel-letters, ה, ו, and י, although rare in early Hebrew documents, are consistently employed in most of the Qumran texts and frequent also in the Hebrew Bible where they were incorporated into the Tiberian system of vocalization.

HEBREW WRITING

VOWEL-LETTERS

	א	ה	ו	ח	י	ע
Square Script	א	ה	ו	ח	י	ע
Biblical Hebrew		final ā final e final ō	ō,ū		ē,ī	
Mishnaic Hebrew	ā	final ā final e final ō	ō,ū		ē,ī	ā
Babylonian pointing	< ā		ˋ u		· i	ע e,a
Greek vowels	A	E	Y	H	I	O
Old Hebrew script	𐤀	𐤄	𐤅	𐤇	𐤉	𐤏

Between the fifth and tenth centuries A.D. a number of more sophisticated vocalization systems were developed. The *Babylonian* system was derived from the four vowel letters א, ו, י, and ע, and like the *Palestinian* system was supralinear, consisting of points and strokes written above the consonantal script. The *Tiberian* system of pointing, a development from the Palestinian system, has survived in three forms, of which that used in Tiberia by the Ben Asher family from the ninth century became the standard for Biblical Hebrew to the present day.

VOCALIZATION SYSTEMS

	ā	*a*	*e*	*ē*	*i*	*ō*	*u*	*ə*
Babylonian	˘	ע (·)		··	·	:	ˋ	/
Palestinian	'	–	.·	·.	:	∴	··	/
Tiberian	ָ	–	∵	··	·	·	⋱	:

BIBLIOGRAPHY

GENERAL

Albright, W.F. & Lambdin, T.O., "The evidence of language" in *Cambridge Ancient History*, Vol.I, Pt.I 3rd ed., Cambridge 1970, pp. 122-155.

Barr, J., *The Semantics of Biblical Language*, Oxford 1961.

" " , *Comparative Philology and the Text of the Old Testament*, Oxford 1968.

Crystal, D., *Linguistics, Language and Religion*, London 1965.

Diringer, D., *The Alphabet. A Key to the History of Mankind*, 2 vols, 3rd ed., London 1968.

Halliday, M.A.K., Macintosh, A., and Strevens, P.D., *The Linguistic Sciences and Language Teaching*, London 1964.

Hospers, J.H., *A Basic Bibliography for the Study of the Semitic Languages*, Leiden 1973.

Lyons, J., *Introduction to Theoretical Linguistics*, Cambridge 1968.

Moscati, S., Spitaler, A., Ullendorff, E., Soden, W. von, *An Introduction to the Comparative Grammar of the Semitic Languages. Phonology and Morphology*, Wiesbaden 1964.

Rabin, Ch.,"Hebrew" in Sebeok, T., ed., *Current Trends in Linguistics*, Vol. VI, The Hague-Paris 1970, pp. 304-46.

Sawyer, J.F.A., *Semantics in Biblical Research. New Methods of Defining Hebrew Words for Salvation*, London 1972.

Würthwein, E., *The Text of the Old Testament*, Oxford 1957.

GRAMMAR

Bergsträsser, G., *Hebräische Grammatik*, Leipzig 1918-29.

Bauer, H. & Leander, P., *Historische Grammatik der hebräischen Sprache*, Halle 1922 (reprinted Hildesheim 1965).

BIBLIOGRAPHY

Gesenius' Hebrew Grammar, ed. Kautzsch, E., 2nd English edition by Cowley, A.E., Oxford 1910 (reprinted London 1966).

Joüon, P., *Grammaire de l'Hébreu Biblique*, 2nd ed., Rome 1947 (reprinted Rome 1962)

Lambdin, T.O., *Introduction to Biblical Hebrew*, London 1973.

Meyer, R., *Hebräische Grammatik*, 4 vols., Berlin 1966-72.

Schneider, W., *Grammatik des Biblischen Hebräisch*, Munich 1974.

DICTIONARIES, ETC.

Brown, F., Driver, S.R., & Briggs, C.A. *A Hebrew and English Lexicon of the Old Testament based on the Thesaurus of Gesenius*, Oxford 1907 (reprinted Oxford 1968).

Davidson, B., *The Analytical Hebrew and Chaldee Lexicon*, reprinted London 1963.

Fohrer, G., *Hebrew and Aramaic Dictionary of the Old Testament* (Eng. transl. by W. Johnstone), London 1973.

Gesenius, W., *Handwörterbuch über das Alte Testament*, ed. Buhl, F., Berlin 1915 (reprinted Berlin 1962).

Holladay, W.L., *A Concise Hebrew and Aramaic Lexicon of the Old Testament*, Leiden 1971.

Köhler, L. and Baumgartner, W., *Lexicon in Veteris Testamenti Libros*, Leiden 1958; 3rd edition, Leiden 1967-.

Langenscheidt's Pocket Hebrew Dictionary to the Old Testament, 13th ed., New York 1961.

Mandelkern, S., *Veteris Testamenti Concordantiae Hebraicae atque Chaldaicae*, Leipzig 1896 (reprinted Jerusalem-Tel Aviv 1962; Graz 1967).

Rabin, Ch. and Radday, Z., *Thesaurus*, 2 vols., Jerusalem 1974.

Watts, J.D.W., *List of Words Occurring Frequently in the Hebrew Bible*, 2nd ed., Leiden 1967.

Young, R., *Analytical Concordance to the Bible*, Edinburgh 1880.

BIBLIOGRAPHY

SOME SPECIAL STUDIES CONSULTED

Andersen, F.I., *The Hebrew Verbless Clause in the Pentateuch,* Nashville New York 1970.

Barr, J., "The Image of God in the Book of Genesis - a Study in Terminology", *BJRL* 51 (1968), pp. 11-26.

Bynon, J. and T., ed. *Hamito-Semitica,* Janua Linguarum, Series Practica 200, The Hague 1975.

Chayen, M.J., *The Phonetics of Modern Hebrew,* The Hague 1973.

Chomsky, W., "The Pronunciation of the Shwa", *JQR* 62 (1971), pp. 88-94.

Driver, S.R., *A Treatise on the Use of the Tenses in Hebrew and Some Other Syntactical Questions,* Oxford 1892.

Hospers, J.H., "Some observations about the teaching of Old Testament Hebrew", *Symbolae Biblicae et Mesopotamicae F.M.Th. de Liagre Böhl Dedicatae,* Leiden 1972, pp. 188-198.

T. Mettinger, "The Hebrew Verb System. A Survey of Recent Research", *ASTI* 9 (1974) (Festschrift Hans Kosmala), pp. 64-84.

Muraoka, T., *Emphasis in Biblical Hebrew,* Oxford 1969.

Rabin, Ch., מלים זרות ("Loan-words"), *Encyclopaedia Biblica,* Vol.IV, Jerusalem 1972, cols. 1070-80.

Sawyer, J.F.A., "Root-meanings in Hebrew", *JSS* 12 (1967), pp.37-50.

" " "An analysis of the context and meaning of the Psalm-headings", *TGUOS* 22 (1970), pp. 26-38.

Ullendorff, E., "Is Biblical Hebrew a language?" *BSOAS* 34 (1971), pp.241-55.

EDITIONS OF THE HEBREW BIBLE *(Codex Leningradensis, 1008 A.D.)*

Dotan, A., תורה נביאים וכתובים (Tel Aviv 1972).

Elliger, K. & Rudolph. W., *Biblia Hebraica Stuttgartensia,* Stuttgart 1968-.

Kittel, R., *Biblia Hebraica,* 7th ed., Stuttgart 1953.

Snaith, N.H., *Hebrew Old Testament,* British and Foreign Bible Society edition, London 1958.

HEBREW-ENGLISH VOCABULARY

This vocabulary includes the citation-forms (I) of all the lexical items introduced in the exercises. The derived stems (X) of verbs of which the simple stem does not occur in the grammar are also listed alphabetically as citation-forms: e.g. נִלְחַם "to fight" under נ; הִצִּיל "to rescue" under ה.

Irregular plurals and pregenitive forms of nouns are frequently given, as also are unusual forms of prepositions. The third masculine singular of the Prefix Conjugation of verbs is given, and references to where each verb-type is discussed.

א.

אָב *āv* (אָבוֹת, אֲבִי-) "father"

אֶבֶן *éven* (אֲבָנִים, אַבְנ-) f. "stone"

אַבְרָהָם *avrāhām* "Abraham"

אָבַד *āvad* (יֹאבַד XII) "to be lost, die" D."to destroy"; H."to destroy".

אֱדֹם, אֱדוֹם *edōm* "Edom, a people or region south of Judah".

אָדָם *ādām* "man, humanity, Adam".

אֲדָמָה *adāmā* f. "earth, land".

אָהֵב *āhēv* (יֶאֱהַב XV) "to love".

אֹהֶל *ṓhel* "tent"

אַהֲרֹן *aharōn* "Aaron, brother of Moses, founder of priestly family".

אוֹיֵב *ōyēv* "enemy"

אוֹר *ōr* (אוֹרוֹת) "light"

אוֹר *ōr* (יָאוֹר XVII) "to shine"; H. "to make bright"

אָז *āz* "then"

אָח *āχ* (אַחִים, אֲחִי-) "brother, kinsman"

אֶחָד *eχād* (fem. אַחַת) "one"

אַחַר *aχar* (cf. אַחֲרֵי) "after, behind"

אַחֵר *aχēr* "other, different".

אַחֲרוֹן *aχarōn* "last, later".

אַחֲרֵי *aχarē* (cf. אַחַר) "after, behind".

אַחַת *aχat* see אֶחָד.

אִיּוֹב *iyōv* "Job".

אֵיךְ *ēχ*, אֵיכָה *éχā* "how?"

אַיִן *áyin* (אֵין) "there is (are) not" (XIV).

אִישׁ *īsh* (אַנְשֵׁי, אֲנָשִׁים) "a man, anyone, each" (XVIII).

אָכַל *āχal* (יֹאכַל XII) "to eat"; H. "to feed".

אֵל *ēl* "God, El".

אַל- *al* "not" (in modal sentences) (XIV).

אֶל- *el* (אֵלַי) "to, towards".

אֵלֶּה *éle* (cf זֶה) "these"

אֱלֹהִים *elōhīm* "God, Elohim".

אֱלִימֶלֶךְ *elīméleχ* "Elimelech, husband of Naomi"

אֶלֶף *élef* "1000".

אֵם *ēm* (-אִמּ, אִמּוֹת) f. "mother".

אִם *im* "if, that" (XIX); particle introducing oath (XX).

אָמַר *āmar* (יֹאמַר XII) "to say".

אֱנוֹשׁ *enōsh* "man" (poetic: XVI).

אֲנַחְנוּ *anáχnū* "we".

אֲנִי *anī* "I".

אָנֹכִי *ānōχī* "I".

אֲנָשִׁים *anāshīm* "men" (plura of אִישׁ).

אָסַף *āsaf* (יֶאֱסֹף XII) "to gather, assemble".

אַרְבַּע *arba* "4".

אַרְבָּעִים *arbā'īm* "40".

אֲרוֹן *arōn* "ark (of the covenant), box".

אַרְנוֹן *arnōn* "Arnon, wadi marking boundary between Ammon and Moab".

אֶרֶץ *érets* (-אֶרֶץ, אֲרָצוֹת) f. "earth, land"

אִשָּׁה *ishā* (נְשֵׁי, נָשִׁים, אֵשֶׁת) f. "woman"

אֲשֶׁר *asher* relative word "that, which, etc." (XX. 4)

אֶת- *et* (-אֹת) object-marker (VIII)

אֶת- *et* (-אִתּ) "with"

אַתְּ *at* "you (fem.)"

אַתָּה *atā* "you (masc)"

אַתֶּם *atem* "you (masc. pl.)"

אֶתְמוֹל *etmōl* "yesterday"

אַתֶּן *aten* "you (fem. pl.)"

ב.

-בְּ *bə*-"in, into, by, with, against" (p.65)

בָּא *bā* (יָבוֹא XVII) "to come, enter"; H. "bring"

בָּבֶל *bāvel* "Babel"

בָּחַר *bāχar* (יִבְחַר XV) "to choose"

בָּטַח *bātaχ* (יִבְטַח XV) "to trust".

בֵּין *bēn* "between, among"

בִּין *bīn* (יָבִין XVII) "to understand"; H. "to gain insight"

בַּיִת *báyit* (בָּתִּים, בֵּית) "house, temple"

בָּכָה *bāχā* (יִבְכֶּה XVIII) "to weep"

בַּל *bal* "not" (XIV)

בִּלְתִּי *biltī* "not" (XIV)

בָּמָה *bāmā* f. "high-place associated with pagan worship"

בֵּן *bēn* (-בֶּן, -בְּנ; בָּנִים, בְּנֵי) "son, member of a group"

בָּנָה *bānā* (יִבְנֶה XVIII) "to build"

בִּקֵּשׁ *bikēsh* D. (יְבַקֵּשׁ) "to seek, look for"

בָּרָא *bārā* (יִבְרָא XIII) "to create (used only of God)"

בָּרוּךְ *bārūχ* "blessed"

בְּרִית *bərīt* f. "covenant, alliance, promise"

בֵּרַךְ *bēraχ* D. (יְבָרֵךְ) "to bless"

בָּשָׂר *bāsār* "meat, flesh, mankind"

בַּת *bat* (בָּנוֹת, בַּת-) f. "daughter, member of a group"

בְּתוֹךְ *bətoχ* "in, in the midst of, among"

ג.

גָּאַל *gā'al* (יִגְאַל) "to redeem"

גִּבּוֹר *gibōr* "hero"

גָּדוֹל *gādōl* "great"

גּוֹי *gōi* "nation, gentile"

גָּלָה *gālā* (יִגְלֶה XVIII) "to go into exile"; D."to reveal, uncover"

גַּם *gam* "also, even"

גֵּר *gēr* "sojourner, alien"

גַּת *gat* f. "Gath, one of the five Philistine cities"

ד.

דָּבָר *dāvār* (דִּבְרֵי, דְּבָרִים) "word, thing"

דִּבֶּר *diber* D (יְדַבֵּר) "to speak"

דָּוִד *dāvīd* "David"

דּוֹר *dor* (דּוֹרוֹת) "generation, lifetime"

דָּם *dam* "blood"

דֶּרֶךְ *déreχ* f. "way, road"

דָּרַךְ *dāraχ* (יִדְרֹךְ XI) "to walk"

דָּרַשׁ *dārash* (יִדְרוֹשׁ XI) "to seek, consult"

ה.

הֶבֶל *hével* "Abel"

הוּא *hū* "he, that, it"

הוֹסִיף *hōsīf* H (יוֹסִיף XVI) "to add, increase, repeat (XV)"

הוֹשִׁיעַ *hōshīa* H (יוֹשִׁיעַ) "to save, help"

הִיא *hī* "she, that, it"

הָיָה *hāyā* (יִהְיֶה XVIII) "to be, become"

הֵיכָל *hēχāl* (הֵיכָלוֹת) "palace, temple"

הִכָּה *hikā* H (יַכֶּה XIX) "to strike, kill"

הֵכִין *hēχīn* H (יָכִין XVII) "to prepare, appoint"

הָלַךְ *hālaχ* (יֵלֵךְ XVI) "to go"; T."to walk"

הֵם *hēm* "they, those"

הֵמָּה *hḗmā* "they, those"

הֵן *hēn* "they, those"

הִנֵּה *hinē* "behold"

הִצִּיל *hitsīl* H (יַצִּיל XIX) "to deliver, rescue"

הַר *har* "mountain, range of mountains, hill-country"

הִתְפַּלֵּל *hitpalēl* T (יִתְפַּלֵּל) "to pray"

ו.

-וְ *və*-"and, but (XIX)"

ז.

זֹאת *zōt* "this" (fem)

זֶבַח *zévaχ* "communion-sacrifice"

זָבַח *zāvaχ* (יִזְבַּח XIII) "to slaughter, sacrifice"

זֶה *ze* "this" (masc)

זָהָב *zāhāv* "gold"

זָכַר *zāχar* (יִזְכֹּר XI) "to remember; H summon, mention"

זָעַק *zā'ak* (יִזְעַק XIII) "to cry, call for help"

זָקֵן *zākēn* "old"

זְרֻבָּבֶל *zerubāvel* "Zerubbabel, royal leader of returning exiles in 520 B.C."

זֶרַע *zéra* (-זְרַע)"seed, descendants"

זָרַע *zāra* (יִזְרַע XIII) "to sow"

ח.

חַג *χag* (-חַג) "feast, pilgrimage (Ex.23:14-17; Deut.16:16)"

חֹדֶשׁ *χódesh*(-חָדְשׁ) "month, new moon"

חָזָק *χāzāk* "strong"

חָזַק *χāzak* (יֶחֱזַק XV) "to be strong; H. seize"

חַטָּאת *χatāt* f. "sin"

חַי *χai* "alive, living"

חָיָה *χāyā* (יִחְיֶה XVIII) "to live"

חַיָּה *χayā* f. "animal"

חַיִל *χáyil* (חֵיל V) "strength, wealth, army"

חָכָם *χāχām* "wise"

חָכְמָה *χoχmā* f. "wisdom"

חֲלוֹם *χalōm* (חֲלֹמוֹת) "dream"

חָמֵשׁ *χāmēsh* (חֲמִשָּׁה) "5"

חֵן *χēn* "charm, favour"

חֶסֶד *χésed* (-חַסְדּ) "loyalty, love"

חֹק *χōk* (-חֻקּ) "obligation, law"

חֶרֶב *χérev* (-חֲרָבוֹת, חַרְבּ) f. "sword"

חָרָה *χārā* (יֶחֱרֶה XVIII) חָרָה-לוֹ "he was angry" (XVI)

חֹתָם *χōtām* "seal"

ט.

טוֹב *tōv* "good"

טוּב *tūv* "well-being, success"

י.

יַבָּשָׁה *yabāshā* f. "dry land"

יָד *yād* "hand" (f.)

יָדַע *yāda* (יֵדַע XVI) "to know"; H. "to make known"

יָהּ *yā* shortened form of יְהוָה (XI)

יְהוּדָה *yəhūdā* f. "Judah, territory around Jerusalem"

יְהוָה *adōnai* "the Lord" (I)

יְהוֹנָתָן *yəhōnātān* "Jonathan, son of Saul, loved by David"

יוֹאָב *yō'āv* "Joab, David's military commander"

יוֹם *yōm* (יְמֵי, יָמִים) "day"; הַיּוֹם "today"

יוֹנָה *yōnā* "Jonah, prophet of the Lord"

יוֹסֵף *yōsēf* "Joseph, Jacob's son, who became governor of Egypt"

יַחְדָּו *yaχdāv* "together"

יִיטַב *yītav* (PC only: XV) "to be good, do well"

יַיִן *yáyin* (יֵין) "wine"

יָכֹל *yāχōl* (יוּכַל XV) "to be able"

יָלַד *yālad* (יֵלֵד XVI) "to have a child"; H. "to beget"

יָם *yām* (יַמִּים) "sea"

יַעֲקֹב *ya'akōv* "Jacob, ancestor of the twelve tribes of Israel"

יָצָא *yātsā* (יֵצֵא XVI) "to go/come out"; H."to take/bring out"

יִצְחָק *yitsχāk* "Isaac, son of Abraham"

יָרֵא *yārē* (יִירָא XV) "to be afraid"

יִרְאָה *yir'ā* "fear" (f.)

יָרַד *yārad* (יֵרֵד XVI) "to go/come down: H."to take/bring down"

יַרְדֵּן *yardēn* "Jordan, largest river in Palestine"

יְרוּשָׁלִַם *yərūshāláyim* "Jerusalem" (f.)

יָרַשׁ *yārash* (יִירַשׁ XVI) "to possess, inherit"

יֵשׁ־ *yesh* "there is(are)" (X)

יִשְׂרָאֵל *yisrā'ēl* "Israel"

יָשַׁב *yāshav* (יֵשֵׁב XVI) "to dwell, sit"; H. "to settle (a people)"

כ

כְּ־ *kə*-"like, as, according to" (XV)

כָּבוֹד *kāvōd* "glory, honour"

כֹּה *kō* "thus, so"

כֹּהֵן *kōhen* "priest"

כֹּחַ *kōaχ* "power, strength"

כִּי *kī* "that, because" (XIX)

כִּי־אִם *kī 'im* "nevertheless, unless, except" (XIX)

כָּכָה *kā́χā* "thus, so"

כֹּל *kōl* (כָּל־) "all, every, any" (XIV)

כָּלָה *kālā* (יִכְלֶה XVIII) "to be finished, perish; D."to complete"

כְּלִי *kəlī* (כֵּלִים) "vessel, equipment, weapon, ornament"

כְּמוֹ *kəmō* (cf. כְּ־) "like, as" (XV)

כְּמוֹשׁ *kəmōsh*"Chemosh, chief god of Moab"

כֵּן *kēn* "thus, so"

כִּסֵּא *kisē* (כִּסְאוֹת) "chair, throne"

כֶּסֶף *késef* (כְּסָפִים, כַּסְפּ-) "silver

כִּפֶּר *kiper* D. (יְכַפֵּר) "to atone"

כָּרַת *kārat* (יִכְרֹת XI) "to cut"; כָּרַת בְּרִית "to make a covenant

כָּתַב *kātav* (יִכְתֹּב XI) "to write"

ל.

-לְ *lə* "to, for, of" (XV)

לֹא *lō* "no, not"

לֵב *lēv* (לִבּוֹת, לִבּ-) "heart, mind"

לֵבָב *lēvāv* see לֵב

לֵוִי *lēvī* "Levi, Levite, ancestor or member of priestly family"

לֶחֶם *léχem* (-לַחְמ) "bread, food"

לַיְלָה *láilā* "night"

לָמַד *lāmad* (יִלְמַד XV) "to learn"; D. "to teach"

לָמָּה *lā́mā* "why?"

לְמַעַן *ləmá'an* "for the sake of, in order that" (XIX)

לִפְנֵי *lifnē* (-לִפְנֵי, -לְפָנ) "before" (XV)

לָקַח *lākaχ* (יִקַּח XIV) "to take"

מ.

מְאוֹד *mə'ōd* "very"

מֵאָה *mē'ā* "100" (f.)

מָגֵן *māgēn* (מְגִנִּים, -מָגִנּ) "shield"

מִדְבָּר. *midbār* "wilderness"

מָה *mā* "what?"

מוּסָר *mūsār* "instruction, chastisement"

מוֹעֵד *mō'ēd* "meeting, appointed time, feast"

מָוֶת *mávet* (מוֹת) "death"

מִי *mī* "who? whom?"

מַיִם *máyim* (מֵי) "water"

מָלֵא *mālē* (יִמְלָא XV) "to be full"; D. "to fill"

מַלְאָךְ *mal'āχ* "angel, messenger"

מִלְחָמָה *milχāmā* "war, battle" (f.)

מֶלֶךְ *méleχ* (מַלְכֵי, מְלָכִים, מַלְכּ־) "king"

מָלַךְ *mālaχ* (יִמְלוֹךְ) "to be king, reign"

מַמְלָכָה *mamlāχā* (מַמְלֶכֶת) f. "reign, kingdom"

מִן־ *min* (מִ־, מֵ־) "from, than, after"

מְנוּחָה *mənūχā* "peace, rest" f.

מִנְחָה *minχā* "cereal offering, gift" (f.)

מַעֲשֶׂה *ma'ase* "deed, activity, work"

מָצָא *mātsā* (יִמְצָא XIII) "to find, reach"

מִצְוָה *mitsvā* "commandment" (f.)

מִצְרַיִם *mitsráyim* "Egypt, Egyptians"

מָקוֹם *mākōm* (מְקוֹמוֹת) "place"

מֹשֶׁה *mōshe* "Moses"

מָשַׁח *māshaχ* (יִמְשַׁח XIII) "to anoint"; מָשִׁיחַ *māshīaχ* "anointed"

מִשְׁכָּן *mishkān* (מִשְׁכָּנוֹת) "dwelling-place, tabernacle (Ex. 25-30)"

מִשְׁפָּחָה *mishpāχā* "family" (f.)

מִשְׁפָּט *mishpāt* "judgment, lawsuit, justice"

מֵת *mēt* (יָמוּת XVII) "to die"; H. "to kill"

נ.

נָבִיא *nāvī* "prophet"

נְבִיאָה *nəvī'ā* "prophetess" (f.)

נָגַע *nāga* (יִגַּע XIV) "to touch, hurt"; H. "to arrive at"

נָח *nāχ* (יָנוּחַ XVII) "to rest" H. "to set down, settle, leave alone"

נֹחַ *nōaχ* "Noah"

נַחַל *náχal* "wadi, stream"

נַחֲלָה *naχalā* "heritage, inheritance" (f.)

נִחַם *niχam* (יִנָּחֵם) N."to relent,console oneself"; D."to comfort"

נָטָה *nātā* (יִטֶּה XIV) "to spread out"; H."to bend down"

נִינְוֵה *nīnəvē* "Nineveh, capital of Assyrian Empire" (f.)

נִלְחַם *nilχam* N (יִלָּחֵם) "to fight"

נָסַע *nāsa* (יִסַּע XIV) "to set out, march"

נָעֳמִי *no'omī* "Naomi, the mother-in-law of Ruth the Moabitess"

נַעַר *ná'ar* "boy, young man"

נָפַל *nāfal* (יִפּוֹל XIV) "to fall"; H. "to bring down"

נֶפֶשׁ *néfesh* (נְפָשׁוֹת, נַפְשׁ-) "person, self, soul" (f.)

נָשָׂא *nāsā* (יִשָּׂא XIV) "to lift, carry, forgive"

נִשְׁבַּע *nishba* (יִשָּׁבַע) "to swear (an oath), promise"

נָתַן *nātan* (יִתֵּן XIV) "to give, put"

ס.

סוּס *sūs* "horse"

סֵפֶר *séfer* (סְפָרִים, סִפְר-) "written document, book"

סָר *sār* (יָסוּר XVII) "to turn aside"; H. "to remove"

ע.

עֶבֶד *éved* (עֲבָדִים, עַבְד-) "servant, slave"

עָבַד *āvad* (יַעֲבוֹד XII) "to serve, worship, work"

עָבַר *āvar* (יַעֲבוֹר XII) "to pass, cross"

עַד- *ad* "until, as far as, up to"

עוֹד *ōd* "still, again" (XV)

עוֹלָם *ōlām* "all time"; לְעוֹלָם "for ever"

עָוֹן *āvōn* (עֲוֹנוֹת) "sin, guilt"

עֹז *ōz* (עֻז-) "might, power"

עֻזִּיָּהוּ *uziyāhū* "Uzziah, king of Judah (783-742 B.C.)"

עַיִן *áyin* (עֵין, עֵינַיִם) "eye, well" (f.)

עִיר *īr* (עָרִים, עָרֵי) "city" (f.)

עַל- *al* (עָלַי) "upon, according to, concerning" (XV)

עָלָה *ālā* (יַעֲלֶה XVIII) "to go/come up"; H. "to take/bring up"

עֹלָה *ōlā* "holocaust" (f.)

עַם *am* (עַמִּים, עַמֵּי) "people"

עִם- *im* (עִמְּ-) "with"

עָמַד *āmad* (יַעֲמוֹד XII) "to stand"; H. "to set up, restore"
עַמּוֹן *amōn* "Ammon, a people living in Transjordan"
עָנָה *ānā* (יַעֲנֶה XVIII) "to answer, testify"
עֵץ *ēts* "tree, wood"
עֵצָה *ētsā* "advice, sagacity" (f.)
עֶרֶב *érev* "evening"
עָשָׂה *āsā* (יַעֲשֶׂה XVIII) "to make, do"
עַתָּה *atā* "now" (XV)

פ.

פֶּה *pe* (פִּי) "mouth, command"; כְּפִי "according to"
פְּלִשְׁתִּים *pəlishtīm* "Philistines, one of the Sea Peoples, who settled in Palestine"
פֶּן- *pen* "lest, in case" (XIX)
פִּנָּה *pinā* "corner" (f.)
פָּנִים *pānīm* (פְּנֵי, פָּנ-) "face"; see לִפְנֵי.
פָּקַד *pākad* (יִפְקוֹד XI) "to call to account, punish"; H."to appoint"
פָּרָה *pārā* (יִפְרֶה XVIII) "to be fruitful"
פַּרְעֹה *par'ō* "Pharaoh, the king of Egypt"
פָּתַח *pātaχ* (יִפְתַּח XIII) "to open"

צ

צָבָא *tsāvā* "army service, host"; יְהוָה צְבָאוֹת "Lord of hosts"
צַדִּיק *tsadīk* "innocent, righteous"
צֶדֶק *tsédek* "righteousness, victory"
צָדַק *tsādak* (יִצְדַּק XV) "to be innocent, righteous"; H."acquit"
צִוָּה *tsivā* (יְצַוֶּה) "to command"
צוּר *tsūr* "rock"
צִיּוֹן *tsiyōn* "Zion (f.), alternative name for Jerusalem"
צָעַק *tsā'ak* (יִצְעַק XIII) cf. זָעַק "to cry for help"

ק.

קֶבֶר *kéver* (קְבָרִים, קִבְר-) "tomb, grave"

קָבַר *kāvar* (יִקְבּוֹר XI) "to bury"
קָדוֹשׁ *kādōsh* "holy"
קֹדֶשׁ *kṓdesh* (קֳדָשִׁים, קָדְשׁ-) "holiness"
קָדַשׁ *kādash* (יִקְדַּשׁ XV) "to be holy"
קָהָל *kāhāl* "congregation"
קוֹל *kōl* (קוֹלוֹת) "voice, sound"
קִיקָיוֹן *kīkāyōn* "gourd"
קָם *kām* (יָקוּם XVII) "to stand, get up"; H."to establish"
קָרָא *kārā* (יִקְרָא XIII) "to call, read aloud"
קָרֵב *kārēv* (יִקְרַב XV) "to draw near, approach"
קָרְבָּן *korbān* "offering, sacrifice"

ר.
רָאָה *rā'ā* (יִרְאֶה XVIII) "to see"; H."to show"; N."to appear"
רֹאשׁ *rōsh* (רָאשִׁים, רָאשֵׁי) "head, top"
רִאשׁוֹן *rīshōn* "first"
רֵאשִׁית *rēshīt* "beginning" (f.)
רַב *rav* (רַבִּים, רַבָּה) "much, many"
רָבָה *rāvā* (יִרְבֶּה XVIII) "to be much, many"; H."to multiply" (XV)
רוּחַ *rūaχ* (רוּחוֹת) "wind, spirit" (f.)
רָם *rām* "high"
רַע *ra* "bad, evil"; **רָעָה** f. "disaster"
רָעָב *rā'āv* "famine"
רַק *rak* "only"

ש.
שְׁאוֹל *shə'ōl* "Sheol, the underworld"
שָׁאוּל *shā'ūl* "Saul, first anointed king of Israel"
שָׁאַל *shā'al* (יִשְׁאַל XIII) "to ask"
שָׁב *shāv* (יָשׁוּב XVII) "to return, turn"; H."to bring back"
שַׁבָּת *shabāt* (שַׁבָּתוֹת) "Sabbath"
שָׂדֶה *sādē* (שָׂדוֹת) "field, territory"

שִׁירָה *shīrā* "song" (f.)

שָׁכַח *shāχaχ* (יִשְׁכַּח XIII) "to forget"

שָׁלוֹם *shālōm* "peace, well-being"

שָׁלַח *shālaχ* (יִשְׁלַח XIII) "to send"

שְׁלֹמֹה *shəlōmō* "Solomon"

שָׁלֹשׁ *shālōsh* (שְׁלֹשֶׁת) "3"

שֵׁם *shēm* (שֵׁמוֹת, שְׁם-) "name"

שָׁם *shām* "there"

שָׂם *sām* (יָשִׂים XVII) "to put, give"

שְׁמוּאֵל *shəmū'ēl* "Samuel, prophet who anointed the first two kings of Israel"

שָׂמֵחַ *sāmēaχ* (יִשְׂמַח XV) "to rejoice"

שִׂמְחָה *simχā* "rejoicing" (f.)

שָׁמַיִם *shāmáyim* "heaven, sky"

שָׁמַע *shāma* (יִשְׁמַע XIII) "to hear"

שָׁמַר *shāmar* (יִשְׁמֹר XI) "to keep, watch"

שֶׁמֶשׁ *shémesh* "sun"

שָׂנֵא *sānē* (יִשְׂנָא XV) "to hate"

שָׁנָה *shānā* (שָׁנִים) "year" (f.)

שַׁעַר *shá'ar* (שְׁעָרִים) "gate"

שָׁפַט *shāfat* (יִשְׁפֹּט XI) "to judge, vindicate"

שָׁר *shār* (יָשִׁיר XVII) "to sing"

שַׂר *sar* "prince, ruler"

שָׂרָה *sārā* "Sarah, wife of Abraham" (f.)

שָׁתָה *shātā* (יִשְׁתֶּה XVIII) "to drink"

שְׁתַּיִם *shtáyim* (שְׁנֵי, שְׁנַיִם: שְׁתֵּי) "2"

ת.

תֹּהוּ וָבֹהוּ *tóhū vāvóhū* "formless waste (Gen. 1:2)"

תּוֹרָה *tōrā* "law, instruction" (f.)

תַּחַת *táχat* "under, instead of"

תָּמִים *tāmīm* "perfect"

תְּפִלָּה *təfilā* "prayer" (f.)

תַּרְדֵּמָה *tardēmā* "deep sleep" (f.)

INDEX OF PREFIXES

א "I" (*1s* PC): normally אֶ אַ אָ (אֲ in D-stem)

בְּ "in, into, by, with, against" with nouns, verbal nouns, and suffix pronouns (also בֶּ בָּ בַּ : p.159)

הַ "the": normally הַ or הָ (occasionally הֶ : p.158).

הֲ interrogative (XI)

ה H-stem Suffix Conjugation, imperative, verbal noun.

ה N-stem imperative, verbal noun: הִ (הֵ before gutturals : p.158).

הִתְ T-stem Suffix Conjugation, imperative, verbal noun.

וְ "and": normally וְ ; often וַ and וּ (p.160).

י "he, it, they" (*3ms*, *3mpl* PC): normally יִ יַ יָ (יְ in D-stem)

כְּ "like, as" with nouns and verbal nouns (also כֶּ כָּ כַּ : p.159).

כְּמ "like, as" with suffix pronouns (variant of כְּ : p.103).

לְ "to, for" with nouns, verbal nouns and suffix pronouns (also לֶ לָ לַ: p. 159).

מִ "from, than" with nouns and verbal nouns : מִ (מֵ before gutturals: p.158).

מ participle of D-stem (מְ): H-stem (מַ, מֵ, מוֹ); and T-stem (מִתְ).

מִמ "from, than" with suffix pronouns (variant of מִ : p.103).

מִתְ participle of T-stem.

נ "we" (*1pl* PC): normally נִ נַ נָ (נְ in D-stem)

נִ N-stem Suffix Conjugation, participle, verbal noun.

שֶׁ "which, that, etc." (cf. אֲשֶׁר).

ת "you (subject: *2s*, *2pl* PC): normally תִּ תַּ תָּ (תְּ in D-stem)

"she, it" (*3fs* PC); "they" (*3fpl* PC).

INDEX OF SUFFIXES

ָה *fs* noun, adjective, participle.
"she, it" (*3fs* SC)
modal suffix (PC, imperative: XIII).
"to, towards" (XV).

ָהּ "her" with nouns, verbs, participles, prepositions.
הָ "her" (variant of ָהּ in post-vocalic position).

הוּ "him" (with verbs); "his (with some nouns).

הֶם "their (masc.)" with plur. nouns; "them (masc.)" with prepositions and plur. participles.
הֶן "their (fem)" with plur. nouns: "them (fem) "with prepositions
and plur. participles.

וֹ "his" with sing. nouns; "him" with verbs and prepositions.
ו "his, him" (variant of וֹ in post-vocalic position).

וּ "they" (*3pl* SC; *3mpl* PC).
"you" (subject: *2mpl* PC; and imperative).
ן or וּן "they, you" (variant of וּ).

וֹת *fpl* noun, adjective, participle.
verbal noun of verbs ending in a vowel (XVIII).
וֹתַי "my" with *fpl* nouns: cf. וֹתֶיךָ "your"; וֹתָיו "his"; etc.

ִי "my" with sing. nouns; "me" with prepositions.
"you" (subject: *2fs* PC; *fs* imperative).
ַי "my" with plur. nouns; "me" with some prepositions

INDEX OF SUFFIXES

ִי PG plural with nouns, adjectives, participles.

ָיו "his" with pl. nouns, participles (pronounced -*āv*).

ִים *mpl* nouns, adjectives and participles.
ַ֫יִם dual nouns.

ִין "you" (subject: *2fs* PC) (variant of ִי)

ךָ "your"(*ms*) with nouns; "you"(*ms*) with verbs, prepositions, participles.
ךְ "your"(*fs*) with nouns; "you"(*fs*) with verbs, prepositions, participles; "your"(*ms*) in pausal forms (p.157).
כֶם "your"(*mpl*) with nouns; "you"(*mpl*) with verbs, prepositions, participles.
כֶן "your"(*fpl*) with nouns; "you"(*fpl*) with verbs, prepositions, participles.

ָם "their"(*mpl*) with sing. nouns; "them"(*mpl*) with verbs, prepositions, participles.
ֵם "them"(*mpl*) with verbs (variant of ָם).
ם "them"(*mpl*) with verbs (variant of ָם)
מוֹ "them"(*mpl*) with prepositions (rare variant of הֶם).

ָן "their"(*fpl*) with sing. nouns; "them"(*fpl*) with verbs, prepositions, participles.
ֵן "them"(*fpl*) with verbs (variant of ָן).

נ combines with other suffixes in variant forms: see ֶ֫נּוּ ִין וּן
ֶ֫נִּי (cf. p.149).

נָה "you" (subject: *2fpl* PC; *fpl* imperative).
נָה "they" (*3fpl* PC).

INDEX OF SUFFIXES

נוּ "we" (*1pl* SC)

ֵ֫נוּ "our" with nouns; "us" with verbs, prepositions, participles.

ֶ֫נּוּ "him" with verbs, quasi-verbals (X), prepositions (variant of הוּ-: cf.p.149); or "us" (variant of ֵ֫נוּ)

ִני "me" with verbs.

ֶ֫נִּי "me" with verbs, quasi-verbals, and prepositions (variant of ִני: cf.p.149).

ת *fs* noun, adjective, participle; especially PG of *fs* nouns in ָה.

ת verbal noun of verbs beginning with נ (XIV) and י (XVI).

תָּ "you" (subject: *2ms* SC).

תְּ "you" (subject: *2fs* SC)

תָה "she" (*3fs* SC) in verbs ending in a vowel (XVIII).

תִּי "I" (*1s* SC)

ַ֫תַיִם fem. dual nouns.

תֶּם "you" (subject: *2mpl* SC)

תֶּן "you" (subject: *2fpl* SC).

GENERAL INDEX

This index includes terms and subjects not covered by the Table of Contents on pp. xi-xiii.

INDEX OF BIBLICAL PASSAGES DISCUSSED